# A Popular History of Priestcraft in All Ages and Nations

*(1833)*

*A Hindu god in copulation*

# William Howitt

ISBN 0-7661-0216-5

Request our FREE CATALOG of over 1,000
# Rare Esoteric Books
## Unavailable Elsewhere

Freemasonry * Akashic * Alchemy * Alternative Health * Ancient Civilizations * Anthroposophy * Astral * Astrology * Astronomy * Aura * Bacon, Francis * Bible Study * Blavatsky * Boehme * Cabalah * Cartomancy * Chakras * Clairvoyance * Comparative Religions * Divination * Druids * Eastern Thought * Egyptology * Esoterism * Essenes * Etheric * Extrasensory Perception * Gnosis * Gnosticism * Golden Dawn * Great White Brotherhood * Hermetics * Kabalah * Karma * Knights Templar * Kundalini * Magic * Meditation * Mediumship * Mesmerism * Metaphysics * Mithraism * Mystery Schools * Mysticism * Mythology * Numerology * Occultism * Palmistry * Pantheism * Paracelsus * Parapsychology * Philosophy * Plotinus * Prosperity & Success * Psychokinesis * Psychology * Pyramids * Qabalah * Reincarnation * Rosicrucian * Sacred Geometry * Secret Rituals * Secret Societies * Spiritism * Symbolism * Tarot * Telepathy * Theosophy * Transcendentalism * Upanishads * Vedanta * Wisdom * Yoga * *Plus Much More!*

## KESSINGER PUBLISHING, LLC
http://www.kessingerpub.com
email: books@kessingerpub.com

A

POPULAR HISTORY

OF

PRIESTCRAFT

IN ALL AGES AND NATIONS.

BY

WILLIAM HOWITT.

Help us to save free Gospel from the paw
Of hireling wolves, whose conscience is their maw.
MILTON.

LONDON:
EFFINGHAM WILSON, ROYAL EXCHANGE.

1833.

Manning and Co., Printers,
London-house Yard

Oh! Truth! immortal Truth! on what wild ground
Still hast thou trod through this unspiritual sphere!
The strong, the brutish, and the vile surround
Thy presence, lest thy streaming glory cheer
The poor, the many, without price, or bound.
Drowning thy voice, they fill the popular ear,
In thy high name, with canons, creeds, and laws,
Feigning to serve, that they may mar thy cause.

And the great multitude doth crouch and bear
The burden of the selfish.   That emprize,—
That lofty spirit of Virtue which can dare
To rend the bands of error from all eyes,
And from the freed soul pluck each sensual care,
To them is but a fable.   Therefore lies
Darkness upon the mental desart still,
And wolves devour, and robbers walk at will.

Yet, ever and anon, from thy bright quiver,
The flaming arrows of thy might are strown;
And rushing forth, thy dauntless children shiver
The strength of foes who press too near thy throne.
Then, like the sun, or thy Almighty Giver,
Thy light is through the startled nations shown;
And generous indignation tramples down
The sophist's web, and the oppressor's crown.

Oh! might it burn for ever!  But in vain—
For vengeance rallies the alarmed host,
Who from men's souls draw their dishonest gain.
For thee they smite, audaciously they boast,
Even while thy sons are in thy bosom slain.
Yet this is thy sure solace—that not lost,
Each drop of blood, each tear,—Cadmean seed,
Shall send up armed champions at thy need.

1827.                                                    W. H.

# ADVERTISEMENT.

This little work is a rapid attempt to present a concise and concentrated view of universal Priestcraft, to assist and strengthen the present disposition to abate that nuisance in England. Had time been allowed, it would have been easy to have worked it up into a most luminous whole, and to have drawn upon many other sources; but what I have here collected from the best authorities, and said from the impulse of my own mind, I think will be sufficient to establish any disinterested person in the conviction, that priestcraft is one of the greatest curses which has afflicted the earth; and in the persuasion, that till its hydra heads are crushed there can be no perfect liberty.

There may be some who will differ from me as to the theory of Bryant—but that does not affect the main question. Whether the Arkite theory be correct or not, nothing is more certain than that Paganism had one common origin, and that that origin lies far back in the early ages of the world. Nothing is more certain than that priests have, in all ages, followed one system—that of availing themselves of the superstitions of the people for their own interested motives; and nothing better attested than the crimes and delusions of that order of men treated of in this volume.

There will be some who will exclaim when I come to the English Church, oh! the author is a dissenter!—I am a dissenter; and therefore, as a looker-on, according to a favourite popular maxim, am likely to have a truer view of the game than they who are playing it. I am a dissenter; and one of the most sturdy, and ceremony-despising class; and therefore, having deserted " the beggarly elements" of state creeds, am more anxious to release my fellow-men from the thraldom of state priests. I am a dissenter; and therefore, feeling the burden and the injustice of being compelled to support a system whose utility I deny, and whose corruptions need little labour of proof, I have the greater reason to raise my voice against it.

I am aware that I shall experience abundance of abuse and hostility; but that is the certain fate of every one who defends the truth. I only say—" Fiat justitia ruat cœlum :" and I thank God that I never yet paused to ask what is *politic*, but what is *right*. I thank God, too, that neither fearing one class of men, nor hoping aught from another, my only motive has been, justice to all, and kindness to the poor,—my only object, the spread of truth and knowledge;—and as for the result—let that be as it may.

*Nottingham, June 4th,* 1833.

# CONTENTS.

### CHAPTER I.

THE two Evil Principles, Kingcraft and Priestcraft, co-eval in their origin—Innumerable Historians of the one, but none singly and entirely of the other—The real and monstrous Character of Priestcraft—Evil Systems attacked in this work without mercy, but not Men - - - - - - - 1

### CHAPTER II.

Paganism distinguished universally by the same great leading Principles—supposed to originate in the corruption of the Patriarchal Worship soon after the Flood—Probable diffusion of Original Population—Origin of the Doctrine of Three Gods, in Greece, Egypt, Persia, Syria, among the Tartars, Chinese, Goths, Americans, etc.—Of the Preservation of the Ark in the Religious Ceremonies of all Pagan Nations—Of the Doctrine of a Succession of Worlds, and of a Deluge—Ancient Mysteries celebrated, especially by the Greeks, Egyptians, Hindoos, and Druids—Advantage taken by Priests of this great system of Superstition - - - - 5

### CHAPTER III.

Mythology of the Assyrians and Syrians—the horrors of Moloch—Chemosh—Baal and Baal-Fires—Bryant's Theory of the Cuthic Tribes agrees with the existence of Castes in all Pagan Nations—Spirit of the Syrian Priests as shewn in the Jewish History—Vile Deceptions of Priests—The Wife of the God—Priestly Arts exposed by Daniel - - - 12

## CHAPTER IV.

Page

The same system of Superstition and Priestcraft which prevailed in Asia, existing also among the Celts and Goths of ancient Europe—Every where the Priests the dominant Caste—In Britain, Gaul, and Germany their state shewn by Cæsar and Tacitus—The Notions, Sacrifices, and Superstitions of Scandinavia. - - 20

## CHAPTER V.

The same system discovered, to the surprise of the learned, in America—The Gods, Doctrines, and Practices of the Northern Indians, Mexicans, and Peruvians—Dominance of the Priests and Nobles, and Slavery of the People—their bloody Sacrifices and fearful Orgies, similar to those of the Asiatics—The amazing number of their Human Sacrifices recorded by the Spanish writers—Striking Picture of Priestcraft in Southey's Madoc. - - - - - - 31

## CHAPTER VI.

The Priest-ridden condition of Egypt notorious—involved in the same system of Priestcraft already noticed—Dr. Robertson's Theory of the Uniformity of Pagan Creeds insufficient, and why—Egyptian Superstitions—Excessive Veneration of Animals, and consequent singular Rites and Facts—Horrid and licentious Customs—Policy of their Priests to conceal Knowledge from the People—place themselves above the Nobles and even the Kings—regulate all the daily actions of the Kings—Striking Illustrations of the verity of the Greek accounts in the History of Joseph—Priests supposed to have been sole Kings in Egypt for ages. - - - - - - 45

## CHAPTER VII.

The popular Theology of the Greeks—Another and more Occult Theology—Effect of the Poetry of Homer on the spirits of his countrymen—his noble Maxims—Priestcraft compelled to adopt a nice policy by the free spirit of the Greeks; yet bloody and licentious Rites introduced, and the people effectually enslaved by means of Festivals, Games, Sacrifices, Oracles, Augury, and Mysteries—The immense influence of

Oracles—Description of the Mysteries—Description of the Egyptian darkness with respect to them—Taliesin's allusions to them—Priestly Avarice - 54

## CHAPTER VIII.

India—Priestcraft in its boldest aspect—Doctrines, Sacrifices, and licentious Rites—Women of the Temple—Immense Wealth accumulated by the Brahmins—seized by the Arabians—Mahmoud of Gazna—his Feast at Canaugha — his Adventure at the Temple of Sumnaut—Eternal Slavery stamped by the Brahmins on the Hindoos by the institution of Castes—Inviolable Sanctity and Immunities of the Brahmins—The Sooders—The Chandelahs—Remarks 74

## CHAPTER IX.

The Hebrews—Comparison of the Old Man of the Sea, and the Old Man of the Church—The Hebrew Priesthood the only one ever divinely ordained, yet evil in its tendency, and fatal to the Nation—began in Aaron in dastardly equivocation—shewed itself in the Sons of Eli, in avarice and lewdness—and finally crucified Christ - - - - - 94

## CHAPTER X.

POPERY—Christ and Christianity—the latter speedily corrupted—Acts by which the Papal Church seized on power - - - - - - 100

## CHAPTER XI.

POPERY CONTINUED: Struggles of the Popes for power—The Emperors favour them on account of their influence with the People—Scandalous transactions between them and the French monarchs—Pepin and Charlemagne—Gregory VII., the notorious Hildebrand, asserts absolute power over Kings—his intercourse with the Countess Matilda — claims the right of installing Bishops—Further enormities of the Popes—This example followed by the Bishops and Clergy, who become Dukes and Nobles—Evil influence of Councils - - - - - 110

## CHAPTER XII.

Establishment of Monkery—Numbers and enormities of the Monks—are the Spies and Champions of Popery—their quarrels—Strange History of Jetzer—Frauds—some gross ones practised in England—Maid of Kent—Pilgrimage of Grace—Forgery of the Decretals—Infinite modes of enslaving the Popular Mind—Relics, Pilgrimages, Crusades, Festivals, Confessions, Purgatory, Pardons, Mass, Excommunications, Inquisition, etc.—Treatment of learned Men - - - - - - - - - - 121

## CHAPTER XIII.

POPISH ARROGANCE AND ATROCITIES: The Pope proclaims himself Lord of the Universe—his Treatment of Dandolo, of Frederick Barbarossa, and of Henry IV.—sets up and dethrones Kings—Imitated by the Clergy—Thomas à Becket—King John's Humiliation—PAPAL ATROCITIES: Galileo—Massacres of Protestants in the Netherlands—Massacre of St. Bartholomew—Bloody Persecutions of the Vaudois—War of Extermination waged by the Pope in Provence—Extinction of the Troubadours—Noble Conduct of the young Count of Bezeirs—Rise of the Inquisition - - - - - - - 136

## CHAPTER XIV.

Jesuits and Inquisitors—Pernicious Doctrines of the Jesuits—Hudibras's Exposition of such Doctrines—Loyola their founder, sets up, under the name of General, another sort of Pope—The success of his Plans—General Character and Progress of the Jesuits—their Mercantile Concerns—their Conduct in China—in Paraguay—in the European Countries—attempts on the Lives of Queen Elizabeth and James I.—their Murder of Henry III. and Henry IV. of France—The Inquisition—Introduced into most Catholic Countries, but permanent in Spain—The Atrocities of the Spanish Inquisition against the Jews, Moors, and Lutherans—Excessive Power of the Inquisitors—Cromwell's Threat—Limborch's Account of the Proceedings of the Inquisition—Tortures—

Auto-da-fé described by Dr. Geddes — Suppression of the Inquisition by Napoleon—its restoration by Ferdinand—Present state of Catholic Countries - 150

## CHAPTER XV.

ENGLISH CHURCH — Unfortunate circumstances under which the Reformation began in England—Regal power fatal to Religion—Arbitrary conduct of the Tudors—Inquisition established in England under the names of the Star Chamber and High Commission Court—Popish bias of Elizabeth—her completion of the Liturgy—Despotism of the Stuarts—their Persecutions in England and Scotland—The arbitrary spirit of Laud conducts himself and Charles I. to the block—Laud's fondness for Popish Mummery—His singular Consecration of St. Catherine's Church — Heterogeneous materials of the English Church, and consequent Schisms—it continues to persecute till the Accession of William III.—Hopeless and unalterable nature of State Religion—State of the Clergy - - - - - - - 178

## CHAPTER XVI.

Ministerial Plan of Irish Church Reform—See of Derry — Statements respecting the Irish Church — its Revenues—Results of State Religion in Ireland—English Church—Injustice of compelling Dissenters to support the Establishment—Tithes—Inalterable nature of State Religions—Curious Anecdotes—Milton's opinion of a Stipendiary Clergy—Remarks 199

## CHAPTER XVII.

Clerical Income—Salaries of the Bishops—Exposure of the Abuse of Queen Anne's Bounty Fund, by the Edinburgh Review—Instances of the continuance of these Abuses—Pluralities, and Curates' Stipends—The Universities—Milton's opinion of College Education—Ecclesiastical Courts—Sir David Lindsey's Satire on them—Absurdity of the popular Belief in the Consecration of Burial Grounds—Fees of Consecration—Awkward facts respecting Family Vaults —Instance of Prelatical Despotism - - - 216

## CHAPTER XVIII.

Evils of the system of Church Patronage—Simony, and almost all the Abuses in the Church flow from it—Strange Defence of the Church by a Clergyman—Proofs of the beneficial effects of moderate Clerical Incomes—Scotch and German Clergy—False notions of Gentility held by our Clergy—Decker's Declaration that Christ was a true Gentleman—What Clergymen might be—Instances of what they are under the private Patronage system—Milton and Spelman's opinions of Surplice Fees - - - - - 245

## CHAPTER XIX.

Confirmation in the Country—its Picturesque and Poetical Appearance—its Licentious Consequences, arising from the Apathy of the Clergy - - - - 261

## CHAPTER XX.

Retrospective View of the Effects of Priestcraft—The great Moral and Political Lesson it teaches—Concluding Remarks - - - - - 270

# PRIESTCRAFT IN ALL AGES.

## CHAPTER I.

### GENERAL VIEW OF PRIESTCRAFT.

THIS unfortunate world has been blasted in all ages by two evil principles—Kingcraft and Priestcraft—that, taking advantage of human necessities, in themselves not hard—salutary, and even beneficial in their natural operation—the necessity of civil government, and that of spiritual instruction, have warped them cruelly from their own pure direction, and converted them into the most odious, the most terrible and disastrous scourges of our race. These malign powers have ever begun, as it were, at the wrong end of things. Kingcraft, seizing upon the office of civil government, not as the gift of popular choice, and to be filled for the good of nations, but with the desperate hand of physical violence, has proclaimed that it was not made for man, but man for it—that it possessed an inherent and divine right to rule, to trample upon mens' hearts, to violate their dearest rights, to scatter their limbs and their blood at its pleasure upon the earth; and, in return for its atrocities, to be worshipped on bended knee, and hailed as a god. Its horrors are on the face of every nation; its annals are written in gore in all civilized climes; and, where pen never was known, it has scored its terrors in the hearts of millions, and left its traces in deserts of everlasting desolation, and in the ferocious spirits of abused and brutalized hordes. What is all the history of this wretched planet but a mass of its bloody wrath and detestable oppressions, whereby it has converted earth into a hell; men into the worst of demons; and has turned the human mind from its natural pursuit of knowledge, and virtue, and social happiness, into a career of blind rage, bitter and foolish prejudices; an entailment of awful and crime-creating ignorance; and has held the universal soul of man in the blackest and most pitiable of bondage? Countless are its historians; we need not add one more to the unavailing catalogue: but, of

> That sister-pest, congrégator of slaves
> Into the shadow of its pinions wide,

I do not know that there has been one man who has devoted himself solely and completely to the task of tracing its course of demoniacal devastation. Many of its fiendish arts and exploits, undoubtedly, are embodied in what is called ecclesiastical history; many are presented to us in the chronicles of kingcraft; for the two evil powers have ever been intimately united in their labours. They have mutually and lovingly supported each other; knowing that individually they are "weak as stubble," yet conjointly,

> Can bind
> Into a mass irrefragably firm
> The axes and the rods which awe mankind.

Thus, through this pestilential influence, we must admit that too much of its evil nature has been forced on our observation incidentally; but no one clear and complete picture of it has been presented to our view. It shall now be my task to supply to the world this singular desideratum. It shall be my task to shew that priestcraft in all ages and all nations has been the same; that its nature is one, and that nature essentially evil; that its object is self-gratification and self-aggrandizement; the means it uses—the basest frauds, the most shameless delusions, practised on the popular mind for the acquisition of power; and that power once gained, the most fierce and bloody exercise of it, in order to render it at once awful and perpetual. I shall shew that nothing is so servilely mean in weakness, so daring in assumption, so arrogant in command,— earth, heaven, the very throne and existence of God himself being used but as the tools of its designs, and appealed to with horrible impudence in the most shameless of its lies. That, professing itself merciful, nothing on this earth, which is by no means wanting in scenes of terror, has ever exhibited itself in shapes of equal cruelty—cruelty, cold, selfish, and impasable; that, claiming sanctity as its peculiar attribute, nothing has been so grossly debauched and licentious; that, assuming the mien of humility, nothing is so impiously proud, so offensively insolent; that, proclaiming to others the utter vanity of worldly goods, its cupidity is insatiable—of worldly honours, its ambition is boundless; that, affecting peace and purity, it has perpetrated the most savage wars, ay, in the very name of heaven, and spread far and wide the contagion of sensuality; that, in Europe, usurping the chair of knowledge, the office of promulgating the doctrines of a religion whose very nature overflows with freedom, and love, and liberal enlightenment, it has locked up the human mind for more than a thousand years in the dens of ignorance; mocked it with the vilest baubles, the most imbecile legends;

made it a prey to all the restless and savage passions of an uncultured and daily irritated soul; robbed it of the highest joys of earth or heaven—those of the exercise of a perfected intellect and a benevolent spirit; and finally, by its tyrannies, its childish puerilities, its inane pomps and most ludicrous dogmas, overwhelmed the middle ages with the horrors of an iron bigotry, and the modern world with the tenfold horrors of infidel heartlessness and the wars of atheism.

This is a mighty and an awful charge. Alas! the annals of all people are but too affluent in proofs of its justice. I shall prove this through the most popular histories, that the general reader may, if he please, easily refer to them, and be satisfied of the correctness of my statements. While I proceed, however, to draw these proofs from the most accessible works, I shall carefully war alone with the principle, not with individual men. The very worst systems have often involved in their blind intricacies the best of men: and in some of those which it will be my duty, as a man, to denounce, there have been, and there are at the present moment, numbers of sincere and excellent beings, who are an honour and a blessing to their race.

## CHAPTER II.

ORIGIN OF PAGANISM.

PRIESTCRAFT and kingcraft began at pretty much the same time, and that at an early age of the world, to exercise their baneful influence over it. Whether they existed, and if so, what they did, in the antediluvian world, we know not, and it concerns us little: but immediately after the flood, they became conspicuous. Nimrod is usually supposed to be the first monarch; the first man who, not satisfied with the mild patriarchal rule over his brethren, is believed to have collected armies, dispossessed the peaceful children of Shem of part of their territories by violence, and swayed all whom he could by the terrors of overwhelming force. Priestcraft, it is evident by many indubitable signs, was busily at work at the same moment. Certain common principles running through idolatrous worship in every known part of the globe, have convinced the most acute and industrious antiquarians, that every pagan worship in the world has the same origin; and that origin could have coincided only with some early period, when the whole human family was together in one place. This fact, now that countries, their habits and opinions, have been so extensively examined, would have led learned men of the present day, had not the Bible been in our possession, to the confident conclusion that mankind had, at first, but one source, and one place of abode: that their religious opinions had been at that time uniform: and that, dispersing from that point of original residence, they had carried these opinions into all regions of the earth, where, through the progress of ages, they had received many modifications, been variously darkened and disfigured, but not to such an extent as to extinguish those great leading features which mark them as the offspring of one primeval parent. But the Bible not only shews that such was the origin of the various human families, not only shews the time when they dwelt in one place, when and how they were thence dispersed, but also furnishes us with a certain key to the whole theory of universal paganism.

We see at once that every system of heathen mythology had its origin in the corruption of patriarchal worship before the dispersion at Babel. There the whole family of man was collected in the descendants of Noah's three sons, Shem, Ham, and Japhat; and thence, at that time, they were scattered abroad by the hand of God over the world. Japhat colonized the whole of Europe; all those northern regions called Tartary and Siberia; and, in process of time, by the easy passage of Behring's Straits, the entire continent of America. His son Gomer seems clearly to have been the father of those who were originally called Gomerians; and by slight variations, were afterwards termed Comarians, Cimmerians, Cymbri, Cumbri, Cambri, and Umbri; and, in later years, Celts, Gauls, and Gaels. These extended themselves over the regions north of Armenia and Bactriana; thence over nearly all Europe, and first planted Britain and Ireland. Magog, Tubal, and Mesech, as we learn from Ezekiel, dwelt far to the north of Judea, and became the ancestors of the great Sclavonic or Sarmatian families; the name of Magog still existing in the appellations of Mogli, Monguls, and

Mongolians; those of Tubal and Mesech, in Tobolski, Moschici, and Moscow and Moscovites: Madai was father of the Medes, and Javan of the original inhabitants of Greece, where we may trace the names of his sons Elishah, Tarshish, Kittim, and Dodanim, in Elis, Tarsus, Cittium, and Dodona.

The posterity of Shem were confined to southern Asia; founding by his sons Elam, or Persia, Ashur, or Assyria, a province of Iran, or Great Assyrian empire of Nimrod, whose son Cush appears to have subdued these descendants of Shem. Arphaxad became the father of the Hebrews and other kindred nations; his descendant Peleg founded Babylonia; and Joktan, stretching far towards the east, probably became the father of the Hindoos. Ophir, one of the sons of Joktan, is often mentioned in Scripture as dwelling in a land of gold, to which voyages were made by ships issuing from the Red Sea, and sailing eastward; but Elam and Cush occupied the whole sea-coast of Persia, as far as the Indus. This, therefore, brings us to the great peninsular of Hindostan for the seat of Ophir. Lud, the fourth son of Shem, is presumed to be the founder of Lydia; and Aram, the fifth, the father of Mesopotamia and Syria.

Ham was at first mixed with Shem throughout southern Asia, and became the sole occupant of Africa. Of his sons, Cush became the founder of Iran, or Central Asia, the great Assyrian empire, and the progenitor of all those called Cushim, Cushas, Cuths, Goths, Scuths, Scyths, Scots, or Gauls. Mizraim peopled Egypt; Phut, the western frontier of Egypt, and thence passing west and south, spread over the greater part of Africa: and Canaan, it is well known, peopled the tract afterwards inhabited by the Israelites.

Thus, it is said, was the world peopled; and that

it was thus peopled, we learn not only from Moses, but from profane writers; and find both accounts confirmed by abundant evidence in the manners, traditions, language, and occupance of the different races at the present day. Sir William Jones found only three great original languages to exist—Arabic, Sclavonic, and Sanscrit: and these three all issue from one point, central Asia, whence, by consent of the most ancient records and traditions of the great primeval nations, their original ancestors spread.

But before they were thus scattered, they had corrupted the religious doctrines they had received from their great progenitor, Noah; or rather, had set them aside, in order to deify Noah and his three sons, whom they had come to regard as a re-appearance of Adam and his three sons, Cain, Abel, and Seth. The singular coincidence of circumstances between Adam and Noah, forced this upon their imaginations. Adam, the first man, and father of the first world,—and Noah, the first man, and father of the second world, had each three sons conspicuous in history; and of these three, one in each case was a bad one—Cain and Ham. Led by this, to consider the second family but an avater of the first, they regarded them as immortal, and worshipped them. Hence we have in all pagan mythologies a triad of principal gods. In the Greek—Jupiter, Neptune, and Pluto; in the Hindoo—Brahma, Vishnu, and Siva; in the Egyptian—Osiris, Horus, and Typhon; one of whom, in each case, is a deity of a dark nature, like Cain and Ham. The Persians had their Ormuzd, Mithras, and Ahriman; the Syrians, their Monimus, Aziz, and Ares; the Canaanites, their Baal-Shalisha, or self-triplicated Baal; the Goths, their Odin, Vile, and Ve, who are described as the three sons of the mysterious cow, a symbol of the ark; the Jakuthi

Tartars, their Artugon, Schugo-teugon, and Tangara, the last, even in name, the Tanga-tanga of the Peruvians: for this singular fact stops not with the great primitive nations; it extends itself to all others, even to those discovered in modern times. Like China and Japan, the Peruvians were found, on the discovery of America, to have their triads, Apomti, Churunti, and Intiquoaqui; or the father-sun, the brother-sun, and the son-sun. The Mexicans had also their Mexitli, Tlaloc, and Tezcallipuca; the last, the god of repentance. The Virginians, Iroquois, and various nations of North-American Indians, held similar notions. The New Zealanders believe that three gods made the first man, and the first woman from the man's rib; and their general term for bone is Eve. The Otaheitans had a similar idea.

Thus, far and wide, to the very hidden ends of the earth, spread this notion of a triad; and hence, in the second century, it found its way, through Justin Martyr, into the Christian church.

The post-diluvians likewise held the Ark in the most sacred veneration. It was that into which their great father and all living things had entered and floated away safely over the destroying waters. It was the type of the earth into which Adam had entered by death; and, as they supposed, re-appeared in Noah. Hence, an ark is to be found in nearly every system of pagan worship. After it were fashioned the most ancient temples. It was borne in the most religious processions of Osiris, Adonis, Bacchus, Ceres, and amongst the Druids; and has been found, to the astonishment of discoverers and missionaries, amongst the Mexicans, the North-American Indians, and the South-sea Islanders.

Hence, also, the doctrine of a succession of worlds, from the supposed re-appearance of Adam and his three sons, in Noah and his three sons, which has expanded itself into the great system of transmigrations and avaters of the Hindoos. Hence, also, the traditions of a universal deluge to be found amongst all the ancient nations; amongst the wild tribes of America; amongst the Hindoos in the east, and the Celts in the west. Hence, the close connexion of lakes with heathen temples; and hence, lastly, the ancient mysteries, which were but a symbolical representation of entering the ark, or great cave of death and life; which, as the old world was purified by the flood, was supposed to purify and confer a new life on those who passed through those mysteries, which were celebrated, with striking similarity in Greece, India, Egypt, and amongst the Druids in these islands. These, and many other general features of paganism—for abundant illustration of which, I refer my reader to the learned works of Calmet, Bryant, Faber, and Spencer, De Legibus Ritualibus Hebræorum—sufficiently testify to the common origin of all heathen systems of worship; and we shall presently find how amply the priests of all ages and all the Gentile nations, have laid hold on these rich materials, and converted them into exuberant sources of wealth, and power, and honour to themselves, and of terror, deception, and degradation to their victims—the people.

It may, perhaps, be said that they themselves were but the slaves of superstition, in common with those they taught; and that it would be unfair to charge them with the wilful misleading of their auditors, when they themselves were blinded by the common delusions of their times and countries. But we must recollect, that though the people were taught by them to believe, and could not, in dark times, easily escape the influence of their doctrines and practices, studiously adapted to dazzle and deceive the senses, yet it was impossible for the priests to enter upon their office, without discovering that those terrors were fictitious,—without finding that they were called upon to maintain a series of utter fallacies. The people might listen to oracles, uttered amid a multitude of imposing pageants, and awful solemnities; in the sacred gloom of temples and groves; and might really believe that a god spoke. But where were the priests? Behind these scenes!—and must soon have found that, instead of the inspiration of a present god, they themselves were the actors of the vilest impositions; which, through the temptations of power, and fame, and wealth, they became the willing means of fixing on their countrymen.

When did any one, in any nation, on discovering that he had entered an order of impostors, renounce their connexion, and abandon his base calling? Never!—the spirit of priestcraft was too subtly potent for him. He either acquiesced readily in measures, which were to him, pregnant with honour, ease, and abundance; or saw that instant destruction awaited him, from the wily and merciless spirit of priestcraft, if he gave but a symptom of abjuring, or disclosing its arcana of gainful deceit. As the entrance of the Adytus of the mysteries, so the vestibule of the priestly office was probably guarded by naked swords, and oaths full of destruction to the backslider. Be that as it may, there is not a fact on the face of history more conspicuous than this—that no order of men has ever clung to the service of its caste, or has fulfilled its purposes, however desperate, or infamously cruel they might be, with the same fiery and unflinching zeal as priests.

## CHAPTER III.

MYTHOLOGY OF THE ASSYRIANS AND SYRIANS.

We have now seen how idolatry was diffused over the globe, forming a field of no less amplitude than the world itself for priestcraft to exercise itself in; full of ignorance, and full of systems prolific in all the wild creation of superstition so auspicious to priestly desires; and we shall soon see that such advantages were not neglected by that evil power, but were eagerly laid hold on, and by its indefatigable activity the earth was speedily overrun by every curse, and horror, and pollution, that can fix itself on unfortunate humanity.

We shall take a hasty survey of its progress in the most ancient nations, Syria and Assyria; we shall then pass rapidly into Scandinavia and the British Isles, following the course of Druidism; and, without regard to the order of time, glance at the confirmation of this ancient state of things, by that which was found to exist at the time of their discovery in America and the isles of the Indian Ocean. By this plan we shall leave our course clear in a direct progress through ancient Egypt, Greece, and Hindostan; where we shall leave the review of priestcraft as it existed in Paganism, and contemplate its aspect in Judea, under the direct ordinances of God; then, under Christianity, in the Romish church; and, finally, in the ecclesiastical establishment of our own country.

The Bible furnishes us with abundant evidences of what idolatry was in Syria, and the neighbouring kingdoms of Philistia, Moab, Amalek and others. The principal gods of these countries were Baal, Moloch, and Chemosh: but the number of false gods altogether was extremely numerous. The more gods the more shrines, the more priestly gains and influence. The principal characteristics of the whole idol dynasty, were horrible cruelty and gross licentiousness. Chemosh was the god of the Moabites, and his rites were particularly distinguished by their lasciviousness. In Syria those of Ashtaroth, or Astarte, the queen of heaven, were similar; but Baal and Moloch were the very impersonations of savage atrocity. Moloch is represented as a huge metallic image in a sitting posture, which, on days of sacrifice, was heated to redness in a pit of fire, and young children were brought as victims, and placed in his extended and burning arms, where they were consumed in the most exquisite agonies, while the devilish band of priests and their retainers drowned their piercing cries with the stunning din of drums, cymbals, horns, and trumpets.

Baal, however, was the principal idol of all those countries; and—associated as he was in idea with the sun, as was the chief god of all pagan nations, from a fanciful process of imagination, treated of at large by writers on this subject, but which we need not trace here—to him, on almost every lofty eminence, fires were kindled at stated periods, and human sacrifices performed in the midst of unbounded and infernal glee. The Beal-fires, or Baal-fires, kindled on the mountains of Scotland and Ireland by the peasantry at Beltane, or May Eve, are the last remains of this most ancient and universal superstition.

When we recollect over what an immense extent of country, in fact over the greater part of the habitable globe, this idolatry extended; and the number of ages, from the time of the flood to the time of Christianity, a period of upwards of two thousand years; what a terrible sum of miseries must have been inflicted on our race by the diabolical zeal and cupidity of pagan priestcraft. From the temple of Buddh and Jaggernath in India, to the stony circles of Druidism in Europe; from the snowy wastes of Siberia and Scandinavia in the north, to the most southern lands in Africa and America, the fires of these bloody deities rejoiced the demoniac priests and consumed the people.

Mr. Bryant contends, and his theory seems both supported by strong facts and is generally admitted by intelligent historians, that the kindred of Nimrod, the tribe of Cush, a haughty and dominant race, disdaining labour or commerce, disdaining all professions but those of arms or the priesthood, followed the progress of diffusive population into all regions, and either subduing the original settlers or insinuating themselves amongst them, as they had been their general corruptors, became their generals, priests, and kings. This theory certainly agrees well with what the researches of late years have made known of the great tribes of emigration from the east; agrees well with what we know of the Gothic or Cuthic nations, and with the establishment of the despotism of the feudal system. Castes, which remain so unbroken to the present day in Hindostan, and on which we shall have presently to remark, prevailed, in a greater or less degree, all over the world. In Egypt, Herodotus shews it to have been the case. None but kings and priests were noble. In Greece they had their race of demi-gods, or descendants of the ancient Pelasgi, or Cuthites, from whom their priests, augurs, and kings were chosen. Such was the case amongst the Gauls and Britons. The Druids were a sacred and noble caste, who disdained to work or mingle with the people; an insult to one of whom was instant death, as it is with the Brahmins at the present day : and the strong spirit of caste throughout all the feudal nations of Europe, not only all past history, but present circumstances, shew us. Be the origin of dominant castes what it may, nothing is more conspicuous than their existence, and the evils, scorns, and ignominious burdens they have heaped upon the people.

Of the rancorous activity of the heathen priesthood to proselyte and extend their influence on all sides, the Jewish history is full. Scarcely had the Hebrews escaped from Egypt and entered the Desert, when the Moabites came amongst them with their harlot daughters, carrying beneath their robes the images of Chemosh, and scattering among the frail Jews the mingled fires of sensual and idolatrous passion. Through the whole period of the administration of the Judges, they were indefatigably at work, and brought upon the backsliding Hebrews the vengeance of their own living and indignant God. The wise and magnificent Solomon they plucked from the height of his peerless knowledge and glory, and rendered the reigns of his successors continual scenes of reproof and desolation, till the whole nation was swept into captivity.

There cannot be a more expressive instance of the daring hardihood and fanatic zeal of the priests of Baal, nor a finer one of their defeat and punishment, than that given on Mount Carmel in the days of Ahab and Jezebel. Those pestilential wretches had actually, under royal patronage, corrupted or destroyed the whole legitimate priesthood. There were but left seven thousand, even of the people, " who had not bowed the knee to Baal, nor kissed him." They were in pursuit of the noble prophet himself, when he came forth and challenged them to an actual proof of the existence of their respective deities.

It may be argued that the readiness with which they accepted this challenge, is sufficient evidence that they themselves were believers in the existence of their deity; and it may be that some were stupid, or fanatic enough to be so; but it is far likelier that, possessing royal patronage, and a whole host of base and besotted supporters, they hoped to entrap the solitary man: that, knowing the emptiness of their own pretensions, they were of opinion that Elijah's were equally empty, and therefore came boldly to a contest, in which if neither party won, an individual against a host would easily be sacrificed to priestly fury and popular credulity. Be it as it might, nothing is more certain than that the ferocious zeal of priestcraft, for its own objects, has been in all ages so audacious as not to fear rushing, in the face of the world, on the most desperate attempts. This event was most illustrative of this blind sacerdotal hardihood; for, notwithstanding their signal exposure and destruction, yet in every successive age of the Hebrew kingdom, the pagan priests ceased not to solicit the Israelites to their ruin. The Hebrew kings, ever and anon, awoke from the trance of delusion into which they drew them, and executed ample vengeance; hewing down their groves, and overturning their altars; but it was not till the general captivity,—till Judah was humbled for a time, before Babylon, and Israel was wholly and for ever driven from the land, that the pest was annihilated.

The mythology of Assyria was of much the same nature;—Baal, however, being there held in far higher honour than all other gods; for the priesthood, according to the servile cunning of its policy, had flattered the royal house by deifying its founder, and identifying him with the sun by the name of Belus, or Bel. What I have already said of this god will suffice; and I shall only state that, as the priesthood there had shewn its usual character of adulation to the high, and cruelty to the low, so it displayed almost more than its customary lewdness. Herodotus tells us, that " at the top of the tower of Belus, in a chapel, is placed a couch magnificently adorned: and near it a table of solid gold; but there is no statue in the place. No man is suffered to sleep here, but a female occupies the apartment, whom the Chaldean priests affirm their deity selects from the whole nation as the object of his pleasures. They declare that their deity enters this apartment by night, and reposes upon this couch. A similar assertion is made by the Egyptians of Thebes; for in the interior part of the temple of the Thebean Jupiter, a woman, in like manner, sleeps. Of these two women, it is presumed, that neither of them have any communication with the other sex. In which predicament, the priestess of the temple of Pateræ, in Lycia, is also placed. Here is no regular oracle; but whenever a divine communication is expected, the woman is obliged to pass the preceding night in the temple." That is, the priests made their god the scape-goat of their own unbridled sensuality; and, under the pretext of providing a sacrifice of beauty to the deity, selected the most lovely woman of the nation for themselves.

This species of detestable deception, seems to have been carried on to an enormous extent in ancient times. If we are to believe all the Grecian stories, and especially the Homeric ones, of the origin of their demi-gods, we can only explain them in this manner. A circumstance of the same nature is related by Josephus; which is curious, because the priests of the temple in that case, were induced by a young noble to inveigle a married lady of whom he had become enamoured, into the temple, under pretence that the god had a loving desire of her company, and shewed that the gratification, not merely of themselves, but of men in power, by frauds, however infamous or diabolical, has been always a priestly practice.

But to return to Assyria. The seeds of licentiousness, sown by their early priests, grew and spread abundantly in after ages. When the Assyrian was merged in the Babylonian empire, the orgies of the temple of Mylitta, the Babylonian Venus, were infamous above all others; so much so, that every woman, whether high or low, was bound by the national practice to present herself before the temple once in her life, and there submit to prostitute herself with whoever first chose her; and the price of her shame was paid into the treasury, to swell the revenues of the priests. So horrible a fact has been doubted; but Herodotus seriously asserts it, and it has been confirmed by other authorities.

That these crafty and voluptuous priests were not amongst those deceived by their own devices, but were solely deceivers, living in honour and abundance by juggling the people, we need no better testimony than that of the story of Bel and the Dragon. They are there represented as setting before the idol splendid banquets, which he was asserted to devour in the night; but Daniel scattering sand on the floor, shewed the people in the morning the footsteps of the priests, their wives and children, who had, as they were regularly accustomed, flocked into the temple at night, and helped the god to dispatch his viands.

Though this story is one of those called apocryphal, it is certainly so far true, that it shews what were the opinions of the wise at that day, of the priests, founded, no doubt, on sufficient observation.

## CHAPTER IV.

### CELTS AND GOTHS.

WITHOUT following minutely the progress of original migration, from east to west, through the great Scythian deserts, we will now at once open upon the human family as it appeared in Europe, when the Romans began to extend their conquests into the great forests and wild lands of its north-western regions: and here, again, we behold with surprise, how exactly the nations had preserved those features of idolatrous superstition which I have before stated to be universal, and which we have been contemplating in central Asia.

Part of southern Europe appears to have been peopled by one great branch of the descendants of Japhet, under the name of Sclavonians, and to have maintained their settlements against all future comers: but another great branch, the Gomerians, or Celts, had been followed by the warlike and domineering Goths, and had, in some cases, received from them teachers and governors; in others, had been totally expelled by them, or lost character, language, and every thing, in their overwhelming tide. The northern parts of Britain, Ireland, Wales, Gaul, and some other districts, retained the Celtic character; while England, Scandinavia, Germany, Belgium, and some other tracts, became decidedly Gothic. Of these facts, the very languages of the respective countries, at the present day, remain living proofs. But, whatever was the name, the language, or the government of the different parts of Europe, everywhere its religion was essentially the same; everywhere the same Cuthic race of domineering priests. Everywhere, says a sagacious antiquarian, "we find, first, an order of priests; secondly, an order of military nobles; thirdly, a subjugated multitude; and institutions, the spirit of which, is that of thrusting the lower orders from all place and authority, and systematically dooming them to an unalterable state of servile depression." Whoever will examine the system of the Druids, as he may in Toland's history of them, in Borlace's Cornwall, or Davis's Celtic Mythology, will be perfectly convinced of its identity with that of Persia, Egypt, and Hindostan. Their triads, their own assumed sanctity of character, their worship of the god Hu, the Buddhu of the east; their traditions of the flood; the ark, which their circular stone temples symbolized; their human sacrifices; their doctrine of transmigration; and other abundant characteristics, are not to be mistaken. Dr. Borlace was so struck with the perfect resemblance of the Druids to the Persian Magi and the Indian Brahmins, that he declared it was impossible to doubt their identity. Mr. Rowland argues in the same manner with regard to the Irish Druids, who, as usual, constituted the first of the three classes into which the community was divided. He feels assured that they must have been Magi. Long indeed before our time, Pliny had made the same remark, applying the very term of Magi to them.

In Gaul, Cæsar found precisely the same state of things—the same dominant class; and has left so lucid an account of them, that his representation will, at once, place before us the actual condition of both Gaul and Britain. "Over all Gaul there are only two orders of men in any degree of honour and esteem: for the common people are little better than slaves; attempt nothing of themselves; and have no share in the public deliberations. As they are generally oppressed with debt, heavy tributes, or the exactions of their superiors, they make themselves vassals to the great, who exercise over them the same jurisdiction that masters do over slaves. The two orders of men with whom, as we have said, all authority and distinctions reside, are the Druids and nobles. The Druids preside in matters of religion, have the care of public and private sacrifices, and interpret the will of the gods. They have the direction and education of the youth, by whom they are held in great honour. In almost all controversies, whether public or private, the decision is left to them; and if any crime is committed, any murder perpetrated, if any dispute arises touching an inheritance, or the limits of adjoining estates, in all such cases they are supreme judges. They decree rewards and punishments; and if any one refuse to submit to their sentence, whether magistrate or private man, they interdict him the sacrifices. This is the greatest punishment that can be inflicted upon the Gauls; because, such as are under this prohibition, are considered as impious and wicked; all men shun them, and decline their conversation and fellowship, lest they should suffer from the contagion of their misfortunes. They can neither have recourse to the law for justice, nor are capable of any public office. The Druids are all under one chief. Upon his death, a successor is elected by suffrage; but sometimes they have recourse to arms before the election can be brought to issue. Once a year, they assemble at a consecrated place in the territories of the Carnutes, whose country is supposed to be in the middle of Gaul. Hither such as have any suits depending, flock from all parts, and submit implicitly to their decrees. Their institution is supposed to have come originally from Britain; and even at this day, such as are desirous of being perfect in it, travel thither for instruction. The Druids never go to war; are exempt from taxes and military service, and enjoy all manner of immunities. These mighty encouragements induce multitudes of their own accord to follow that profession, and many are sent by their parents. They are taught to repeat a great number of verses by heart, and often spend twenty years upon this institution; for it is deemed unlawful to commit their statutes to writing, though on other matters, private or public, they use Greek characters. They seem to have adopted this method for two reasons,—to hide their mysteries from the knowledge of the vulgar, and to exercise the memory of their scholars. It is one of their principal maxims, that the soul never dies, but after death, passes from one body to another. They teach likewise many things relative to the stars, the magnitude of the world and our earth, the nature of things, and the power and prerogative of the immortal gods.

"The other order of men is the nobles, whose study and occupation is war. Before Cæsar's arrival in Gaul, they were almost every year at war, offensive or defensive; and they judge of the power and quality of their nobles, by the vassals and number of men they keep in pay.

"The whole nation of the Gauls is extremely addicted to superstition, whence, in threatening distempers, and the imminent danger of war, they make no scruple to sacrifice men, or engage themselves by vow to such sacrifices; in which case, they make use of the ministry of the Druids; for it is a prevalent opinion amongst them, that nothing but the life of man can atone for the life of man, insomuch that they have established even public sacrifices of this kind. Some prepare huge Colossuses of osier twigs, into which they put men alive, and setting fire to them, those within expire amongst the flames. They prefer for victims such as have been convicted of theft, robbery, or other crimes, believing them the most acceptable to the gods: but when such are wanting, the innocent are made to suffer.

"The Gauls fancy themselves to be descended from the god Pluto, which, it seems, is an established tradition amongst the Druids; and for this reason they compute time by nights, not by days.

"The men have power of life and death over their wives and families; and when any father of a family of illustrious rank dies, his relations assemble, and upon the least ground of suspicion, put even his wives to the torture, like slaves. Their funerals are magnificent and sumptuous, according to their quality. Everything that was dear to the deceased, even animals, are thrown into the fire; and formerly, such of their slaves and clients that they loved most, sacrificed themselves at the funeral of their lords."

In this valuable account, the striking resemblance of the Druids to the Brahmins, must impress every one,—not the least their funeral rites, and doctrine of metempsychosis. But there are some other things equally curious. We have here the BAN,—that tremendous ecclesiastical engine, which the Romish church most probably borrowed of the Goths; and which we shall find it hereafter wielding to such appalling purpose. The tradition of the Druids, that they are descended of Pluto, is, too, a most remarkable circumstance; agreeing so perfectly with the theory of Bryant, that they were Cuths, the descendants of Ham, the Pluto of mythology.

Cæsar proceeds to give Roman names to Gallic gods. This was the common practice of the Romans; a fact, which, as it is known from other sources that the Druids never gave them such names, only proves that the Romans named them from their obvious attributes; again confirming Bryant's theory, that however the ethnic gods be named, they are essentially identical. Cæsar also adds, that the Germans differed widely from the Gauls, having no Druids, and troubling not themselves about sacrifices: but Tacitus, who is better evidence than Cæsar, where the Germans are concerned, assures us that they had priests and bards. That "jurisdiction is vested in the priests; it is theirs to sit in judgment on all offences. By them delinquents are put in irons, and chastised with stripes; the power of punishing is in no other hands." He adds, "to impress on their minds the idea of a tutelar deity, they carry with them to the field of battle certain images and banners, taken from their usual depositaries, the groves; and that one of these symbols was a ship—the emblem of Isis." This, from what we now know of mythologies, is a certain evidence of the eastern origin of their religion:—the ship being the ark, or ship of the world; and Isis, the great mother of all things, the earth. He assures us that they had also human sacrifices.

The last European country we will now notice, shall be Scandinavia. M. Mallet's most interesting antiquities of those regions were written before our eastern knowledge was so much enlarged, and before Mr. Bryant had promulgated his theory of the origin of paganism; and, therefore, when we come to open his volumes, we are proportionably astonished and delighted to find all the curious particulars he has collected of the Scandinavian gods and religious rites so absolutely confirmatory of that theory. Here again we have the same gods, under the different names of Odin, Thor, Loke, with Frigga or Frea, the goddess of the earth, the great mother. Here again we have the same dominant caste of priests reigning amid the same assemblage of horrors and pollution.

The priests, he says, of these inhuman gods were called Drottes, a name equivalent to Druids. They were frequently styled prophets, wise men, divine men. At Upsal, each of the three superior deities had their respective priests, the principal of whom to the number of twelve, presided over the sacrifices, and exercised an unlimited authority over every thing which seemed to have connexion with religion. The respect shewn to them was suitable to their authority. Sprung, for the most part, *from the same family*, like those of the Jews, they persuaded the people that this family had God himself for its founder. They often united the priesthood and the sovereignty in their own persons, after the example of Odin their progenitor. The goddess Frigga was usually served by kings' daughters, whom they called prophetesses and goddesses. These pronounced oracles; devoted themselves to perpetual virginity; and kept up the sacred fire in the temple. The power of inflicting pains and penalties, of striking and binding a criminal, was vested in the priests alone; and men so haughty that they thought themselves dishonoured if they did not revenge the slightest offence, would tremblingly submit to blows, and even death itself, from the hand of a pontiff, whom they took for the instrument of an angry deity. In short, the credulity of the people, and the craft and presumption of the priests went so far, that these pretended interpreters of the divine will, dared even to demand, in the name of heaven, the blood of kings themselves, and obtained it! To succeed in this, it was requisite only for them to avail themselves of those times of calamity, when the people, distracted with fear and sorrow, laid their minds open to the most horrid impressions. At these times, while the prince was slaughtered at one of the altars of the gods, the others were covered with the offerings, which were heaped up on all sides for their ministers.

But the general cause which regulated these sacrifices, was a superstitious opinion, which made the northern natives regard the number THREE as sacred and peculiarly dear to the gods. Thus every ninth month they renewed this bloody ceremony, which was to last nine days, and every day they offered up nine victims, whether men or animals. But the most solemn sacrifices were those which were offered at Upsal in Sweden, every ninth year. Then the king, the senate, and all the principal citizens were obliged to appear in person, and to bring offerings, which were placed in the great temple. Those who could not come, sent their presents by others, or paid their value in money to priests, whose business it was to receive the offerings. Strangers flocked there in crowds from all parts, and none were excluded except those whose honour was stained, and especially such as had been accused of cowardice. Then they chose amongst the captives, in time of war, and amongst the slaves in time of peace, nine persons to be sacrificed. The choice was partly regulated by the opinion of by-standers, and partly by lot. The wretches upon whom it fell were then treated with such honours by all the assembly; they were so overwhelmed with caresses for the present, and promises for the life to come, that they sometimes congratulated themselves on their destiny. But they did not always sacrifice such mean persons. In great calamities, in a pressing famine, for example, if the people thought they had some pretext to impute the cause of it to the king, they sacrificed him without hesitation, as the highest price they could pay for the divine favour. In this manner the first king of Vermland was burnt in honour of Odin, to put away a great dearth. The kings in their turn did not spare the blood of their people; and many of them even that of their children. Hacon, king of Norway, offered his son in sacrifice to obtain a victory over his enemy, Harold. Aune, king of Sweden, devoted to Odin the blood of his nine sons, to prevail on the god to prolong his life. The ancient history of the north abounds in similar examples.

These abominable sacrifices were accompanied with various ceremonies. When the victim was chosen, they conducted him towards the altar, where the sacred fire was kept burning night and day. It was surrounded by all sorts of iron and brazen vessels. Among them one was distinguished by its superior size; in this they received the blood of their victim. When they offered up animals, they speedily killed them at the foot of the altar; then they opened their entrails and drew auguries from them, as among the Romans: but when they sacrificed men, those they pitched upon were laid upon a large stone, and quickly strangled or knocked on the head. Sometimes they let out the blood, for no presage was more respected than that which they drew from the greater or less degree of impetuosity with which the blood gushed out. The bodies were afterwards burnt, or suspended in a sacred grove near the temple. Part of the blood was sprinkled upon the people, on the grove, on the idol, altar, benches and wall of the temple, within and without.

Sometimes the sacrifices were varied. There was a deep well in the neighbourhood of the temple; the chosen person was thrown headlong in, commonly in honour of Goya, or the earth. If it went at once to the bottom, it had proved agreeable to the goddess; if not, she refused it, and it was hung up in a sacred forest. Near the temple of Upsal there was a grove of this sort, every tree and every leaf of which was regarded as the most sacred thing in the world. This, which was named Odin's grove, was full of the bodies of men and animals which had been sacrificed. The temple at Upsal was as famous for its *oracles* as its sacrifices. There were also celebrated ones at Dalia, a province of Sweden, in Norway, and Denmark. It should seem that the idols of the gods themselves delivered the oracles *viva voce*. In an ancient Icelandic chronicle, we read of one Indred, who went from home to wait for Thorstein, his enemy. Thorstein, upon his arrival, went into the temple. In it was a stone, probably a statue, which he had been accustomed to worship. He prostrated himself before it, and prayed it to inform him of his destiny. Indred, who stood without, heard the stone chant forth these verses—" It is for the last time : it is with feet drawing near to the grave, that thou art come to this place, for it is most certain that before the sun riseth the valiant Indred shall make thee feel his hatred."

The people persuaded themselves sometimes that these idols answered by a gesture, or nod of the head. Thus in the history of Olave Tryggeson, king of Norway, we see a lord, named Hacon, who enters into a temple, and prostrates himself before an idol which held in its hand a great bracelet of gold. Hacon, adds the historian, easily conceiving that so long as the idol would not part with the bracelet, it was not disposed to be reconciled to him, and having made some fruitless efforts to take the bracelet away, began to pray afresh, and to offer it presents; then getting up a second time, the idol loosed the bracelet, and he went away very well pleased.

But they had not only their bloody sacrifices, and their oracles, but their orgies of licentiousness. These occurred on the occasion of the feast of Frigga, the goddess of love and pleasure; and at Uulel, the feast of Thor, in which the license was carried to such a pitch as to become merely bacchanalian meetings, where, amidst shouts, dancing, and indecent gestures, so many unseemly actions were committed as to disgust the wiser part of the community.

## CHAPTER V.

NORTHERN INDIANS, MEXICANS, AND PERUVIANS.

We have just seen that the same baleful superstitions extended themselves from the east to the very extremities of Europe; but we must now share in the astonishment of the discoverers of America, to find them equally reigning and rendering miserable the people there. A new world was found, which had been hidden from the day of creation to the fifteenth Christian age; yet there, through that long lapse of time, it was discovered, the same dominant spirit, and the same terrible system of paganism had been existing. The learned of Europe, on this great event, were extremely puzzled for a time, to conceive how and whence this distant continent had been peopled. The proven proximity of Asia at Behrings Straits, solved the mystery. But had not this become apparent, so identical are the superstitions, the traditions and practices of the Americans, with those of ancient Asia, that we might have confidently pronounced them to have come from that great seminary of the human race.

The North-American Indians, who preserved both most of their liberty, their simplicity of life and of sentiment, worshipping only the Great Spirit, and refusing to have any image of deity; having in general no priests, yet retained many, and very clear, traditions of the primeval world. So striking were these facts, combined with the Asiatic aspects of the Indians in their better days, before European oppressions and European vices had wasted and degraded them, that the early missionaries and visitants of America, Adair, Branaird, Charlevoix, nay, William Penn himself, were strongly persuaded that they had found the lost ten tribes of Israel. When they saw them carrying before them to battle an ark; saw them celebrating feasts of new moons, and heard them talk of the times when the angels of God walked upon earth with their ancestors; talk of the two first people; of the two first brothers, one of whom slew the other; of the flood, and similar traditionary facts; it is not wonderful that they should have adopted such a notion,—not perceiving, as we do now, that these are familiar features of the Asiatic nations; and that though they did not prove them to be Hebrews, they did to a certainty prove them to be Asiatics.

I must here passingly notice one inference, which seems unaccountably to have escaped the minds of antiquarians, connected with the peopling of this continent. In the North-American wilds, exist strange mounds and foundations of old fortifications, cairns, or burying-places, in which earthern vessels and other artificial remains are found, which prove that some people occupied these forests long before the present race of Indians; a people who had more of the arts of civilized life amongst them than these ever possessed. In certain caves of Kentucky, mummies have even been found. Now connecting these facts with the universal traditions of the Mexicans and South Americans, that they came originally from a country far to the north-west, does it not seem clear enough that these remains were the traces of the earlier

Asiatics who entered America, and who, if the same as the Mexicans and Peruvians, unquestionably possessed more of civilization and its arts than the northern tribes?—that other tribes more savage and warlike followed them; and that they themselves gradually sought fresh settlements, in accordance with their own traditions. This simple theory seems to solve the problem which has so long puzzled both the European and American antiquarians.

The Natchez, who had advanced far before other tribes in their civil institutions, worshipped the sun, and maintained, like the Persians, the perpetual fire, his symbol, in their temples. They burnt, on the funeral pile of their chiefs, human victims; giving them, according to M. Dumont, large piles of tobacco to stupify them, as the Brahmins intoxicate their victims to the same hideous custom. Ministers were appointed to watch and maintain the sacred fire: the first function of the great chief, every morning, was an act of obeisance to the sun; and festivals, at stated periods, were held in his honour. Amongst the people of Bogota, the sun and moon were likewise the great objects of adoration. Their system of religion was more regular and complete, though less pure than that of the Natchez. They had temples, altars, priests, sacrifices, and that long train of ceremonies which superstition introduces, wherever she has fully established her influence over the human mind. But the rites of their worship were bloody and cruel: they offered human victims to their deities, and nearly resembled the Mexicans in the genius of their religion.

To the Mexicans and Peruvians we shall, indeed, principally confine our observations. These nations had grown to comparative greatness, and assumed a decided form of civil polity, and many of the rites of what is called civilized life; and in such nations the combined power of kingcraft and priestcraft has been always found to be proportionably strong. In those conspicuous nations there were found all the great features of that superstition which they had brought with them from Asia, and which we have already seen spread and tyrannized over every quarter of the old world. They had their triads of gods; their worship of the sun; their worship of the evil and vindictive principle; and worship of serpents. They had the same dominant caste of priests and nobles; the same abject one of the common people; human sacrifices; the burning of slaves and dependants on the funeral pile; they had the ark; the doctrine of successive worlds; and the patriarchal traditions.

In the first place, their castes.—Robertson, on the authority of Herrera, says,—" In tracing the great lines of the Mexican constitution, an image of feudal policy rises to our view, in its most rigid form; and we discern, in their distinguishing characters, a nobility possessing almost independent authority; a people depressed into the lowest state of dejection; and a king entrusted with the executive power of the state. Its spirit and principles seem to have operated in the new world in the same manner as in the ancient. The jurisdiction of the crown was extremely limited; all real and effective authority was retained by the nobles. In order to secure full effect to these constitutional restraints, the Mexican nobles did not permit the crown to descend by inheritance, but disposed of it by election. The great body of the people was in a most humiliating state. A considerable number, known by the name of Mayeques, could not change their place of residence without permission of the superior to whom they belonged.

They were conveyed, together with the lands on which they were settled, from one proprietor to another; and were bound to cultivate the ground, and perform several kinds of servile work. Others were reduced to the lowest form of subjection, that of domestic servitude, and felt the utmost rigour of that wretched state. Their condition was held to be so vile, and their lives deemed of so little value, that a person who killed one of them was not subjected to any punishment. Even those considered as freemen were treated by their haughty lords as beings of an inferior species. The nobles, possessed of ample territories, were divided into various classes, to each of which peculiar titles of honour belonged. The people, not allowed to wear a dress of the same fashion, or to dwell in houses of a form similar to those of the nobles, accosted them with the most submissive reverence. In the presence of their sovereign they durst not lift their eyes from the ground, or look him in the face. The nobles themselves, when admitted to an audience, entered barefooted, in mean garments, and, as slaves, paid him homage approaching to adoration. The respect due from inferiors to those above them in rank, was prescribed with such ceremonious accuracy, that it incorporated with the language, and influenced its genius and idiom. The style and appellations used in the intercourse between equals, would have been so unbecoming in the mouth of an inferior to one of higher rank, that it would have been deemed an insult."

What a lively picture of that system of domination in the few, and slavery in the multitude, which we have seen, or soon shall see, to have prevailed in all regions; in the feudal lands of Europe; in India and Egypt! and how perfect is the resemblance, when we find, as we shall, that at the head of all these were the priests, who, says Faber, formed a regular hierarchy, and dwelt together in cloisters attached to their temples. So likewise in Peru, the royal family, that which constituted the nobility, were viewed as an entirely distinct race by the abject plebeians: and they studiously preserved the purity of their high blood, by intermarrying solely amongst themselves. With these in the government of the commonalty were associated the priesthood, who, as in Mexico, were no straggling body, but a well-organized fraternity.

With respect to their triads, the same author says, the Peruvians supposed Viracocha to be the creator of the gods: subordinate to him, they believed two triads; connecting, like the natives of the eastern continent, the triple offspring of the great father with the sun; and, as in the case of Jupiter, with the thunder. The first consisted of Chuquilla, Catuilla, and Intyllapa; or the father-thunder, the son-thunder, and the brother-thunder; the second of Apomti, Churunti, and Inti-quaoqui; as the father-sun, the son-sun, and the brother-sun. Nor were they satisfied with these two principal triads. So strongly were they impressed with the notion of three deities inferior to that primeval god who sprung from the sea, that they had likewise three images of Chuquilla, himself a person of the first triad; as the Persian Mythras was not only one with Oromasdés and Ahriman, but was also said to have triplicated himself. They had also an idol Tangatanga, which they said was one-in-three and three-in-one. Added to these, they venerated, like the pagans of the eastern hemisphere, a great universal mother; and what shews further the genuine character of this great demiurgic man of the sea, Noah, the superior of their multiplied triad, the badge of the Inca, was a rainbow and two snakes; the one allusive to the deluge, the other the symbols of the two great parents of both gods and men. Purchas, in his Pilgrimage, quaintly calls this triad, an apish imitation of the Trinity brought in by the devil. Their worship was sufficiently diabolical, being debased with all the abominable impurities of the Arkite superstitions.

Remarks not dissimilar might be made on the deity of the Mexicans, believed to be the creator of the world. They call him Mexitli, or Vitzliputzli. His image was seated on an azure-coloured stool, placed in a litter; his complexion was also azure; and in his hand he held an azure staff, fashioned in the shape of a waving serpent. Their next deity they named Tlaloc; their third Tezcallipuca. Him they esteemed the god of repentance. As for the superior divinity of this triad, he was placed on a high altar, in a small box, decked with feathers and ornaments of gold; and the tradition of the Mexicans was, that when they journeyed by different stations, from a remote country to the north-west, they bore this oracular image along with them, seated in a coffer made of reeds. Whenever they rested, they placed the ark of their deity on an altar; and at length, by his special direction, they built their principal city in the midst of a lake.

They went forwards, says Purchas, "bearing their idol with them in an ark of reeds, supported by four of their principal priests, with whom he talked, and communicated his oracles and directions. He likewise gave them laws, and taught them the sacrifices and ceremonies they still observe. And even as the pillar of cloud and of fire conducted the Israelites in their passage through the wilderness, so this apish devil gave them notice when to advance and when to stay."

Every particular of this superstition shews its diluvian origin; and proves the supposed demiurge to be no other than the great father. The ark of Mexitli is the same machine as that in which the Hammon, or Osiris of Egypt was borne in his procession; the same as the ark of Bacchus; the ship of Isis, and the Argha of Iswara. His dark complexion is that of the Vishnu of the Indian, and Cneph of the Egyptian triads. He was oracular, like the ship Argo of the Greeks; the Baris of Hammon; the chief arkite gods of all Gentile nations. He connects his city with a lake, like the ancient Cabiri, like that of Buto on the lake Chemmis in Egypt; and has evident connexion with the lake and floating islands of all the pagan mythologies.

It is a curious circumstance, that we find the doctrine of the succession of worlds, and of the death and revival of the hero-gods, also amongst the Mexicans. They doubtless brought it out of eastern Asia, with a mythology which is substantially the same as that of the larger continent, agreeably to their standing tradition respecting the route of their ancestors. They supposed the world to have been made by the gods, but imagined that since the creation, four suns have successively appeared and disappeared. The first sun perished by a deluge; the second fell from heaven when there were many giants in the country: the third was consumed by fire; the fourth was dissipated by a tempest of wind. Three days after the last sun became visible, all the former gods died: then, in process of time, were produced those whom they have since worshipped. This resemblance to the tradition of the Hindoos, is striking enough, as well as to that of the Egyptians, who told Herodotus that the same sun had four times deviated from his course, having twice risen in the west, and twice set in the east.

When the Mexicans brought their arkite god out of Asia, they also brought with him the ancient mysteries of that deity. Like the idolaters whom they had left behind, they sacrificed on the tops of mountains in traditional commemoration of the sacrifice on Ararat; and adored their bloody gods in dark caverns, similar to those of the worship of Mythras. Their orgies, like all the other orgies of the Gentiles, appear to have been of a peculiarly gloomy and terrific nature; sufficient to strike with terror, even the most undaunted hearts. Hence their priests, in order that they might be enabled to go through the dreadful rites without shuddering, anointed themselves with a peculiar ointment, and used various fantastic ceremonies to banish fear. Thus prepared, they boldly sallied forth to celebrate their nocturnal rites in wild mountains and the deep recesses of obscure caves, much in the same manner as the nightly orgies of Bacchus, Ceres, and Ceridwen were celebrated by their respective nations. A similar process enabled them to offer up those hecatombs of human victims, by which their blood-stained superstition was more eminently distinguished than even those of Moloch, Cali, Cronus, or Jaggernath. They had also their vestal virgins; and both those women and the priests were wont frantically to cut themselves with knives, while engaged in the worship of their idols, like the votaries of Baal and Bellona.

Of their bloody sacrifices, the Spanish writers are full; particularly Herrera, Acosta, and Bernal Diaz. Fear, says those authors, was the soul of the Mexican worship. They never approached their altars without sprinkling them with blood, drawn from their own bodies. But of all offerings, human sacrifices were deemed the most acceptable. This belief, mingling with the spirit of vengeance, added more force to it; every captive taken in war was brought to the temple, and sacrificed with horrid cruelties. The head and the heart were devoted to the gods: the body was carried off by the warrior who took the captive, to feast himself and his friends. Hence, the spirit of the Mexicans became proportionally unfeeling; and the genius of their religion so far counteracted the influence of policy and arts, that, notwithstanding their progress in both, their manners, instead of softening, became more fierce. Those nations in the New World, who had made the greatest progress in the arts of social life, were, in several respects, the most ferocious; and the barbarity of their actions, exceeded even those of the savage state.

The Spanish writers have been charged with exaggerating the number of human victims annually sacrificed by the Mexicans. Gomara says, there was no year in which twenty thousand were not immolated. The skulls of those unhappy persons were ranged in order, in a building erected for that purpose; and two of Cortes's officers who had counted them, told Gomara they amounted to a hundred and thirty six thousand. Herrera declares that five and twenty thousand have been sacrificed in one day. The first bishop of Mexico, in a letter to the chapter-general of his order, states the annual average at twenty thousand. On the other hand, Bernal Diaz asserts that the Franciscan monks, who were sent into New Spain, immediately after the conquest, found, on particular inquiry, that they did not exceed annually two thousand five hundred. Probably the numbers varied with the varying circumstances of war and other occurrences; but from all authorities, it appears that their bloody rites were carried to an enormous extent.

But enough of these terrible and revolting trophies of priestcraft. We might follow the course of this pestilence into Africa and the South Sea Isles; but I shall rather choose to refer all those who may be curious on the subject, to the narratives of our travellers and missionaries, in which they will see the same causes operating the same effects. I prefer to give a concluding page or two in this chapter, to the vivid picture of priestcraft which Mr. Southey has drawn in his noble poem of Madoc. No man has felt and described the true spirit of this terrible race of men more forcibly than Mr. Southey. His Madoc was a Welch prince, who, according to Cambrian tradition, first discovered America, and there settled with a colony of his countrymen. On this foundation Mr. Southey has formed one of his most delightful poems; full of nature, of the working of strong affections, and of the spirit of the subject.

Madoc discovers land, and falls in with a native who had fled from his country to avoid being sacrificed by the priests. This youth, Lincoya, leads Madoc to his native land, where he is soon introduced to Erillyab, the widowed queen, who sits before her door, near the war-pole of her deceased husband;— a truly noble woman. Madoc, in his own narrative, says,—

>                         She welcomed us
> With a proud sorrow in her mien; fresh fruits
> Were spread before us, and her gestures said
> That when he lived whose hand was wont to wield
> Those weapons,—that in better days,—that ere
> She let the tresses of her widowhood
> Grow wild, she could have given to guests like us
> A worthier welcome. Soon a man approached,
> Hooded with sable; his half-naked limbs
> Smeared black: the people at his sight drew round;

> The women wailed and wept; the children turned
> And hid their faces in their mothers' knees.
> He to the queen addressed his speech, then looked
> Around the children, and laid hands on two
> Of different sexes, but of age alike,
> Some six years old, who at his touch shrieked out.
> But then Lincoya rose, and to my feet
> Led them, and told me that the conqueror claimed
> These innocents for tribute; that the priest
> Would lay them on the altar of his god,—
> Tear out their little hearts in sacrifice,
> Yea, with more cursed wickedness himself,
> Feast on their flesh.

Madoc defends the children; sends away the disappointed priest; and, in consequence, gets into war with the Azticas, the powerful tribe which has seized upon Aztlan, the city of the Hoamen, the people of queen Erillyab. He soon, however, obliges them to come to terms; to renounce their bloody rites, and, having put things into a fair train, returns to Europe for fresh stores and emigrants. In his absence, the priests of Aztlan, according to the wont of all priests, stir up the king of Aztlan again to war. They cry, if not exactly " Great is Diana of the Ephesians," great is Mexitli of the Azticas. They pretend to hear voices and see prodigies; they pretend the gods cry out for the blood of their enemies, and forebode all manner of destruction from them, if they be not appeased. Madoc does but just arrive in time to save his colony. A desperate war is commenced; an occasion is given for the full display of the reckless atrocity, the perfidy, and vile arts of the priests, and for many noble and touching incidents arising out of the contact of better natures with the casualties of battle and stratagem. Hoel, a child, the nephew of Madoc, is carried off, at the instigation of the priests, to be sacrificed. Madoc in following his captives, falls himself into an ambush, and is doomed a victim to Mexitli; but escapes through a national custom of allowing a great warrior to fight for his life at the altar-stone, by the timely arrival of his friends, and by the assistance of a native maiden, to whom also Hoel owes his rescue from the den of Tlaloc, where he was left to starve. The Azticas are defeated, and finally abandon their territory, going onward and founding Mexico: calling it after the name of their chief deity.

To quote all the passages which seem especially made for our purpose, would fill this volume; but I must select one or two. The description of the idol:

> On a huge throne, with four huge silver snakes
> As if the keeper of the sanctuary
> Circled, with stretching neck and fangs displayed,
> Mexitli sate; another graven snake
> Belted with scales of gold his monstrous bulk.
> Around his neck a loathsome collar hung
> Of human hearts; the face was masked with gold;
> His specular eyes seemed fire; one hand upreared
> A club, the other, as in battle, held
> The shield; and over all suspended hung
> The banner of the nation.

The chief priest, Tezozomoc, when about to present little Hoel to the idol, and the child, terrified at his hideous appearance, shrieks and recoils from him:—

> His dark aspect,
> Which nature with her harshest characters
> Had featured, art made worse. His cowl was white;
> His untrimmed hair, a long and loathsome mass,
> With cotton cords entwisted, clung with gum,
> And matted with the blood which every morn
> He from his temples drew before the god,
> In sacrifice; bare were his arms, and smeared
> Black; but his countenance a stronger dread
> Than all the horrors of that outward garb
> Struck, with quick instinct, to young Hoel's heart.
> It was a face whose settled sullenness
> No gentle feeling ever had disturbed:
> Which when he probed a victim's living breast,
> Retained its hard composure.

The whole work is alive with the machinations, arts, and fanatic deeds of the priesthood. The king of the Azticas, in an early conference with Madoc, says, speaking of the priests,—

> Awe them, for they awe me:

and his queen, after he has been killed in battle, and she is about to perish on his funeral pile, calls out to his brother and successor,—

> Take heed, O king!
> Beware these wicked men! They to the war
> Forced my dead lord... Thou knowest, and I know,
> He loved the strangers; that his noble mind,
> Enlightened by their lore, had willingly
> Put down these cursed altars! As she spake
> They dragged her to the stone... Nay: nay! she cried,
> There needs not force! I go to join my lord!
> His blood and mine be on you! Ere she ceased,
> The knife was in her breast. Tezozomoc,
> Trembling with wrath, held up toward the sun
> The reeking heart.

When the war is terminated, Madoc declares,

> No priest must dwell among us,—that hath been
> The cause of all this misery!

And that, indeed, has been the cause of at least half the miseries in the world, as I shall hereafter shew. With this sentiment let us close this chapter.

## CHAPTER VI.

### EGYPT.

We have now traversed an immense space of country, and of time; and found one great uniform spirit of priestcraft, one uniform system of paganism, presiding over and oppressing the semi-barbarous nations of the earth; it remains for us to inquire whether the three great nations of antiquity, Greece, Egypt, and India, so early celebrated for their science, philosophy, and political importance, were affected by the same mighty and singular influence; and here we shall find it triumphing in its clearest form, and existing in its highest perfection.

The priest-ridden condition of Egypt is notorious to all readers of history. Lord Shaftesbury calls it, "the motherland of superstitions." So completely had the lordly and cunning priesthood here contrived to fix themselves on the shoulders of the people, so completely to debase and stupify them with an overwhelming abundance of foolish veneration, that the country swarmed with temples, gods, and creatures, which, in themselves most noxious, or loathsome, were objects of adoration. Juvenal laughs at them, as making gods of their onions; growing gods in their garden-beds by thousands—

> O sanctas gentes, quibus hæc nascunter in hortis
> Numina!

and dogs, cats, lizards, and other creatures were

cherished with extraordinary veneration. Diodorus Siculus says, that a Roman soldier having by accident killed a cat, the common people instantly surrounded his house with every demonstration of fury. The king's guards were immediately dispatched to save him from their rage, but in vain; his authority and the Roman name were equally unavailing.

The accounts we possess, of the extreme populousness of ancient Egypt; of the number and splendour of their temples; of the knowledge and authority of their priests; and the mighty remains of some of their sacred buildings, sufficiently testify to the splendour and absolute dominance of this order in this great kingdom.

To shew that the priestcraft of this ancient realm was part of the same system that we have been tracing, a part of that still existing in India, will require but little labour. We shall see that the Greek philosophers themselves assert the derivation of their mythology from Egypt; and so strikingly similar are those of India and Egypt, that it has been a matter of debate amongst learned men, which nation borrowed its religion from the other. The fact appears to be, that neither borrowed from the other, but that both drew from one common source, a source we have already pointed out—that of the Cuthic tribes. Egypt was peopled by the children of Ham: and by whomsoever India was peopled, the great priestly and military caste early found its way there, and introduced the very same superstitions, founded on the worship of Noah and his sons; and shadowed out with emblems and ceremonies derived from the memory of the flood. Both nations are of the highest antiquity; both arrived at extraordinary knowledge of astronomy, of architecture, of many of the mechanic arts, of government, and of a certain moral and theologic philosophy, which the priests retained to themselves, and made use of as a mighty engine to enslave the people. Their knowledge was carefully shrowded from the multitude; the populace were crammed with all sorts of fabulous puerilities; and were made to feel the display of science in the hands of the priesthood, as evidence of supernatural powers.

Dr. Robertson, in his Disquisition on Ancient India, and in his History of America, has endeavoured to explain the uniformity of pagan belief, by supposing that rude nations would everywhere be influenced by the same great powers and appearances of nature;—by the beneficial influence of the sun and moon; of the fruitful earth; by the contemplation of the awfulness of the ocean, of tempests, and thunder; and would come to adore those great objects as gods. But this will, by no means, account for the striking identity of the great principles and practices of paganism, as we have seen them existing. Different nations, especially under the different aspects of widely divided climates, would have imagined widely different deities; and the ceremonies in which they would have adored them, would have been as infinite as the vagaries of the human fancy. But would they have all produced gods so positively of the same family, that, whoever went from one nation to another, however distant, amongst people of totally different habits and genius, would have immediately recognized their own gods, and have given them their own names? Would Cæsar and Tacitus have beheld Roman gods in Germany and Gaul? Herodotus, Pluto, and Pythagoras, have found those of Greece in Egypt? Would these gods be, in every country, attended by the same traditionary theory of origin,—the three sons of one great father, multiplying themselves into the eight persons of the original gods—the precise number of those enclosed in the ark? Would traditions of the flood in all countries, most full and remarkable, and, in the oldest Hindoo writings, almost word for word with the one in the Bible, have existed, as may be seen in the histories of the various countries; and as may be found carefully collected by Faber and Bryant in their works on the pagan mythologies? This could not be;—nor would so many nations, in different parts of the world, retain the ark; nor celebrate mysteries, substantially the same, in the same terrific manner in caves; nor would they have all hit on the horrid sacrifice of men; nor the same doctrine of transmigration; nor have permitted an imperious caste of priests and nobles to rule over them with absolute domination. To suppose all this to happen, except from one great and universal cause, is as rational as to suppose the system of earth and heaven to be the work of chance: and the farther we go, the more clearly shall we see this demonstrated.

The Egyptians, like all other nations, had their triad of gods;—Horus, Osiris, and Typhon. This was the popular one; but the priests had another of a more intellectual nature, Emeph, Eicton, and Phtha. They had also their great mother Isis, Ceres, or the earth: but they had besides many inferior deities, which we need not enumerate. Every god had his shrine; every shrine its train of priests; besides which there were the shrines of the oracles, so that there was plenty of influence and profit for the priesthood. They bore the ark of Osiris once a year in procession; setting it afloat on the Nile at a certain place, and lamenting it for a time as lost. It was taken up at another place, with great rejoicings that the god was found again. It was said to be pursued by the great evil serpent Typhon in the ocean; but, in time was triumphant over him—a direct allusion to the going of Noah into the ark, and being driven by the great power of waters for a time; when he returned to land, and peopled the world anew.

Their doctrine of transmigration, Herodotus tells us, some of his countrymen, whom he could name but does not choose (meaning, however, Pythagoras and others), carried thence into Greece. The Egyptians, says the venerable Greek, believe that, on the dissolution of the body, the soul immediately enters into some other animal; and that, after using as vehicles every species of terrestrial, aquatic, and winged creatures, it finally enters a second time into a human body. They affirm that it undergoes all these changes in the space of three thousand years.

This is precisely the doctrine of the Hindoos, and of those nations we have already noticed; and hence proceeded that excessive veneration of the people for every species of animal; fearing to hurt or destroy them, lest they should dislodge the soul of a relative or friend. We have noticed their fury about a cat: their veneration for dogs was equally extreme till after the celebrated expedition of Cambyses, the Persian, who, with the zeal of his country against all images of deity, threw down their idols, and slew their sacred animals, which the dogs devoured, and thereby became objects of abhorrence to the Egyptians.

Their laws, says Herodotus, compel them to cherish animals. A certain number of men and women are appointed to this office, which is esteemed so honourable that it descends in succession from father to son. In the presence of these animals the inhabitants of the cities perform their vows. They address themselves as supplicants to the divinity which is supposed to be represented by the animal in whose presence they are. They then cut off their childrens' hair; sometimes the whole; sometimes the half; at others a third. This they weigh in a balance against a piece of silver. As soon as the silver preponderates, they give it to the woman who keeps the beast. It is a capital offence to kill one of these animals. To destroy one accidentally is punishable by a fine paid to the priests; but he who kills an ibis or a hawk, however involuntarily, cannot by any means escape death. Whenever a cat dies there is universal mourning in a family; and every member of it cuts off his eyebrows: but when a dog dies, they shave their heads and every part of their bodies. This, after the days of Cambyses, would, of course, be somewhat altered. The cats, when dead, are carried to sacred buildings, salted, and afterwards buried in the city of Bubastes. Female dogs are buried in sacred chests, wherever they happen to die, as are ichneumons; shrew-mice and hawks are buried at Butos; bears and wolves where they die. Otters and eels also excited great veneration. The crocodile was held to be divine by one part of the kingdom; by another it was execrated. Where it was reverenced, it had temples, a large train of attendants, and, after death, was embalmed. Maximus Tyrius says, a woman reared a young crocodile, and the Egyptians esteemed her highly fortunate as the nurse of a deity. The woman had a child which used to play with the crocodile, till the animal one day turned fierce, and ate it up; the woman exulted, and counted the child's fate blessed in the extreme, to have been the victim of her domestic god. Such is the melancholy stupidity into which priestcraft can plunge the human mind!

I shall not pursue the superstitions of this people

farther, but refer my readers to Herodotus, Plutarch, Diodorus, and Porphyrius, for all further particulars; except to state that the Egyptians, were we to credit Herodotus, were singular in one respect—having no human sacrifices, save, perhaps, in the very earliest ages. This, however, is so remarkable an exception to the universality of the system, that we find it difficult of belief; and, on turning to Strabo, we are assured that they annually sacrificed to the Nile a noble virgin; a statement confirmed by the Arabian writer, Murtadi, who relates that they arrayed her in rich robes, and hurled her into the stream. Diodorus affirms, that they sacrificed red-haired men at the tomb of Osiris, because his mortal enemy, Typhon, was of that colour. Busiris sacrificed Thracians to appease the angry Nile; and three men were daily sacrificed to Lucina at Heliopolis; instead of which Amasis afterwards humanely substituted waxen images.

They not only practised these horrors, but the Phallic rites in all their loathsomeness; and engrafted a vulgar and indecent character on the national manners. They propagated the abominations of Priapis, and the Bacchanalian and Saturnalian orgies amongst the Greeks. The priests had so fast bound the people in the strongest bonds—knowledge in their own order, and ignorance in the multitude; in puerile forms and ceremonies, and the serpent-folds of sensuality; that they had established themselves in the most absolute manner on their shoulders. Rome and India can alone present similar examples.

As we have seen in all other countries, so here they were the lordly caste. The nation, say the authorities I have above quoted, is divided into three castes—priests, nobles, and people; the latter of whom are confined to mechanic or rural employments, utterly excluded from knowledge, advancement, and power. As in India to this day, the son must succeed his father in his trade. "I know not," says Herodotus, "whether the Greeks have borrowed this custom from them, but I have seen the same thing in various parts of Thrace, Scythia, Persia, and Lydia. It seems, indeed, to be an established prejudice amongst nations, even the least refined, to consider mechanics and their descendants as the lowest sort of citizens, and to esteem those most noble who are of no profession. The soldiers and the priests are the only ranks in Egypt which are honourably distinguished; these, each of them, receive from the public a portion of land of twelve acres, free from all taxes: besides this, the military enjoy, in their turn, other advantages; one thousand are every year, in turn, on the king's guard, and receive, besides their land, a daily allowance of five pounds of bread, two of beef, and four austeres of wine."

Plato, Plutarch, and Diodorus agree with him in this particular. A prince, say they, cannot reign in Egypt if he be ignorant of sacred affairs. The king must be either of the race of priests or soldiers; these two classes being distinguished, the one by their wisdom, the other by their valour. When they have chosen a warrior for king, he is immediately admitted into the order of priests, who instruct him in their mysterious philosophy. The priests may censure the king; give him advice; and regulate his actions. By them is fixed the time when he shall walk, bathe, or even visit his wife. The sacred ministers possess, in return, many and great advantages. They are not obliged to consume any part of their domestic property; each has a moiety of sacred viands, ready dressed, assigned him, besides a large daily allowance of beef, and geese, and wine.

What a striking illustration is this of what we find in Genesis, cap. xlvii. v. 22, of the doings of Joseph, who adopted a policy towards the Egyptians more despotic than one would have expected from his patriarchal character; or from a simple Canaanitish shepherd—first of gathering up the corn from all the land of Egypt, and then selling it out, in the horrors of famine, to the people for their possessions, whereby the whole kingdom became the purchased property of Pharaoh, except that of the priests—" only the land of the priests bought he not, for the priests had a portion assigned them of Pharaoh."

The priests, indeed, were too powerful for Joseph, or even for Pharaoh himself. Darius wished only to place a statue of himself in a temple; the priests violently resisted it, and Darius was obliged to submit. Herodotus tells us that the priests shewed him the images of their predecessors for three hundred and forty-one descents: and M. Larcher even supposes that these priests were, for many ages, the sole princes of this strange country; a most triumphant reign of priestcraft indeed! Let us now turn to Greece.

## CHAPTER VII.

### GREECE.

THE popular theology of this noble and celebrated nation, as it existed during its most enlightened ages, has been made familiar to every mind by its literature being taught in all schools, and furnishing perpetual allusions and embellishments to all writers. Herodotus says that Hesiod and Homer invented the theogony of Greece; that is, they, no doubt, methodized the confused traditions of their ancestors, and organized them into that very beautiful system, which we still admire, when it has become the most fabulous of fables, more than the kindred creations of all other people. Though it had the same origin as all other mythologies, yet, passing through the glorious minds of these poets, it assumed all those characters of grace and beauty which they conferred on their literature, their philosophy, and on all the arts and embellishments of life. Familiar as Homer has made us all with that hierarchy of gods which figure so conspicuously in his writings, we are continually furnished by him with glimpses of a more ancient dynasty, and with theories of their origin, which clash with his more general one, and at first puzzle and confound us. When we come, however, to trace up these casual revealings, we soon find ourselves in a new world. These gods, which he at first taught us were all the offspring of Saturn, and of his three sons

Jupiter, Neptune, and Pluto, we discover, to our astonishment, are the gods of all other nations,—gods assuming all the character of the highest antiquity, and deriving their being in a manner totally at variance with the more modern system. His Hercules, Bacchus, Apollo, Ceres, Venus, &c., instead of being the comparatively recent children of Jove, are found to blend and become synonimous with him or the great Mother. Surprised at this strange discovery, we pursue the inquiry, and are led into those very regions where we have lately been—into central Asia, and to the period of the Flood. The tombs of the gods were existing in Greece; they were, therefore, but deified men,—and whence came these men? From the Flood. Traditions of floods were the most familiar of things in Greece; and they agreed, both that of Deucalion and others, with all the particulars of the real one. Herodotus tells us that the Egyptians, into whose religion he was initiated, invented the names of the twelve great gods; but we have already seen whence the Egyptians drew their deities. Plutarch contends that they came from Phœnicia. And who were the gods of the Phœnicians? Ilus, or Ark-Ilus, or Hercules, i.e. Noah; and Dagon; the old man, On, or Oannes, who, according to Sanconiatho, came out of the sea, and taught them to plant corn and the vine. Others say, that the gods came into Greece from Samothrace, with the Pelasgi, an ancient wandering people, who bore in an ark with them the Cabíri, or mighty ones. These Cabiri have been the subject of much contention; but all writers admit that they were three, or eight, that is, the three sons of Noah, or the eight people of the ark. It is most likely that from all these sources portions of the same great system of corrupted worship were derived. So conspicuous is the real origin of all the Grecian traditions, that I shall not dwell upon it. It is enough to state that they celebrated the same mysteries, practised the same human sacrifices, were contaminated with the same Phallic abominations, as all the other nations of paganism; in fact, all the characters of the great Noachic superstitions were engrafted upon them. The bold and free genius of the nation; that splendid and extraordinary emanation of intellect, which not only made it the wonder of the ancient world, but has constituted it the well-spring of knowledge to all ages, and almost the creator of the universal modern mind, saved it from the utmost horrors and degradations of priestcraft. The national spirit operating in the soul of Homer, again through him operated with tenfold force on the minds of his countrymen. In all other countries the priests were the monopolists of knowledge. " Immured," says Maurice, in his Indian Antiquities, " in the errors of Polytheism, as was the great body of the Egyptian nation, it has been incontestibly proved by the immortal Cudworth, that the hierophant, or arch-priest, in the secret rites of their religion, taught the doctrine of the unity of the Godhead; but this noble sentiment, though they had the magnanimity to conceive, they wanted the generosity to impart to the deluded populace; for it was thought dangerous both to the church and state, to shake the foundations of the reigning superstitions." This, if I have not already shewn, it would be easy to shew, was the practice the world over; but this knowledge falling on the mind of Homer, he disdained to make it an instrument of slavery, but poured it abroad like light through the earth; and his countrymen, listening to his glorious poems with enthusiasm, became imbued with the same dauntless, untameable spirit, alike intolerant of the despotism of the throne or the altar.

Many of his more timid compatriots, indeed, were terrified at the freedom of his treatment of the gods. Everywhere we perceive that he regarded them but as convenient poetical machinery. Ever and anon we find him rising into such sublime notions of Deity and the Divine government, that we feel that he possessed that true knowledge of the Creator which Socrates and Plato, and Cicero, in Rome, afterwards displayed. So strikingly, indeed, does he evince this, that many have thought that in his wanderings he had come in contact with the Hebrew doctrines. I doubt this. I believe, rather, it came to him from the earliest ages, by other sources; but, be it as it may, his description of the gods exerting their power is almost worthy of Isaiah.

> Mars shouts to Simois from his beauteous hill:
> The mountain shook, the rapid stream stood still.
> Above, the sire of gods his thunder rolls,
> And peals on peals redoubled rend the poles.
> Beneath, stern Neptune shakes the solid ground;
> The forests wave, the mountains nod around:
> Through all their summits tremble Ida's woods,
> And from their sources boil her hundred floods.
> Troy's turrets totter on the rocking plain,
> And the tossed navies beat the heaving main.
> *Pope's Translation*, B. xx.

The sentiments that abound in the Odyssey are worthy, not merely of a Hebrew, but of a Christian;—as this fine and just opinion of slavery:—

> Jove fixed it certain, that whatever day
> Makes man a slave, takes half his worth away.—B. xviii.

This noble description of the power of conscience:—

> Pirates and conquerors of hardened mind,
> The foes of peace, and scourges of mankind,
> To whom offending men are made a prey,
> When Jove in vengeance gives a land away:

> Even these,—when of their ill-got spoils possessed,
> Find sure tormentors in the guilty breast;
> Some voice of God, close whispering within—
> "Wretch! this is villany; and this is sin!"

And those many declarations of God's guardianship of the poor and the stranger:—

> 'T is Jove unfolds our hospitable door;
> 'T is Jove that sends the stranger and the poor.—B. xiv.

> Let first the herald due libations pay
> To Jove, who guides the wanderer on his way.—B. vii.

> By Jove the stranger and the poor are sent,
> And what to them we give, to Jove is lent.

> Low at thy knee, thy succour we implore;
> Respect us human, and relieve us poor;
> At least some hospitable gifts bestow,
> 'T is what the happy, to the unhappy owe.
> 'T is what the gods require:—those gods revere,—
> The poor and stranger are their constant care.
> To Jove their cause, and their revenge belongs—
> He wanders with them, and he feels their wrongs.—B. ix.

From Homer's mind, truth glanced abroad with a divine and dreadless honesty; unlike that of poor Herodotus, who at the utterance of a bolder sentiment, hopes he has not given offence to gods or men.

We see in his writings not only continual indications of great moral truths, but the same integrity evinced in sketching the manners of the early ages of his country. We see his favourite hero dragging his noble foe at his chariot, and immolating men at the funeral of his friend. What Greece would have been in the hands of priests, but for its own elastic spirit, and for the mighty influence of its poets and sages, we have seen pictured in other nations; what it was, we have now to see. Priestcraft here did not rule with the same unmasked mien, and unrestrained hand, as in other countries;—it adapted its policy to the spirit of the people. It gratified their curiosity after philosophic knowledge, and after the future, by mysteries and oracles; their love of grace and festivity, by beautiful processions and joyous festivals; it captivated and awed their sensitive imaginations, by calling to its aid the fine arts, as the papal church did afterwards by its adherents,—erecting the most magnificent temples, and setting before their eyes those miracles of paintings now lost, except in the eulogiums of antiquity; and of sculpture, some of which remain to command the admiration, if not the worship of the world. By these means they attained their end,—immense wealth and influence,—an influence, the strength of which, on the common mind, may be estimated by facts about to be given, but perhaps more by the circumstance of Socrates, the most sagacious of their philosophers, at the hour of his death, and when he was delivering the most sublime sentiments, enjoining his friends to sacrifice on his behalf, a cock to Æsculapius.

Let us now briefly run over the great features of priestcraft in Greece; and first, of human sacrifices. Archbishop Potter, in his Antiquities of Greece, chap. iv., says, "Neither was it lawful to sacrifice oxen only, but also men. Examples of this sort of inhumanity were very common in most of the barbarous nations. Among the primitive Grecians it was accounted an act of so uncommon cruelty and impiety, that Lycaon, king of Arcadia, was feigned by the poets to have been turned into a wolf, because he offered a human sacrifice to Jupiter. In latter days it was undoubtedly more common and familiar. Aristomenes, the Messinian, sacrificed three hundred men; among whom was Theopompus, one of the kings of Sparta, to Jupiter of Ithome. Themistocles, in order to procure the assistance of the gods against the Persians, sacrificed some captives of that nation, as we find in Plutarch. Bacchus had an altar in Arcadia, upon which young damsels were beaten to death with bundles of rods; something like to which was practised by the Lacedemonians, who scourged the children, sometimes to death, in honour of Diana Orthia. To the Manes and infernal gods, such sacrifices were very often offered. Hence we read of Polyxena's being sacrificed to Achilles; and Homer relates how that hero butchered twelve Trojan captives at the funeral of Patroclus. Æneas, whom Virgil celebrates for his piety, is an example of the same practice:—

> Sulmone creatos
> Quatuor hic juvenes, totidem, quos educat Ufens,
> Viventes rapit; inferias quos immolet umbris,
> Captivoque rogi perfundat sanguine flammas.—*Lib.* x.

"Whoever desires to see more instances of human sacrifices, may consult Clemens of Alexandria, Eusebius, and other Christian apologists."

To this, we may add the well-known sacrifice of Iphygenia, by the assembled Grecian powers on their way to Troy; the sacrifice of two children by Menelaus, related by Herodotus, and what Plutarch says, that the Greeks sacrificed many children annually to Saturn; so that we see this famous people was sufficiently infected by this bloody superstition.

Of their Phallic rites we shall, for decency's sake, say no more than refer to their own writers, whose descriptions of the Bacchic and Priapic orgies, are astonishing.

For their religious festivals and processions; we refer to Potter; and shall only say that in these, every charm of grace, every intoxication of festivity was exhausted, to fascinate a people so alive to such influences; and they were made to contribute abundantly to the coffers of the priests.

Another potential source of power and wealth was augury. Augurs were a class of men frequently priests, but always bearing much the same relation to the pagan priesthood, that the monks did to those of the papal hierarchy. They were but varieties of the same class of animals of prey. They pretended to discern and declare the will of the gods, by the flight of birds, by the intestines of animals, and by various other signs; but it was through the medium of the oracles that priestcraft awed, and practised on, the public mind most effectually. These were situated in solemn temples, or fearful, sacred groves; were surrounded by everything which could terrify and confound the imagination; and, accompanied by dread and mysterious sounds, and by the cries and contortions of the priest or priestess, were supposed to proclaim the dicta of the gods. They were, consequently, a mine of wealth and power to the priests. "Of all sorts of divination," says Potter, "oracles had always the greatest repute, as being thought to proceed in an immediate manner from the gods; whereas, others were delivered by men, and had a greater dependence on them, who might, either out of ignorance, mistake, or out of fear, hope, or other unlawful and base ends, conceal, or betray the truth; whereas, they thought the gods, who were neither obnoxious to the anger, nor stood in need of the rewards, nor cared for the promises of mortal, could not be prevailed upon to do either of them. Upon this account, oracles obtained so great credit and esteem, that, in all doubts and disputes, their determinations were held sacred and inviolable. Whence, as Strabo reports, vast numbers flocked to them to be resolved in all manner of doubts, and to ask counsel about the management of their affairs; insomuch, that no business of great consequence was undertaken; scarce any war waged, peace concluded, new form of government instituted, or new laws enacted, without the advice and approbation of an oracle. Crœsus, before he durst venture to declare war against the Persians, consulted not only all the most famous oracles of Greece, but sent ambassadors to Lybia, to ask advice of Jupiter Hammon. Minos, the Cretan lawgiver, conversed with Jupiter, and received instructions from him, how he might new-model his government. Lycurgus also made visits to the Delphian Apollo, and received from him that platform which he afterwards communicated to the Lacedemonians. Nor does it matter whether these things were true or not, when lawgivers, and men of the greatest authority, were forced to make use of these methods to win them into compliance. My author also goes higher, and tells us that inspired persons were thought worthy of the greatest honour and trusts: insomuch, that we sometimes find them advanced to the throne, and invested with the royal power;—for that, being admitted to the councils of the gods, they were best able to provide for the welfare of men.

"This representation stood the priests, who had their dependence on the oracle, in no small stead; for finding their credit thus thoroughly established, they allowed no man to consult their gods before he had offered costly sacrifices, and made rich presents to them. Whereby it came to pass that few besides great and wealthy men were admitted to ask their advice; the rest being unable to pay the charges required on that account, which contributed very much to raise the esteem of oracles among the common people; men being generally apt to admire the things they are kept at some distance from, and, on the other hand, to contemn what they are familiarly acquainted with. Wherefore, to keep up their esteem with the better sort, even they were only admitted on a few stated days: at other times, neither the greatest prince could purchase, nor persons of the greatest quality any way obtain an answer. Alexander himself was peremptorily denied by the Pythia, till she was by downright force compelled to ascend the tripos, when, finding herself unable to resist any longer, she cried out, ' Thou art invincible!' which words were thought a very lucky omen, and accepted instead of a further oracle."

Thus we see how artfully and triumphantly the priests had managed to enslave this great and most intelligent of people, holding them in abject and utter thraldom even while they imagined themselves free. To the priests they were obliged to come for their original civil constitutions, and these they took care so to frame as to make themselves necessary in every act and hour of existence, as they have done through the universal world. Our author might have told us however, what tricks statesmen were suffered to play with the oracles when it suited them so to do; he might have added what prodigies and portents Themistocles caused to appear in these oracular temples, when he wished to rouse the Greeks against Persia. The arms of the temple at Delphi were shifted from the interior to the front of the fane in the night, as if done by divine hands; they were heard to clash as if by invisible power; rocks fell, and thundered down in the faces of the enemy as they approached these sacred defiles, and friends and foes were impressed with an idea that the gods were present to defend their sanctuaries. These and similar facts he might have told us;—but let us proceed.

Their sacred festivals, games, and celebration of mysteries, we have already heard were almost innumerable; some occurring yearly, others monthly, so that they were seldom without something of the kind to occupy their attention, and bind them to the national religion. To their mysteries only can we devote a few passages.

These have occupied much 'of the curiosity of the learned; and their researches have shewn incontestibly, that the mysteries celebrated in all ages and nations were substantially the same. Whether they were celebrated in Egypt, in honour of Isis and Osiris; in Syria of Baal; in Phrygia, in Crete, in Phenicia, in Lemnos, in Samothrace, in Cypress, in India, or the British Isles; or in the Mythratic caves of Persia; they had all the same object, and were attended by the same ceremonies. In Greece there might be differing particulars in the orgies of Bacchus, Ceres, Jupiter, Pan, Silenus, Rhea, Venus, or Diana, yet their leading traits were the same. Their objects have been stated variously; but they appear, in fact, to have been various, yet all subservient to one great object,—which was, to teach the primal unity of the Deity, notwithstanding the popular multitude of gods, and to shadow out the grand doctrine of the fall and repurification of the human soul. They appear evidently derived from the flood; representing a descent into the darkness of that death which Noah's entrance into the ark indicated to the world, and his subsequent return to life. In all, there was a person lost, and sought after with lamentation; whether Isis was seeking Osiris, Ceres seeking Proserpine; or Thammuz, Bacchus, Pan, Jupiter, or some other, was lamented with tears, and sought through terrors, and afterwards rejoiced in as found. In all, the aspirants descended to darkness as of death, passed over a water in an ark or boat, and came into Elysium. The accounts in Homer and Virgil of the descent of Hercules, Ulysses and Æneas, into hell, are considered to be but details of what is represented in the mysteries. In whatever mode they were celebrated, we invariably find a certain door or gate, viewed as of primary importance. Sometimes it was the door of the temple; sometimes the door of the consecrated grotto; sometimes it was the hatch-way of the boat within which the aspirant was enclosed; sometimes a hole, either natural or artificial, between rocks; and sometimes a gate in the sun, moon, or planets. Through this the initiated were born again; and from this the profane were excluded. The notion evidently originated from the door in the side of the ark through which the primary epopts were admitted, while the profane antediluvians were shut out. So sacred and secret were these mysteries in all countries, that whoever revealed any portion of them was instantly put to death. The scrupulosity of the Romans with regard to the orgies of the Bona Dea, at which women only were admitted, is familiar to every reader of Cicero, by his harangue against Clodius, who violated this custom. Those who consulted the oracle of Trophonius had to pass through darkness, and descend by a ladder into the cave, with offerings of cakes of honey; and drank of the waters of oblivion to forget all past cares, and of the waters of remembrance, to recollect what they were about to see.

They who had been initiated into the mysteries were held to be extremely wise, and to be possessed of motives to the highest honour and purity of life; yet it cannot be denied that they were made, by the introduction of the Phallic obscenities, a means as much of debauchery as of refining the people. A little reflection, says Mr. Maurice, will soon convince us, that as persons of either sex were promiscuously allowed to be initiated, when the original physical cause came to be forgotten, what a general dissipation—what a boundless immorality, would be promoted by so scandalous an exhibition as awaited them. The season of nocturnal gloom in which these mysteries were performed, and the inviolable secresy which accompanied the celebration of them, added to the inviting solitude of the scene, conspired at once to break down all the barriers of restraint, to overturn all the fortitude of manly virtue, and to rend the veil of modesty from the blushing face of virgin innocence. At length licentious passion trampled upon the most sacred obstacles which law and religion united to raise against it. The bacchanal, frantic with midnight intemperance, polluted the secret sanctuary, and prostitution sate throned upon the very altars of the gods.

The effect upon the vulgar multitude cannot be doubted, however different it might be upon the few of higher intellect and higher pursuit. By them the most sublime portions of the ancient mysteries would be awfully felt. Nothing can be conceived more solemn than the rites of initiation into the greater mysteries as described by Apuleius and Dion Chrysostome, who had both gone through the awful ceremony,—nothing more tremendous than the scenery exhibited before the eyes of the terrified aspirant. After entering the grand vestibule of the mystic shrine, he was led by the hierophant, amid surrounding darkness and incumbent horrors, through all those extended aisles, winding avenues, and gloomy adyta, equally belonging to the mystic temples of Egypt, Eleusis, and India. "It was," says Stobæus, as quoted by Warburton, in his Divine Legation of Moses, "a wide and fearful march through night and darkness. Presently the ground began to rock beneath his feet, the whole temple trembled, and strange and dreadful voices were heard through the midnight silence. To these succeeded other louder and more terrific noises, resembling thunder; while quick and vivid flashes of lightning darted through the cavern, displaying to his view many ghastly sights and hideous spectres, emblematical of the various vices, diseases, infirmities, and calamities, incident to that state of terrestrial bondage from which his struggling soul was now going to emerge, as well as of the horrors and penal torments of the guilty in a future state. The temple of the Cecropian goddess roared from its inmost recesses; the holy torches of Eleusis were waved on high by mimic furies; the snakes of Triptolemus hissed a loud defiance, and the howling of the infernal dogs resounded through the awful gloom, which resembled the malignant and imperfect light of the moon when partially obscured by clouds. At this period, all the pageants of vulgar idolatry—all the train of gods, supernal and infernal, passed in awful succession before him; and a hymn, called the Theology of Idols, recounting the genealogy and functions of each, was sung: afterwards the whole fabulous detail was solemnly recanted by the mystagogue; a divine hymn, in honour of ETERNAL AND IMMUTABLE TRUTH, was chanted, and the profounder mysteries commenced. And now, arrived on the verge of death and initiation, everything wears a dreadful aspect; it is all horror, trembling, and astonishment. An icy chilliness seizes his limbs; a copious dew, like the damp of real death, bathes his temples; he staggers, and his senses begin to fail, when the scene is of a sudden changed, and the doors of the interior, and splendidly illumined temple are thrown wide open. A miraculous and divine light discloses itself, and shining plains, and flowering meadows open on all hands before him. 'Accessi confinium mortis,' says Apuleius, 'et calcato Proserpinæ limine, per omnia vectus elementa remeavi; nocte medio SOLEM candido coruscantem lumine.' Arrived at the bourn of mortality, after having trod the gloomy threshold of Proserpine, I passed rapidly through all the surrounding elements, and, at deep midnight, beheld the sun shining in meridian splendour. The clouds of mental error, and the shades of real darkness being now alike dissipated, both the soul and the body of the initiated experienced a delightful vicissitude; and, while the latter, purified with lustrations, bounded in a blaze of glory, the former dissolved in a tide of overwhelming transport. At that period of virtuous and triumphant exaltation, according to the divine Plato, they saw celestial beauty in all the dazzling radiance of its perfection; when, joining with the glorified chorus, they were admitted to the *beatific vision*, and were initiated into the most blessed of all mysteries."

The author of the apocryphal WISDOM OF SOLOMON has preserved a most curious Jewish tradition, relative to the nature of the Egyptian plague of darkness, which intimates that the votaries of Osiris were visited with the very terrors which they employed in his mysteries. The passage is not only strikingly illustrative of what is gone before, but is extremely sublime.—

"When unrighteous men thought to oppress the holy nation, they, being shut up in their houses, the prisoners of darkness and fettered with the bonds of a long night, lay there, fugitives from the Eternal Providence. For, while they were supposed to lie hid in their secret sins, they were scattered under a dark veil of forgetfulness, being horridly astonished, and troubled with strange apparitions. For, neither might the corner that held them keep them from fear, but noises, as of waters falling down, sounded about them, and sad visions appeared unto them with heavy countenances. No power of the fire might give them light, neither could the bright flames of the stars endure to lighten that horrible night. Only there appeared unto them a fire kindled of itself, very dreadful; for being much terrified, they thought the things they saw to be worse than the sight they saw not. As for the illusions of art magic, they were put down, and their vaunting in wisdom was reproved with disgrace; for they who promised to drive away terrors and troubles from a sick soul, were sick themselves of fear, worthy to be laughed at. For though no terrible thing did fear them, yet, being scared with beasts that passed by, and hissing of serpents, they died for fear, refusing to look upon the air, which could on no side be avoided; they sleeping the same sleep that night, wherein they could do nothing, and which came upon them out of the bottoms of inevitable hell, were partly vexed with monstrous apparitions, and partly fainted, their heart failing them —for sudden fear, and unlooked-for, came upon them. So, then, whosoever fell down, was straitly kept, shut up in a prison without iron bars. Whether it were a whistling wind or a melodious noise of birds among the spreading branches, or a pleasing fall of water running violently, or a hideous noise of stones cast down, or a running that could not be seen of skipping beasts, or a roaring voice of most savage wild beasts, or a rebounding echo from the hollow mountains; these things made them to swoon for fear. For the whole world shined with light, and none were hindered in their labour; over them only was spread a heavy night, an image of that darkness which should afterwards receive them."

On this interesting subject it would be easy to follow through the mysteries of all nations, and write a volume; but after merely stating that the initiatory ceremonies of Freemasons, and those of the Vehme Gericht, or secret tribunal, once existing in Germany, seem to derive their origin from this source, I shall merely give a few words of Taliesin, relative to their celebration in Britain, and return to the regular order of my subject.

Among the apparatus of the *art magic* which the Druids used in this ancient ceremony of being born again, was a cauldron; and, as in all other mysteries, and in the initiation of a Freemason, men with naked swords stood within the portal to cut down every coward who would fain turn back before he had passed through the terrors of inauguration; the Druids also, it appears, had to sail over the water in this ceremony.

" Thrice the number," says Taliesin, " that would have filled Prydwen (the magic shield of Arthur, in which he sailed with seven champions), we entered upon the deep,—excepting seven, none have returned from Caer Sidi. Am I not contending for the praise of that lore which was four times reviewed in the quadrangular enclosure? As the first sentence, was it not uttered from the cauldron? Is not this the cauldron of the ruler of the deep? With the ridge of pearls around its border, it will not boil the food of a coward who is not bound by his oath. Against him will be lifted the bright-gleaming sword, and in the hand of the sword-bearer shall he be left; and before the gates of hell shall the horns of light be burning. When we went with Arthur in his splendid labours, excepting seven, none returned from Caer Vediwid. Am I not contending for the honour of a lore which deserves attention? In the quadrangular enclosure, in the island with the strong door, the twilight and the pitchy darkness were mixed together, while bright wine was the beverage placed before the narrow circle. Thrice the number that would have filled Prydwen we embarked upon the sea;—excepting seven, none returned from Caer Rigor. I will not redeem the multitudes with the ensign of the governor. Beyond the enclosure of glass they beheld not the prowess of Arthur. They knew not on what day the stroke would be given, nor at what hour in the serene day the agitated person would be born, or who preserved his going into the dales of the possession of the waters. They knew not the brindled ox with the thick headband. When we went with Arthur of mournful memory, excepting seven, none returned from Caer Vandwy."

Caer Rigor, Sidi, Vediwid, etc., are but different names for the Druidical enclosure of Stonehenge, or, as they styled it, the Ark of the World. The number seven have evidently reference to the seven persons of the ark; Noah himself being represented, according to custom, by Arthur.

In another place Taliesin alludes to the doctrine of the Metempsychosis, which was taught in those mysteries. "I was first modelled in the form of a pure man, in the hall of Ceridwen (the ship goddess), who subjected me to penance. Though small within my ark and modest in my deportment, I was great. A sanctuary carried me above the surface of the earth. Whilst I was enclosed within its ribs the sweet awen rendered me complete; and my law, without audible language, was imparted to me by the old giantess darkly smiling in her wrath; but her claim was not regretted when she set sail. I fled in the form of a fair grain of pure wheat; upon the edge of a covering cloth she caught me in her fangs. In appearance she was as large as a proud mare, which she also resembled (the Ceres-Hippa of the Greeks, who similarly received Bacchus into her womb); then was she swelling-out, like a ship upon the waters. Into a dark receptacle she cast me. She carried me back into the sea of Dylan. It was an auspicious omen to me when she happily suffocated me; God, the Lord, freely set me at large."

To a timid aspirant, the hierophant says, "Thy coming without external purity, is a pledge that I will not receive thee. Take out the gloomy one. Out of the receptacle which is thy aversion, did I obtain the rainbow."—See *Davis's Celtic Mythology*.

It may seem widely wandering from Greece to Britain; but it only shews more strikingly the oneness of the Pagan faith. And now to return.

The priests, thus providing for the tastes of all parties, wealth, power, and unlimited influence became their own. All these things were sources of gain; and whoever would form some idea of the wealth of the Grecian priesthood, let him read in Herodotus of the immense riches conferred on the oracular temples by Crœsus and other monarchs. Let him also learn the following particulars from Diodorus Siculus: "The principal hoards of treasure, both in bullion and coined money, were in their temples, which were crowded with presents of immense value, brought by the superstitious from every part of Greece. These temples were considered as national banks; and the priests officiated as bankers,—not always, indeed, the most honest, as was once proved at Athens, where the state treasurers, having expended or embezzled the public money, had the audacity to set fire to that part of the temple of Minerva where the treasure was contained; by which sacrilegious act that magnificent fane was near being wholly consumed. Their purpose, however, was fully answered, since the registers of the temple were reported to have perished with the treasures, and all responsibility precluded."

The temple just mentioned, the superb fane of

Jupiter Olympius, at Elis, and that of Apollo at Delphi, were the principal of the three sacred depositories. The priests at all times concealed the total sum of the treasures lodged in them with too much caution for us to know the amount; yet, when the Phocenses, urged to despair by the exactions of the Thebans, seized on the treasures of Delphi, they amounted to 10,000 talents—above 2,250,000*l.* sterling—and probably that was but a small portion of what holy perfidy had previously secured. The deposits at the great temple of Ephesus, considered through all ages as inviolable, probably far exceeded those of the three last mentioned.

The spirit of avarice, which in all times characterized the priesthood, and prompted them to such immense accumulation, is not more detestable than dangerous; for, let any one reflect what must be the consequence to a nation where the monarch and the priest are in coalition, as is usually the case, and the monarch, as is usually the case too, is watching to extinguish every spark of popular freedom;—what, I say, must be the consequence when such overwhelming resources are within his reach? The fate of Greece is a melancholy warning on the subject. These immense treasures were eventually seized upon by rapacious conquerors, and their soldiers paid by them to enslave these renowned states; and thus the coin drained from the people by the hands of priestcraft, became in the hands of kingcraft, the means of their destruction. So has it been in every country. So was it in Palestine—so in ancient Rome—in Constantinople; and so pre-eminently in India. To that country let us now proceed.

## CHAPTER VIII.

### INDIA.

The ancient and venerable Hindostan furnishes our last and most triumphant demonstration of the nature of *pagan* priestcraft. In Greece we have seen that, notwithstanding the daring, restless, and intellectual character of the people, it contrived to obtain a most signal influence; but in India, with a people of a gentler temperament, and where no bold spirits, like Homer and the philosophers of Greece, had ventured to make the national theology popularly familiar, priestcraft assumed its most fearless and determined air. In all other lands it did not fail to place itself in the first rank of honour and power; in this it went a step further,—and promulgating a dogma diametrically opposite to the humanizing doctrine of the Bible, that, " God made of one blood all the nations of the earth;" it riveted its chains indissolubly on the mind of that mighty empire. Priestcraft here exhibits a marvellous spectacle. The perfection of its craft, and the utter selfishness of its spirit, are proclaimed by the fact of millions on millions bound, from the earliest ages to the present hour, in the chains of the most slavish and soul-quelling castes, and in the servility of a religious creed so subtilly framed, that it almost makes hopeless the moral regeneration of the swarming myriads of these vast regions. I have already repeatedly stated that it partakes, in common with the whole pagan world, in one general mythological system, and I shall not dwell on its features more particularly. In Maurice's copious Indian Antiquities, whence I shall chiefly draw what I have to say, may be found ample details of the Hindoo religion. It is well known, from a variety of works, that this venerable empire claims the highest antiquity, not merely of national existence, but of the possession of knowledge in philosophy, literature, and the arts; it is equally known, too, since Sir William Jones laid open the antique stores of the Sanscrit language, that this religion has all the common features of those mythologies, on which I have already dwelt. It has its triad of gods, its doctrine of Metempsychosis, its practice of the Phallic licentiousness, and the horrors of human sacrifice and self-immolation. Who has not heard of the burning of Indian widows—of the bloody and wholesale self-slaughter at the temple of Jaggernath—of the destruction of children, now restrained by British interference—and of the absolute dominance of the Brahmins? I shall pass, therefore, hastily over these matters, and confine myself principally to the task of displaying, in the Brahminical hierarchy, an example of priestcraft in its most decided, undisguised, subtle, and triumphant character,—priestcraft, at once in full flower and full fruit; in that state at which it has always aimed, but never, not even in the bloody reign of the Papal church, ever attained elsewhere,—stamping itself on the heart of a great nation in its broadest and most imperishable style, in all its avowed despotism, icy selfishness, imperturbable pride, and cool arrogance of fanatical power.

Two great sects exist here,—those of Buddh and Brahma, which preserve an inviolable separation, except in the temple of Jaggernath, where, seeming to forget all their former prejudices, they unite in the commission of lust and cruelty.

It is to the Brahminical sect, as the most predominant, that I shall principally confine my remarks. These profess the mildest of doctrines, refuse to kill any living creature for food, and subsist on milk, fruit, and vegetables. Yet, what is at first sight most remarkable, and what cannot be accounted for by any other means than that of the immutable nature of corrupted religion, they not only inflict on themselves, under the character of Yogees, the most horrible austerities; but have for ages encouraged the destruction of female children; do to the present time encourage, and under the influence of the most powerful social causes, render almost necessary the immolation of widows; sanction and stimulate, annually, thousands of simple victims to destroy themselves at the shrine of the monstrous Jaggernath; and, till recently, sacrificed, not only animals but men.

Of human sacrifices, the express ordination of the Rudhiradhyaya, or sanguinary chapter of the Calica Purana, in the fifth volume of the Asiatic Researches, is sufficient testimony. No precepts can be conceived more express, nor, indeed, more horrible, than those which this tremendous chapter enjoins.

" By a human sacrifice, attended with the forms here laid down, Deva, the goddess Cali, the black goddess of destruction, is pleased 1000 years.

" By a human sacrifice, Camachya, Chandica, and Bhairava, who assume any shape, are pleased 1000 years. An oblation of blood which has been rendered pure by holy texts, is equal to ambrosia; the head and flesh also afford much delight to Chandica. Let, therefore, the learned, when paying adoration to the goddess, offer blood and the head; and when performing the sacrifice to fire, make oblations of flesh."

Here follow numerous minute directions, none of which I shall quote, except one;—itself sufficiently horrid.

"Let the sacrificer say, Hrang, hring! Cali, Cali! O, horrid-toothed goddess! eat, cut, destroy all the malignant; cut with this axe; bind, bind; seize, seize; drink blood! spheng, spheng! secure, secure! salutations to Cali!"

For the Phallic contaminations, let this pasage from Maurice suffice. Abundant matter of the like nature might be added; but the less said on this subject the better. Of the recent existence of such things, Buchanan's account of the temple of Jaggernath may satisfy the curious reader.

"What I shall offer on this head will be taken from two authentic books, written at very different periods, and therefore fully decisive as to the general prevalence of the institution from age to age,—the Anciennes Rélations, and Les Voyages de M. Tavernier,—the former written in the 9th, the latter in the 17th century.

"Incited, unquestionably, by the hieroglyphic emblems of vice so conspicuously elevated and strikingly painted in the temple of Mahadeo, the priests of that deity industriously selected the most beautiful females that could be found, and, in their tenderest years, with great pomp and solemnity, consecrated them, as it is impiously called, to the service of the divinity of the pagoda. They were trained in every art to delude and delight; and, to the fascination of external beauty, their artful betrayers added the attractions arising from mental accomplishments. Thus was an invariable rule of the Hindoos, that *women have no concern with literature*, dispensed with on this infamous occasion. The moment these hapless creatures reached maturity, they fell victims to the lust of the Brahmins. They were early taught to practise the most alluring blandishments, to roll the expressive eye of wanton pleasure, and to invite to criminal indulgence by stealing upon the beholder the tender look of voluptuous languishing. They were instructed to mould their elegant and airy forms into the most enticing attitudes, and the most lascivious gestures, while the rapid and most graceful motion of their feet, adorned with golden bells and glittering with jewels, kept unison with the exquisite melody of their voices. Every pagoda has a band of these young syrens, whose business on great festivals is to dance in public before the idol, to sing hymns in his honour, and in private to enrich the treasury of the pagoda by the wages of prostitution. These women are not, however, regarded in a dishonourable light; they are considered as *wedded to the idol*, and they partake the veneration paid to him. They are forbidden ever to desert the pagoda where they are educated, and are never permitted to marry; but the offspring, if any, of their criminal embraces, are considered sacred to the idol: the boys are taught to play on the sacred instruments used at the festivals; and the daughters are devoted to the abandoned occupation of their mothers.

"The reader has, doubtless, heard and read frequently of the degeneracy and venality of PRIESTS; and we know from Herodotus, what scandalous prostitutions were suffered in honour of Mylitta; but a system of corruption, so systematical, so deliberate, and so nefarious,—and that professedly carried on in the name, and for the advantage of religion,—stands perhaps unrivalled in the history of the world, and the annals of infamy. It was by degrees that the Eleusinian worship arrived at the point of its extreme enormity; and the obscenities, finally prevalent, were equally regretted and disclaimed by the institutors; but in India we see an avowed plan of shameless seduction and debauchery: the priest himself converted into a base procurer; and the pagoda itself a public brothel. The devout Mahometan traveller, whose journey in India, in the ninth century, has been published by M. Renaudot, and from which account this description is partly taken, concludes the article by a solemn thanksgiving to the Almighty, that he and his nation were delivered from the errors of infidelity, and were unstained by the enormities of so criminal a devotion."

In a country so immensely rich, and so obedient to the dictations of priestcraft, the avarice of the sacerdotal tribe would accumulate enormous treasures. We have recently alluded to the hordes gathered by priestly hands into the temples of Greece. In the temple of Belus in Assyria, there were three prodigious statues, not of cast, but of beaten gold, of Jupiter, Juno, and Rhea. That of Jupiter was erect, in a walking attitude; forty feet in height; and weighed a thousand Babylonian talents. The statue of Rhea was of the same weight, but sitting on a throne of gold, with two lions standing before her, and two huge serpents in silver, each weighing thirty talents. Juno was erect; weighed eight hundred talents; her right hand grasped a serpent by the head, and her left a golden sceptre, encrusted with gems. Before these statues stood an altar of beaten gold, forty feet long, fifteen broad, and five hundred talents in weight. On this altar stood two vast flagons, each weighing thirty talents; two censers for incense, each five hundred talents; and, finally, three vessels for the consecrated wine, weighing nine hundred talents.

The statue of Nebuchadnezzar, in the plain of

Dura, formed of the gold heaped up by David and Solomon, Dr. Prideaux calculated at one thousand talents of gold, in value three millions and a half sterling.

Herodotus tells us, that Crœsus frequently sent to Delphi amazing presents; and burnt, in one holocaust, beds of gold and silver, ornamental vessels of the same metals, purple robes, silken carpets, and other rich furniture, which he consumed in one pile, to render that oracle propitious; while the wealthiest citizens of Sardis threw into the fire their most costly furniture: so that out of the melted mass, one hundred and seventeen golden tiles were cast; the least, three spans long, the largest six, but all one span in thickness; which were placed in the temple.

When Cambyses burnt the temple of Thebes in Egypt, there were saved from the flames three hundred talents of gold, and two thousand three hundred talents of silver; and amongst the spoils of that temple was a stupendous circle of gold, inscribed with the Zodiacal characters, and astronomical figures, which encircled the tomb of Oxymandias. At Memphis he obtained still greater sacred wealth.

These seem astounding facts; but before the sacerdotal wealth and templar splendour of India, they shrink into insignificance. The principal use which the Indians seem to have made of the immense quantities of bullion, from age to age, imported into their empire, was to melt it down into statues of their deities; if, indeed, by that title we may denominate the personified attitudes of the Almighty, and the elements of nature. Their pagodas were crowned with these golden and silver statues; they thought any inferior metal must degrade the divinity. Every house too, was crowded with statues of their ancestors; those ancestors that were exalted to the stars for their piety, or valour. The very altars of the temples were of massy gold; the incense flamed in censers of gold, and golden chalices bore their sacred oil, honey, and wine. The temple of Auruna, the day-star, had its lofty walls of prophyry internally covered with broad plates of gold, sculptured in rays, that, diverging every way, dazzled the beholder; while the radiant image of the deity burned in gems of infinite variety and unequalled beauty, on the spangled floor. The floor of the great temple of Naugracut, even so late as in the time of Mandesloe, was covered with plates of gold; and thus the Hindoo, in his devotion, trampled upon the god of half mankind.

In the processions also, made in honour of their idols, the utmost magnificence prevailed. They then brought forth all the wealth of the temple; and every order of people strove to outvie each other in displaying their riches, and adding to the pomp. The elephants marched first, richly decorated with gold and silver ornaments, studded with precious stones; chariots overlaid with those metals, and loaded with them in ingots, advanced next; then followed the sacred steers, coupled together with yokes of gold, and a train of the noblest and most beautiful beasts of the forest, by nature fierce and sanguinary, but rendered mild and tractable by the skill of man: an immense multitude of priests carrying vessels, plates, dishes, and other utensils, all of gold, adorned with diamonds, rubies, and sapphires, for the sumptuous feast of which the gods were to partake, brought up the rear. During all this time, the air was rent with the sound of various instruments, martial and festive; and the dancing girls displayed in their sumptuous apparel, the wealth of whole provinces, exhausted to decorate beauty devoted to religion.

The Arabians burst upon India, like a torrent;—their merciless grasp seized the whole prey! The western provinces first felt their fury. The Rajah of Lahore, when taken, had about his neck sixteen strings of jewels; each of which was valued at a hundred and eighty thousand rupees: and the whole at three hundred and twenty thousand pounds sterling. A sum, however, comparatively trifling, when compared with that of which the Sultan of Gazna afterwards became master in his eruption into that province; and which Mirkhond states at seven millions of coin in gold, seven hundred maunds of gold in ingots, together with an inestimable quantity of pearls and precious stones. The maund is a Persian weight, never estimated at less than forty pounds.

Let us attend this valiant marauder on another or two of his plundering expeditions into Hindostan. At the holy fane of Kreeshna, at Mathura, he found five great idols of pure gold, with eyes of rubies, of immense value. He found also three hundred idols of silver, which being melted down, loaded as many camels with bullion; the usual load of a camel being from seven hundred to one thousand two hundred pounds weight. At the great temple of Sumnaut, he found many thousands of gold and silver idols of smaller magnitude; a chain of gold, which was suspended from the roof, and weighed forty maunds; besides an inestimable horde of jewels of the first water. This prince, a day or two before his death, ordered his whole treasury to be placed before him; and having for some time, from his throne, feasted his eyes on the innumerable sacks of gold, and caskets of precious stones, burst into tears—perhaps from the recollection of the bloodshed and atrocities by which they had been accumulated—but more probably from the feeling of the vanity of all human cupidity and power,—a dismal conviction that they could not save him, but that they must pass to other hands, and he to the doom of eternity.

Immense quantities of the beautiful coins of Greece and Rome are supposed to have passed to India in the great trade of the ancients with it, for spices, silks, gems, and other precious articles, and to have been melted down in the crucible, without the least regard to the grandeur of their design, the majesty of the characters impressed, or the beauty of their execution, and went to swell the magnificence of the pagodas. We are well assured, that all the great pagodas of India had complete sets, amounting to an immense number, of the avaters and deities, which were deemed degraded if they were of baser metal than silver and gold; except in those instances where their religion required their idol to be of stone, as Jagger-nath; which had, however, the richest jewels of Golconda for eyes; and Vishnu, in the great basin of Catmandu, in Nepaul. Such was the wealth gathered by the Tartars in this wonderful country, that Mahmoud of Gazna made feasts that lasted a month; and the officers of his army rode on saddles of gold, glittering with precious stones; and his descendant, Timur, made a feast on a delightful plain, called Canaugha, or the treasury of roses, at which was exhibited such a display of gold and jewels, that in comparison, the riches of Xerxes and Darius were trifling. The treasures which Timur took in Delhi, were most enormous;—precious stones, pearls, rubies, and diamonds, thousands of which were torn from the ears and necks of the native women; and gold and gems from their arms, ancles, and dress: gold and silver vessels, money, and bullion, were carried away in such profusion by the army, that the common soldiers absolutely refused to encumber themselves with more; and an abundant harvest of plunder was left to future invaders.

Mahmoud of Gazna hearing astonishing accounts of the riches of the great pagoda of Sumnaut, whose roof was covered with plates of gold and encircled with rubies, emeralds, and other precious stones, besieged the place, and took it. On entering the temple, he was struck with astonishment at the inestimable riches it contained. In the fury of his Mahommedan zeal against idols, he smote off the nose of the great image. A crowd of Brahmins, frantic at his treatment of their god, offered the most extravagant sums for his desistance; but the soldiers of Mahmoud only proceeded with greater ardour to demolish it, when behold! on breaking its body, it was found to be hollow, and to contain an infinite variety of diamonds, rubies, and pearls of a water so pure, and a magnitude so uncommon, that the beholders were overwhelmed with astonishment. But the riches accumulated by the priests of this affluent region were so immense, that they exceed the power of the imagination to grasp them; and I shall leave this subject with what Mr. Orme, in his History of Hindostan, tells us:—that the Brahmins slumbered in the most luxurious repose in these splendid pagodas; and that the numbers accommodated in the body of the great ones, was astonishing. He acquaints us that pilgrims came from all parts of the Peninsula to worship at that of Seringham, but none without an offering of money; that a large part of the revenue of the island is allotted for the maintenance of the Brahmins who inhabit it; and that these, with their families, formerly composed a multitude, not less in number than forty thousand souls, supported without labour, by the liberality of superstition.

So much for the ease and affluence of the Brahminical life; now for a glance at that system which they had rendered so prolific of good things;—a system, the most awful that ever proceeded from the genius of priestcraft, fertile in cunning and profitable schemes. I have already shewn that in all nations the priests placed themselves at the head, and even controlled the king, as they often chose him. But in India, the Brahmins went, as I have remarked, still further. Here, in order to rivet for ever their chains on the people, they did not merely represent themselves as a noble and inviolable race, but they divided the whole community into four castes. They wrote a book, and entitled it, "The Institutes of Menu," the son of Brahma. This book contained the whole code of their religious laws, which, as proceeding from the divinity, were to last for all time,—be for ever and indissolubly binding on every Hindoo; and not to be violated in the smallest degree, except on pain of forfeiting all civil privileges and enjoyments, of life itself, and of incurring the torments of hell. These castes were to preserve for ever their respective stations. Those born in one, were not only not to pass into another, but every man was bound to follow the profession of his father. Whatever might be the difference of genius, it must be crushed; whatever desire to amend the condition of life, it must be extinguished; all variety of mind, all variations of physical constitution, all unfitness for one trade, station, or pursuit, went for nothing:—to this most infernal of priestly impositions, man, with all his hopes and desires, his bodily weaknesses, his mental aspirations, or repugnances, must succumb, and be lulled, or rather, cramped into an everlasting stupor, that the privileged Brahmin might tax him and terrify him, and live upon his labours, in the boundless enjoyment of his own pride, and insolence, and lust. " By this arrangement," says Mr. Maurice, " it should be remembered, the happiness and security of a vast empire was preserved through a long series of ages under their early sovereigns; by curbing the fiery spirits of ambitious individuals, intestine feuds were, in a great measure, prevented; the wants of an immense population were amply provided for by the industry of the labouring classes; and the several branches of trade and manufacture were carried to the utmost degree of attainable perfection." A singular kind of happiness, and one which none but a priest could have a conception of. To plunge a great nation into the everlasting sleep and sluggishness of ecclesiastical despotism, is to secure its happiness!—the happiness of beasts maintained for the value of their labour, and fattened for the butcher;—a happiness, which in the very sentence preceding, the writer terms " a barbarous attempt to chain down the powers of the human soul, to check the ardour of emulation, and damp the fire of genius."

To establish this system the Brahmins resorted to the daring fraud of representing Menu—supposed to be Noah—as not "making all men of the same blood," but as producing four different tribes of men. The first, the Brahmins, from his mouth; the second, the Kettri, or Rajahs, from his arm; the third, the Bice, or merchants, from his thigh; and the fourth, the Sooder, or labouring tribe, from his foot! Thus this doctrine, once received as true, an everlasting and impassable bar was placed between each tribe—divine authority. That it should not be endangered, the land of India was declared holy; and the Hindoos were forbidden, by all the terrors of temporal and eternal penalties, to go out of it. The Brahmins having thus, in the early ages of superstitious ignorance, taken this strong ground, proceeded to fortify it still further. The Rajahs, or provincial rulers were all chosen from their own, or the war-tribe; and the Marajah, or supreme King, was always chosen by them, often from themselves, and was entirely in their hands. By them he was educated, and moulded to their wishes; they were appointed, by these divine institutes, his guardians, and perpetual, inalienable counsellors.

Having thus firmly seized and secured the whole political power, they had only to rule and enrich themselves out of a nation of slaves, at their pleasure; paying them with promises of future happiness, or terrifying them by threats of future vengeance, into perfect passiveness; and so completely had this succeeded that, for thousands of years, their system has continued; and it is the opinion of Sir William Jones, that so ingeniously is it woven into the souls of the Hindoos, that they will be the very last people converted to Christianity. For what, indeed, can be done with a nation who, from time immemorial, have been accustomed to regard their priests as beings of a higher nature,—their laws as emanations from Heaven,—and themselves as the creatures of an unescapable destiny : who, on the one hand, are stunned with fear of future torments, and, on the other, are exposed to the dagger of the first man they meet, authorized by those pretendedly divine institutes to cut down every apostate that he encounters? From such a consummate labyrinth of priestly art nothing short of a miracle seems capable of rescuing them.

The Brahmins, like the popish priests, for the arts of priests are the same everywhere, reserve to themselves the inviolable right of reading the Vedas, or holy books, and thus impose on the people what doctrines they please. So scrupulously do they guard against the exposure of their real contents, that it is only in comparatively modern times that they have become known. A singular story is told of the Emperor Akbar, who, desiring to learn the Hindoo tenets, applied to the Brahmins, and was refused. Hereupon he had the brother of his faithful minister, Abul Fazil, a youth, brought up with a Brahmin, under a feigned character: but, after a residence of ten years, and at the moment of being about to return to court, owing to his attachment to the Brahmin's daughter, he confessed the fraud, and would have been instantly stabbed by his preceptor, had he not entreated him for mercy on his knees, and bound himself by the most solemn oaths, not to translate the Vedas, nor reveal the mysteries of the Brahmin creed. These oaths he faithfully kept during the life of the old Brahmin; but afterwards he conceived himself absolved from them, and to him we owe the publication of the real contents of those sacred volumes.

But let us look at the system a little more at large. "Though," says Maurice, "the functions of government by the laws of Menu devolved on the Kettri, or Rajah tribe; yet it is certain that in every age of the Indian empire, aspiring Brahmins have usurped and swayed the imperial sceptre. But, in fact, there was no necessity for the Brahmin to grasp at empire,—he wielded both the empire and the monarch. By an overstrained conception of the priestly character, artfully encouraged, for political purposes, by the priest himself, and certainly not justified by any precept given by Noah to his posterity, the Brahmin stood in the place of deity to the infatuated sons of Indian superstition; the will of heaven was thought to issue from his lips; and his decision was reverenced as the fiat of destiny. Thus boasting the positive interposition of the Deity in the fabrication of its singular institutions; guarded from infraction by the terror of exciting the divine wrath; and directed principally by the sacred tribe, the Indian government may be considered as a theocracy —a theocracy the more terrible, because the name of God was perverted to sanction and support the most dreadful species of despotism;—a despotism which, not content with subjugating the body, tyrannized over the prostrate faculties of the enslaved mind.

" An assembly of Brahmins sitting in judgment on a vicious, a tyrannical king, may condemn him to death; and the sentence is recorded to have been executed; but no crime affects the life of a Brahmin. He may suffer temporary degradation from his caste, but his blood must never stain the sword of justice; he is a portion of the Deity. He is inviolable! he is invulnerable! he is immortal!

" In eastern climes, where despotism has ever reigned in its meridian terror, in order to impress the deeper awe and respect upon the crowd that daily thronged around the tribunal, the hall of justice was anciently surrounded with the ministers of vengeance, who generally inflicted in presence of the monarch the sentence to which the culprit was doomed. The envenomed serpent which was to sting him to death; the enraged elephant that was to trample him beneath its feet; the dreadful instruments that were to rend open his bowels, to tear his lacerated eye from the socket, to impale alive, or saw the shuddering wretch asunder, were constantly at hand. The audience chamber, with the same view, was decorated with the utmost cost and magnificence, and the East was rifled of its jewels to adorn it. Whatever little credit may in general be due to Philostratus, his description of the palace of Musicanus too nearly resembles the accounts of our own countrymen, of the present magnificence of some of the rajahs, to be doubted, especially in those times when the hoarded wealth of India had not been pillaged. The artificial vines of gold, adorned with buds of various colours in jewellery, and thick set with precious stones, emeralds, and rubies, hanging in clusters to resemble grapes in their different stages to maturity: the silver censers of perfume constantly borne before the ruler as a god: the robe of gold and purple with which he was invested; and the litter of gold fringed with pearls, in which he was carried in a march, or to the chase,—these were the appropriate ornaments and distinctions of an Indian monarch.

"In short, whatever could warmly interest the feelings, and strongly agitate the passions of men; whatever influences hope; excites terror; all the engines of a most despotic superstition and a most refined policy, were set at work for the purpose of chaining down to the prescribed duties of his caste the mind of the bigoted Hindoo. Hence his unaltered, unalterable attachment to the national code, and the Brahminical creed. As it has been in India from the beginning, so will it continue to the end of time. For the daring culprit who violates either, heaven has no forgiveness, and earth no place of shelter or repose!

"An adultress is condemned to be devoured alive by dogs in the public market-place. The adulterer is doomed to be bound to an iron bed, heated red-hot, and burned to death. But what is not a little remarkable, for the same crime a Brahmin is only to be punished with ignominious tonsure.

"For insulting a Brahmin, an iron style, ten fingers long, shall be thrust, red-hot, down the culprit's mouth. For offering only to instruct him in his profession, boiling oil shall be dropped in his mouth and ears. For stealing kine, belonging to priests, the offender shall instantly lose half one foot. An assaulter of a Brahmin, with intent to kill, shall remain in hell for a hundred years; for actually striking him, with like intent, a thousand years. But though such frequent exceptions occur in favour of Brahmins, none are made in favour of kings! The Brahmin,—eldest-born of the gods,—who loads their altars with incense, who feeds them with clarified honey, and whose, in fact, is the wealth of the whole world, ever keeps his elevated station. To maintain him in holy and voluptuous indolence, the Kettri, or Rajah, exposes his life in front of battle; the merchant covers the ocean with his ships; the toiling husbandman incessantly tills the burning soil of India. We cannot doubt, after this, which of the Indian castes compiled this volume from the *remembered Institutes* of Menu.

"The everlasting servitude of the Soodra tribe is riveted upon that unfortunate caste by the laws of destiny; since the Soodra was born a slave, and even when emancipated by his indulgent master, a slave he must continue: *for, of a state which is natural to him,* by whom can he be divested? The Soodra must be contented to *serve;* this is his unalterable doom. To serve in the family of a Brahmin is the highest glory, and leads him to beatitude."

There is, however, a fifth tribe,—that of the outcasts from all the rest,—the Chandelahs; those who have lost caste, and the children of mixed marriages, that abhorrence of the Hindoo code, for, if once permitted, it would overturn the whole artful system. It is ordained that the Chandelah exist remote from their fellow-creatures, amid the dirt and filth of the suburbs. Their sole wealth must consist in dogs and asses; their clothes must be the polluted mantles of the dead; their dishes for food, broken pots; their ornaments, rusty iron; their food must be given them in potsherds, at a distance, that the giver may not be defiled by the shade of their outcast bodies. Their business is to carry out the corpses of those who die without kindred; they are the public executioners; and the whole that they can be heirs to, are the clothes and miserable property of the wretched malefactors. Many other particulars of this outcast tribe are added by authors on India, and they form in themselves no weak proof of the unrelenting spirit of the Hindoo code, that could thus doom a vast class of people,—a fifth of the nation,—to unpitied and unmerited wretchedness. An Indian, in his bigoted attachment to the Metempsychosis, would fly to save the life of a noxious reptile; but, were a Chandelah falling down a precipice, he would not extend a hand to save him from destruction. In such abomination are the Chandelahs held on the Malabar side of India, that if one chance to touch one of a superior tribe, he draws his sabre and cuts him down on the spot. Death itself, that last refuge of the unfortunate, offers no comfort to him, affords no view of felicity or reward. The gates of Jaggernath itself are shut against him; and he is driven, with equal disgrace, from the society of men and the temples of the gods.

Such is the picture of priestcraft in India; such the terrible spectacle of its effects, as they have existed there from nearly the days of the Flood. Towards this horrible and disgusting goal, it has laboured to lead men in all countries and all ages; but here alone, in the whole pagan world, it has succeeded to the extent of its diabolical desires. We might add numberless other features: the propitiatory sacrifice of cows, and trees of gold, prescribed by the avaricious Brahmins; the immunities and privileges with which they have surrounded themselves; the bloody rites they have laid on others, especially among the Mahrattas, where, even at the present day, human sacrifices are supposed to abound; the tortures they have induced the infatuated Yogees to inflict on themselves—some going naked all their lives, suffering their hair and beard to grow till they cover their whole bodies,—standing motionless, in the sun, in the most painful attitudes, for years, till their arms grow fast above their heads, and their nails pierce through their clenched hands,—scorching themselves over fires,—enclosing themselves in cages,—and enacting other incredible horrors on themselves, for the hope, inspired by the Brahmins, of attaining everlasting felicity. But the subject is too revolting; I turn from it in indignation, and here close my review of priestcraft in the pagan world.

## CHAPTER IX.

### THE HEBREWS.

We have now gone to and fro in the earth, and have walked up and down in it; not, like a certain celebrated character, seeking whom we might devour, but inquiring who have been devoured of priests; and everywhere we have made but one discovery; everywhere, in lands, however distant, and times, however remote, a suffering people, and a proud and imperious priesthood have been found. Sinbad the sailor, in his multifarious and adventurous wanderings, once chanced to land in a desert island, in which a strange creature, the Old Man of the Sea, leapt upon his shoulders, and there, spite of all his efforts to dislodge him, night and day, for a long time, maintained his station. By day, he compelled poor Sinbad, by a vigorous application of his heels to his ribs, to go where he pleased,—beneath the trees, whence he plucked fruit, or to the stream, where he drank. By night, he still clung, even in his sleep, with such sensitiveness to his neck, that it was impossible to unseat him. At length a successful stratagem presented itself to Sinbad. He found a gourd, and squeezed into it the juice of the grape, and set it in a certain place till it had fermented, and became strong wine. This he put to the mouth of the Old Man of the Sea, who drank it greedily, became drunk, and fell asleep so soundly, that Sinbad unfolded his clinging legs from his breast, hurled him from his shoulders, and, as he lay, crushed his head with a stone. The adventure of Sinbad was awkward enough, but that of poor human nature has been infinitely worse. THE OLD MAN OF THE CHURCH, from age to age, from land to land, has ridden on the shoulders of humanity, and set at defiance all endeavours and all schemes to dislodge him. Unlike the Old Man of the Sea, whose best beverage was a brook, he is too well inured to strong drinks to be readily overcome by them. He is one of those drinkers called deep-stomached, and strong-headed; who sit out all guests, dare and bear all spirituous potations, and laugh, in invulnerable comfort, over the intoxication of the prostrated multitude. And what wonder? His seat has ever been at the boards of princes. The most sparkling cup has not passed him by untasted; the most fiery fluid has not daunted him. He has received the vintages reserved solely for kings and their favourites; and though there was blood in it, he has not blenched. The tears of misery dropped into it, could not render it too bitter; the bloody sweat-drops of despair too poisonous: though the sound of battle was in his ears, he ceased not to grasp the flagon,—it was music,—though martyrs burned at their stakes before him, and the very glow of their fires came strongly upon him, he interrupted not his carouse, but only cooled more gratefully his wine. He has quaffed the juice of all vines; presided at the festivities of all nations; poured libations to all gods: in the wild orgies of the ancient German and British forests he has revelled; in the midnight feast of skulls he has pledged the savage and the cannibal; the war-feast of the wilderness, or the sacred banquet of the refined Greek, alike found him a guest; he has taken the cup of pollution from the hand of the Babylonian harlot; and pledged, in the robes of the Gallic Primate, renunciation of the Christian religion with the Atheist. Lover of all royal fetes; delighter in the crimson-cushioned ease of all festivals in high places; soul of all jollity where the plunderers and the deluders of man met to rejoice over their achievments; inspirer of all choice schemes for the destruction of liberty and genuine knowledge ·when the vintage of triumphant fraud ferments in his brain, till the wine of God's wrath, in the shape of man's indignation, confound him,—what shall move him from his living throne? From the days of the Flood to those of William the Fourth of England he has ridden on, exultingly, the everlasting incubus of the groaning world.

We have perambulated the prime nations of paganism. It would have been easy to have extended our researches further, to have swelled our details to volumes; but the object was only to give a sample from the immense mass of ecclesiastical enormities. We now come to the Holy Land; and to the only priesthood ever expressly ordained of heaven. It might have been expected that this would prove a splendid exception to the general character of the order; but alas!—as the Jewish dispensation was formed under the pressing necessity of guarding against the idolatry of surrounding nations, and as merely preparatory to a more spiritual one, so it would seem as if one design of the Almighty had been to shew how radically mischievous and prone to evil an ecclesiastical order is, under any circumstances. The Jewish priests had this advantage over all others whatever, that they were one tribe of a great family, to whom, in sharing out the land given to them of God, the altar was made their sole inheritance,—the whole country being divided amongst the other eleven tribes. But, notwithstanding this fair title, so strongly did the universal spirit of priestcraft work in them, that their history may be comprised in a few sentences, and is one of the most striking in the world. It began in Aaron with idolatry, accompanied by most pitiful evasions; it shewed itself in its prime, in the sons of Eli, in shameless peculation and lewdness; and it ended in the crucifixion of Christ! Such a beginning—a middle—and an end—the world besides cannot shew.

When we hear Aaron telling the people, in the face of the most astounding miracles,—when the sound of God's trumpets, which had shaken them to the earth, in terror, had yet scarcely ceased to ring in their ears,—when God himself, in a fiery majesty, that made the mountain before them smoke and tremble to its base, was at hand delivering to Moses his eternal law—hear him telling them to bring their golden ornaments, and he would make a god to go before them; and, in the next moment, telling Moses that the people constrained him, and he threw the gold into the fire, and "out came this calf," as if by accident,—we are filled with contempt for sacerdotal sycophancy and time-serving.

When we read that "the sons of Eli were the sons of Belial,—they knew not the Lord:—and the priests' custom was, that when any man offered sacrifice, the priests' servant came while the flesh was in seething, with a flesh-hook of three teeth in his hand; and he strook it into the pan, or kettle, or cauldron, or pot;—all that the flesh-hook brought up, the priest took for himself. So they did in Shiloh, to all the Israelites that came thither. Also, before they burnt the fat the priests' servant came, and said to the man that sacrificed, 'give flesh to roast for the priest, for he will not have sodden flesh of thee, but raw.' And if any man said unto him, 'let them not fail to burn the fat presently, and then take as much as thy soul desireth;' and then he would answer him,—'Nay, but thou shalt give it me *now;* and if not, I will take it by force.' Therefore the sin of the young men was very great before the Lord; for men abhorred the offering of the Lord. Now Eli was very old, and heard all that his sons did unto all Israel; and how they lay with the women that assembled at the door of the tabernacle of the congregation." When we read this, we are on fire with indignation. But when we hear the chief priests crying out against Christ—the hope, nay, the great object of the formation of their nation,—the most meek, and pure, and beneficent being that ever existed—"away with this fellow! he is not fit to live! Away with him! crucify him!" we are thunderstruck with astonishment!—we are silenced and satisfied for ever, of the rooted and incurable malignancy of priestcraft. If God himself descended from heaven, and charged a priestly hierarchy with corruption, they would tell him to his face, that he lied. They would assail him as a slanderer and misrepresenter of the good, and raise, if possible, his own world in arms against him! If the fate of all other nations spoke to us in vain—that of the Jews should be an eternal warning. The very priests which God ordained, first corrupted, and then destroyed the kingdom. They began with idolatry, and ended with killing the Son of God himself. Their victims, the Jews, still walk before our eyes, a perpetual and fearful testimony against them. It was the priests who mainly contributed to annihilate them for ever as a people, and to disperse them through all regions, the objects of the contempt, the loathing, and the pitiless persecution of all ages, and of every race.

## CHAPTER X.

### POPERY.

---

O that the free would stamp the impious name
    Of Pope into the dust! or write it there,
So that this blot upon the page of fame
    Were as a serpent's path, which the light air
Erases, and the flat sands close behind!
        Ye the oracle have heard;
        Lift the victory-flashing-sword,
And cut the snaky knots of this foul Gordian word,
    Which, weak itself as stubble, yet can bind
        Into a mass, irrefragably firm,
    The axes and the rods which awe mankind.
        The sound has poison in it—'t is the sperm
Of what makes life foul, cankerous, and abhorred;
    Disdain not then, at thine appointed term,
    To set thine armed heel on this reluctant worm.
                                SHELLEY.

---

CHRIST appeared;—the career of Paganism was checked;—the fate of Judaism was sealed. A character and a religion were placed before the eyes of men hitherto inconceivable in the beauty and philanthropy of their nature. Unlike all other founders of a religious faith, Christ had no selfishness, no desire of dominance; and his system, unlike all other systems of worship, was bloodless, boundlessly beneficent, inexpressibly pure, and, most marvellous of all, went to break all bonds of body and soul; and to cast down every temporal and every spiritual tyranny. It was a system calculated for the whole wide universe;—adapted to embrace men of all climes, all ages, all ranks of life, or intellect; for the rich and for the poor; for the savage and the civilized; for the fool and the philosopher; for man, woman, and child;—which, recognizing the grand doctrine, that " God made of one blood all the nations of the earth," represented the Almighty as the father, and all men as brethren born to one universal love,—to the same inalienable rights,—to the same eternal hope. He himself was the living personification of his principles. Demolishing the most inveterate prejudices of men, by appearing a poor man amongst the poor; by tearing from aristocratic pride and priestly insolence their masks of most orthodox assurance; by proclaiming, that the truth which he taught should make all men free; by declaring that the Gentiles lorded it over, and oppressed one another, but that it should not be so with his followers; by pulling down with indignation spiritual pride in high places, and calling the poor and afflicted, his brethren, and the objects of his tenderest regard,—he laid the foundations of civil and religious freedom, of mental power growing out of unrestrained mental energies, and of love and knowledge co-equal in extension with the world. This perfect freedom of universal man he guarded by leaving no DECREES; but merely great, and everlasting principles, intelligible to the mind and conscience of the whole human race; and on which, men in all countries, might found institutions most consonant to their wants. By declaring that " wherever two or three were met together in his name, he would be in the midst of them," he cut off, for ever, every claim, the most specious, of priestly dominance; and by expressing his un-qualified and indignant abhorrence of every desire of his disciples "to call down fire from heaven upon his enemies," or to forbid those to preach and work miracles in his name, who did not immediately follow him, and conform to their notions, he left to his church a light more resplendent than that of the sun, on the subject of non-interference with the sacred liberty and prerogatives of conscience.

One would have thought that from this epoch, the arm of priestcraft would have been broken; that it would never more have dared to raise its head;—but it is a principle of shameless avidity and audacity; and it is exactly from this time that we trace the most amazing career of its delusions and atrocities, down to the very day of our own existence.

Who is not familiar with the horrors and arrogant assumptions of the papal church? Scarcely had the persecutions of the pagan emperors ceased, when the Christian church became inundated with corruptions and superstitions of every kind. Constantine embraced Christianity; and almost the whole world embraced it nominally with him. From a conversion of such a kind, the work of regal example and popular interested hopes, what effects were to be expected? The martial tyranny of ancient Rome, which had subdued the world, was coming to an end. The wealth of which a thousand states had been stripped, had turned to poison in her bosom, and brought upon the stern mistress of bloodshed and tears that retribution, from which national rapine and injustice never eventually escape. But as if the ghost of departed despotism hovered over the Seven Hills, and sought only a fresh body to arise in a worse shape, a new tyranny commenced in the form of priestcraft, ten times more terrible and hateful than the old,—because it was one which sought to subjugate not merely the persons of men, but to extinguish knowledge; to crush into everlasting childishness the human mind; and to rule it, in its fatuity, with mysteries and terrors. The times favoured the attempt. With the civil power of the Roman empire, science and literature were disappearing. A licentious army controlled the destiny of a debauched and effeminated people; and the Gothic and Hunnish nations, rushing in immense torrents over the superannuated states of Europe, scattered, for a time, desolation, poverty, and ignorance. At this crisis, while it had to deal with hordes of rough warriors, who, strong in body and boisterous in manner, had yet minds not destitute of great energies, and many traditional maxims of moral and judicial excellence, but clothed in all the simple credulity of children,—up rose the spirit of priestcraft in Rome, and assumed all its ancient and inflated claims. As if the devil, stricken with malice at the promulgation of Christianity, which threatened to annihilate his power, had watched the opportunity to inflict on it the most fatal wound, and had found no instrument so favourable to his purpose as a priest,—such a glorious and signal triumph never yet was his from the creation of the world. Had he devised a system for himself, he could not have pitched upon one like popery;—a system which, pretending to be that of Christ, suppressed the Bible,—extinguished knowledge,—locked up the human mind,—amused it with the most ludicrous baubles,—and granted official licenses to commit all species of crimes and impurity. Satan himself became enthroned on the Seven Hills in the habit of a priest, and grinned his broadest delight amidst the public and universal reign of ignorance, hypocrisy, venality, and lust.

As if the popes had studied the pagan hierarchies, they brought into concentrated exercise all their various engines of power, deception, and corruption.

They could not, indeed, assert, as the pagan priesthood had done, that they were of a higher origin than the rest of mankind; and therefore entitled to sit as kings, to choose all kings, and rule over all kings; for it was necessary to preserve some public allegiance to the doctrines of Christianity,—but they took ground quite as effective. They declared themselves the authorized vicegerents of heaven; making Christ's words to Peter their charta—" On this rock I will build my church,"—hence asserting themselves to be the only true church, though they never could shew that St. Peter ever was at Rome at all. On this ground, however—enough for the simple warriors of the time—they proceeded to rule over nations and kings. On this ground they proclaimed the infallibility of the pope and his conclave of cardinals, and thus excluded all dissent. Their first act, having once taken this station, was that which had been the practice of priests in all countries,—to shut up the true knowledge amongst themselves. As the priests of Egypt and Greece inclosed it in mysteries, they wrapt the simple truths of the gospel in mysteries too; as the Brahmins forbid any except their own order to read the sacred Vedas,—they shut up the Bible,—the very book given to enlighten the world;—the very book which declared of its own contents, that " they were so clear that he who ran might read them;" that they taught a way of life so perspicuous that " the wayfaring man, though a fool, could not err therein." This was the most daring and audacious act the world had then seen; but this act once successful, the whole earth was in their power. The people were ignorant; they taught them what they pleased. They delivered all sorts of ludicrous and pernicious dogmas as scripture; and who could contradict them? So great became the ignorance of even their own order, under this system, so completely became the Bible a strange book, that when, in after ages, men began to inquire, and to expose their delusions, a monk warned his audience to beware of these heretics who had invented a new language, called Greek, and had written in it a book called the New Testament, full of the most damnable doctrines. By every act of insinuation, intimidation, forgery, and fraud, they not only raised themselves to the rank of temporal princes, but lorded it over the greatest kings with insolent impunity. The BANN, which we have seen employed by the priests of Odin in the north, they adopted, and made its terrors felt throughout the whole Christian world. Was a king refractory—did he refuse the pontifical demand of money—had he an opinion of his own—a repugnance to comply with papal influence in his affairs?— the thunders of the Vatican were launched against him; his kingdom was laid under the bann; all people were forbidden, on pain of eternal damnation, to trade with his subjects; all churches were shut; the nation was of a sudden deprived of all exterior exercise of its religion; the altars were despoiled of their ornaments; the crosses, the reliques, the images, the statues of the saints were laid on the ground; and, as if the air itself were profaned, and might pollute them by its contact, the priests carefully covered them up, even from their own approach and veneration. The use of bells entirely ceased in all churches; the bells themselves were removed from the steeples, and laid on the ground with the other sacred utensils. Mass was celebrated with shut doors, and none but the priests were admitted to the holy institution. The clergy refused to marry, baptise, or bury; the dead were obliged to be cast into ditches, or lay putrefying on the ground; till the superstitious people, looking on their children who died without baptism as gone to perdition, and those dead without burial amid the ceremonies of the church and in consecrated ground as seized on by the devil, rose in rebellious fury and obliged the prince to submit and humble himself before the proud priest of Rome.

> Realms quake by turns: proud arbitress of grace,
> The church, by mandate shadowing forth the power
> She arrogates o'er heaven's eternal door,
> Closes the gates of every sacred place.
> Straight from the sun and tainted air's embrace
> All sacred things are covered; cheerful morn
> Grows sad as night—no seemly garb is worn,
> Nor is a face allowed to meet a face
> With natural smile of greeting. Bells are dumb;
> Ditches are graves—funereal rites denied;
> And in the church-yard he must take his bride
> Who dares be wedded! Fancies thickly come
> Into the pensive heart ill fortified,
> And comfortless despairs the soul benumb.
> WORDSWORTH.

But not merely kings and kingdoms were thus circumstanced, every individual, every parish was liable to be thus excommunicated by the neighbouring priest. The man who offended one of these powerful churchmen, however respected and influential in his own neighbourhood over night, might the next morning behold the hearse drawn up to his hall door,—a significant emblem that he was dead to all civil and religious rights, and that if he valued his life, now at the mercy of any vile assassin, he must fly, and leave his family and his property to the same tender regards which had thus outlawed himself.

The invention of monkery was a capital piece of priestly ingenuity. By this means the whole world became inundated with monks and friars,

> Black, white, and grey, with all their trumpery.

confess his sins to the priest. Thus the priest was put into possession of everything which could enslave a man to him. Who was so pure in life and thought that, after having unbosomed himself to his confessor—made him the depository of his most secret thoughts, his weakest or worst actions, dare any more to oppose or offend him? But the chains of shame and fear were not all; those of hope were added. The priest had not only power to hear sins, but to pardon them. He could shut up in hell, or let out; he was not content with enslaving his follower in this world—he carried on his influence to the next, and even invented a world, from the tortures of which no man could escape without his permission.

How all this could be built on the foundation of Christianity might be wondered at; but it should never be forgotten that the Bible was locked up, and everything was directed to the acquisition of power and gain. Everything was a source of gain. Besides the direct tribute to the popedom, every shrine had its offerings; every confession, every prayer had its price. Escape from purgatory and indulgence in sin were regulated by a certain scale of payment. The rich, the foolish, and the penitent were wheedled out of their property to maintain the endless train of pope, cardinals, priests, monks, nuns, confessors, and their subordinates. By them abbeys, cathedrals, and churches were endowed with ample lands; and every one who incurred the censure of the church, added also by fines to its funds. For a thousand years this system was triumphant throughout Europe;

> Thou heaven of earth! what spells could pall thee then,
>   In ominous eclipse! A thousand years
> Bred from the slime of deep oppression's den,
>   Dyed all thy liquid light with blood and tears.

Over a great part of it, it reigns still.

Millions of monks and secular priests, all forbidden to marry; all pampered in luxurious ease and abundance to voluptuousness, were let loose on the female world as counsellors and confessors, with secresy in one hand, and amplest power of absolution from sin in the other; and the effect on domestic purity may be readily imagined. So, smoothly ran the course of popery for many a century: but when, spite of all its efforts to the contrary, the human mind again began to stir; when knowledge again revived; and the secrets of the church were curiously pried into; then this terrible hierarchy, calling itself Christian, let loose its vengeance. Fire and fagot, chains and dungeons, exterminating wars, and inquisitions, those hells on earth, into which any man might, at a moment's notice, be dragged from his family, his fireside, or his bed, at the instigation of malice, envy, cupidity, or holy suspicion, to tortures and death. These were the tender mercies of the papal priestcraft in the hour of its fear.

This is a brief sketch of what the popish church was: we will now go on to give evidence of its spirit and proceedings from the best authenticated histories.

1. Of the means employed to obtain power.
2. Of the uses of that power.
3. Of the arrogance of the popish priesthood in power.
4. Of their atrocities.

The evidence I shall select must necessarily be a very small portion from the immense mass of the deeds of this church; for its history is such a continued tissue of ambition, cupidity, and vice in its most hateful shapes,—dissensions, frauds, and bloodshed, that nothing but the desire to draw from it a great moral and political lesson, could induce me to wade through it.

## CHAPTER XI.

#### POPERY CONTINUED.

---

They willeth to be king's peres,
And higher than the emperour;
And some that weren but pore freres
Now woollen waxe a warriour.—CHAUCER.

But, Lorde, we lewed men knowen no God but thee, and we, with thyne help and thy grace, forsaken Nabugodonosor and hys lawes. For he, in his prowd estate, wole have all men onder hym, and he nele be onder no man. He ondoeth thy lawes that thou ordenest to be kept, and maketh hys awne lawes as hym lyketh, and so he maketh hym kynge aboven all other kynges of the erth; and maketh men to worschupen hym as a God, and thye gret sacryfice he hath ydone away.
THE PLOWEMAN'S PRAIER.

---

THE earliest means which the bishops of Rome employed to acquire power was, to assert their supremacy over all other bishops of the Christian church. This was not granted at once, but led to many quarrels with their cotemporaries. The bishop of Constantinople, in particular, contended with them for the superiority; the emperor Constantine having shifted there the seat of civil government. These odious squabbles I must necessarily pass over, and confine myself entirely to the Romish church, as being more intimately connected with our object. I may state, once for all, that the patriarchs of Constantinople maintained the contest with Rome through every age to the very time of the Reformation; and many disgraceful expositions of priestly wrath were made on both sides. Of the Greek church, it will be sufficient to say, that its prelates partook largely in the arts and vices of priests in general, and plunged that church into an abundance of ceremonious puerilities, in which it remains to this day.

The attempts of the Romish pontiffs to grasp at power were not crowned with instant success, either over their fellow priests or cotemporary princes. It was a work of time, of continual stratagem, and the boldest acts of assumption. The full claims of papal dominion over the Christian world in Europe were not admitted, indeed, till the 11th century.

In the 4th century, Mosheim says, in the episcopal order the bishop of Rome was the first in rank; and was distinguished by a sort of pre-eminence over all other bishops. Prejudices, arising from a variety of causes, contributed to establish this superiority; but it was chiefly owing to certain circumstances of grandeur and opulence, by which mortals, for the most part, form their ideas of pre-eminence and dignity, and which they generally confound with the reasons of a just and legal authority. The bishop of Rome surpassed all his brethren in the magnificence and splendour of the church over which he presided; in the riches of his revenues and possessions; in the number and variety of his ministers; in his credit with the people; and in his sumptuous and splendid manner of living. These dazzling marks of human power; these ambiguous proofs of true greatness and felicity, had such an influence on the minds of the multitude, that the see of Rome became, in this century, a most seducing object of sacerdotal ambition. Hence it happened, that when a new pontiff was to be elected by the suffrages of the presbyters and the people, the city of Rome was generally agitated with dissensions, tumults, and cabals, whose consequences were often deplorable and fatal. One of these, in 366, gave rise to a civil war, which was carried on within the city of Rome with the utmost barbarity and fury, and produced the most cruel massacres and depopulations.

The picture of the church which Milton makes Michael foreshew to Adam was speedily realized.

> The Spirit
> Poured first on his apostles, whom he sends
> To evangelize the nations, then on all
> Baptized, shall them with wond'rous gifts endue
> To speak all tongues, and do all miracles,
> As did their Lord before them. Thus they win
> Great numbers of each nation, to receive
> With joy the tidings brought from Heaven: at length,
> Their ministry performed, and race well run,
> Their doctrine, and their story written left,
> They die; but in their room, as they forewarn,
> Wolves shall succeed for teachers, grievous wolves,
> Who all the sacred mysteries of Heaven
> To their own vile advantages shall turn
> Of lucre and ambition: and the truth
> With superstitions and traditions taint,
> Left only in those written records pure,
> Though not but by the Spirit understood.
> Then shall they seek to avail themselves of names,
> Places and titles, and with these to join
> Secular power; though feigning still to act
> By spiritual; to themselves appropriating
> The Spirit of God, promised alike and given
> To all believers; and, from that pretence
> Spiritual laws by carnal power shall force
> On ev'ry conscience; laws which none shall find
> Left them enrolled, or what the Spirit within
> Shall on the heart engrave. What will they then
> But force the Spirit of Grace itself, and bind
> His consort Liberty? What but unbuild
> His living temple, built by Faith to stand,
> Their own faith, not another's? For, on earth,
> Who against faith and conscience can be heard

Infallible? Yet many will presume:
Whence heavy persecution shall arise
On all, who in the worship persevere
Of spirit and truth; the rest, far greater part,
Will deem, in outward rites and specious forms,
Religion satisfied: truth shall retire
Bestuck with slanderous darts, and works of faith
Rarely be found: so shall the world go on,
To good malignant, to bad men benign:
Under her own weight groaning: till the day
Appear of respiration to the just,
And vengeance to the wicked.

In this century many of those steps were laid by which the bishops of Rome afterwards mounted to the summit of ecclesiastical power and despotism. These steps were laid, partly by the imprudence of the emperors, partly by the dexterity of the Roman prelates. In the fifth century the declining power of the emperors left the pontiff at liberty to exercise authority almost without control; and the irruptions of the barbarians contributed to strengthen this authority; for, perceiving the subserviency of the multitude to the bishop, they resolved to secure his interest and influence by loading him with benefits and honours.

This was the second mode by which they acquired power,—flattering the surrounding kings; serving them occasionally, without regard to honour or principle, or, as they grew stronger, subduing them by menaces to their will. In the seventh century the Roman pontiffs used all sorts of methods to maintain and enlarge the authority and pre-eminence they had acquired by a grant from the most odious tyrant that ever disgraced the annals of history. Boniface III. engaged Phocas, that abominable despot, who waded to the imperial throne through the blood of the Emperor Mauritius, to take from the Patriarch of Constantinople the title of Æcumenical, or Universal

Bishop, and confer it upon him. In the next century a still more glaring stretch of assumed priestly power was exhibited. We observe, says Mosheim, in the French annals, the following remarkable and shocking instance of the enormous power that was, at this time, invested in the Roman pontiff. Pepin was mayor of the palace to Childeric III.; and, in exercise of that high office, was possessed, in reality, of the royal power; but, not content with this, he formed the design of dethroning his sovereign. He therefore sent ambassadors to Rome to inquire, *whether the divine law did not permit a valiant and warlike people to dethrone a pusillanimous and indolent monarch, who was incapable of performing any of the functions of royalty, and to substitute in his place one more worthy to rule?* Zachary had need of the aid of Pepin; and his answer was all that could be wished. When this decision of the pope was published in France, Pepin stripped poor Childeric of his royalty; and stepped immediately into his throne. This decision was solemnly confirmed by his successor, Stephen II., who went to France; and being under the necessity of soliciting Pepin's aid against the Lombards, dissolved the act of allegiance and fidelity the usurper had sworn to Childeric; and, to render his title as firm as possible, anointed and crowned him, his wife, and two sons.

This compliance of the Roman pontiffs' proved an abundant source of opulence and credit to them. Pepin marched into Italy, subdued all the pope's enemies, and put him in possession of the Grecian provinces in Italy. The Exarch of Ravenna, when Pepin retired, threw off the yoke, and besieged Rome; but Pepin returned, and compelled him again to deliver up the exarchate of Ravenna and Pentapolis to the pontiff; and thus raised the Bishop of Rome to the rank of a temporal prince. After Pepin's death a new attack was made upon the papal territory, by Dideric, king of the Lombards. The then pope, Adrian I., fled to Charlemagne, the son of Pepin; who, having need of the pope's sanction to seize on the Eastern Roman Empire, hastened to Rome; repelled the pope's foes, and in consideration of his sanction of his ambitious views, added fresh territories to the papal see. Thus, by the most shameless and unprincipled trafficking between the pretended Vicar of Christ, and these bold bad kings, did the popes acquire royalty and dominion, and gave to treason and regal robbery the assumed sanction of heaven! Once placed by kings on temporal thrones, these audacious priests soon shewed their royal cotemporaries what companions they had admitted amongst them. Not contented with what royal robbery had given them, they speedily assailed their princely neighbours; sought to hurl them from their throne, and stirred up some of the most bloody wars on record.

The notorious Hildebrand, a Tuscan monk, of mean origin, having arrived at the pontificate, styled himself Gregory VII., and displayed to the world the full measure of the priestly spirit. He was a man, says Mosheim, of uncommon genius, whose ambition in forming the most arduous projects, was equalled by his dexterity in bringing them into execution. Sagacious, crafty, and intrepid, he suffered nothing to escape his penetration, defeat his stratagems, or daunt his courage. Haughty and arrogant beyond all measure; obstinate, impetuous, and intractable; he looked up to the summit of universal empire with a wistful eye; and laboured up the steep ascent with uninterrupted ardour, and invincible perseverance. Void of all principle, destitute of every virtuous feeling; he suffered little restraint in his audacious pursuits from the dictates of religion, or the remonstrances of conscience. Not content to enlarge the jurisdiction and augment the opulence of the see of Rome, he strove to render the universal church subject to its despotism; to dissolve the jurisdiction of kings and princes over the various orders of the clergy; and exclude them from the management of the revenues of the church. Nay, he would submit to his power the kings, emperors, and princes themselves; and render their dominions tributary to Rome. Such were the pious and apostolic exploits that employed Gregory VII. during his whole life; and which rendered his pontificate a continual scene of tumult and bloodshed. His conduct to France was worthy of the country which had first given princely power to the Roman priests, and of himself. It was just that the realm which had put power into such hands for such purposes as it did, should be bitten by a fiendish ingratitude. Hildebrand declared France tributary to the see of Rome; and ordered his legates to demand yearly, in the most solemn manner, the payment of that tribute. Nothing can be more insolent than the language in which the priest addressed himself to Philip of France, recommending an humble and obliging carriage, from this consideration, that *both his kingdom and his soul were under the dominion of St. Peter*, i. e., *his vicar, the pope, who had power to bind and to loose him both on earth and in heaven.* Nothing escaped his all-grasping ambition. He drew up an oath for the emperor of the Romans, from whom he demanded a profession of subjection and obedience. He pretended Saxony was a feudal tenure, having been a pious offering of Charlemagne to the see of Rome. He claimed Spain: maintained it had been the property of the apostolic see from the earliest times of the church; and the Spanish princes paid him tribute. He made the like attempts on England: but found in William the Conqueror a different subject. William granted his Peter-pence, but refused to do homage for his crown. He wrote circular letters to the German princes, to Geysa, King of Hungary, and Sweno, King of Denmark, demanding submission. The son of Demetrius, Czar of the Russias, went to Rome, in consequence of his letters, to obtain the kingdom which would devolve to him on his father's death, as a gift from St. Peter, after professing subjection and allegiance to the prince of the Apostles,—a gift readily granted by the officious pope, who was extremely liberal of what did not belong to him. Demetrius Suinimer, Duke of Croatia and Dalmatia, was raised to royalty by him in the year 1076; and solemnly proclaimed King at Salona, on condition that he should pay annually two hundred pieces of gold to St. Peter, at the Easter festival. Boleslaus II., King of Poland, having killed Stanislaus, Bishop of Cracow, Gregory not only excommunicated him, but hurled him from his throne; dissolved the oath of allegiance which his subjects had taken; and forbid, by an express, imperious edict, the nobles and clergy of Poland from electing a new king without his leave.

In Italy his success was transcendant. Matilda, the daughter of Boniface Duke of Tuscany, the most powerful and opulent princess of that country, found that neither ambition nor years had extinguished the tender passion in the heart of Gregory,—and as a testimony of the familiarity which existed between them, settled all her possessions in Italy and elsewhere upon the church of Rome; an act, however, strongly resisted by her successor, and the cause of many struggles and much bloodshed.

To complete his despotic power over every Christian prince, this odious priest claimed the sole right of installing bishops in their office. It had been the custom of every prince to appoint the bishops of his own land. At the death of any one of these, the ring and crosier, the insignia of his office, were sent to the monarch, and were by him delivered to the one he appointed. This right Gregory claimed as the sole prerogative of the pope; thus designing to make the whole church dependent on him, and entirely subservient to all the papal views—powerful instruments in the pontifical hands against both prince and people, the world over. The resistance this claim met with, led to terrible wars; and we shall have occasion to mention that with the Emperor of Germany, and his humiliation before the haughty priest, under the head of priestly arrogance.

Thus did this race of most shameless and audacious men, while they called themselves the pastors of the flock of the meek and tender Christ, daringly and recklessly advance to a pitch of the most amazing, enduring, and universal despotism over the loftiest and most powerful monarchs. But to display effectively the full character of the Roman pontiffs, we must write volumes on their deeds in the thirteenth and fourteenth centuries, which were filled with their arrogant demands from, and assumptions over, the sovereign powers of Europe; for, at once, Conrad Duke of Suabia, and Frederick of Austria, were actually beheaded at Naples by order of Clement IV.; and another emperor, Henry IV., is supposed to have been poisoned by a wafer, in taking the sacrament from a Dominican monk. Their excommunications,—their wars,—their vindictive quarrels with kings, and with each other,—these things swell the numerous volumes of ecclesiastical history. Nothing, indeed, is so revolting in all the annals of the world as the malignant bitterness of these vicars of Christ against each other upon different occasions. Their unbridled ambition led more than once to the election of two popes at the same time, and to the consequent tearing asunder of all Europe with their petty factions.

The example of the pontiffs was not lost on the bishops, abbots, and inferior clergy. These, even in the time of Charlemagne, had actually obtained for their tenants and their possessions an immunity from the jurisdiction of the counts and other magistrates; as also from taxes and imposts of all kinds. But in this century they carried their pretensions still further,—aimed at the civil government of the cities and territories in which they exercised a spiritual dominion; and even aspired to the honours and authority of dukes, marquises, and counts of the empire. The nobles were for ever resisting, in their respective domains, the assumptions of the clergy in matters of jurisdiction and other affairs. These, therefore, seized the opportunity which was offered them by the superstition of the times, to obtain from the kings these, the ancient rights of the nobles; and, as the influence of the bishops over the people was greater than that of the nobility, the kings, to secure the services of so powerful a priesthood, generally granted their requests. Thus they became bishops and abbots clothed with titles and dignities so foreign to their spiritual office,—reverend dukes, marquises, counts, and viscounts!

It was not however by these means only that they sought dominion over the world. They had a thousand arts to rivet their power into the souls of the people. COUNCILS were one of them. As if the sacerdotal name and inculcations were not influential enough, they sought, by collecting together all the dignities of the church into one place, to invest them with a more awful character; and to render the enactments of these priestly congresses everlasting and indissoluble laws. These enactments were such as—the worship of images, decreed in the council of Nice 787; the holding of a festival to the virgin mother, instituted by the council of Mentz in the 9th century; taking the cup of the sacrament from the laity; and a declaration of the lawfulness of breaking the most solemn engagements made to heretics, by the council of Constance in the fifteenth century, with a thousand other despotic or absurd decrees against all sects, and all freedom of opinion; and for the institution of exclusive rites and festivals.

## CHAPTER XII.

### POPERY CONTINUED.

---

*(Chastity speaks).*
I blame the Emperour Constantine,
That I am put to sic ruine,
   And baniest from the kirk:
For since he maid the Paip an king,
In Rome, I could get na lodging:
   But headlong in the dark.
But ladie Sensualitie,
Since then, has guidit this cuntrie,
   And monie of the rest:
And now scho reulis all this land
And has decreed, at her command,
   That I should be supprest.
Sir David Lyndsay's Satyre of the Three Estaites.

---

THE establishment of monkery was another means of building up a perfect despotism by the papists. These orders orginated in the third century, and, multiplying through successive ages, became, not only various in name, but countless in number; spreading in swarms throughout every part of Christendom; propagating superstition, lewdness, and ignorance; acting as spies and supporters of the papal dominion; fixing themselves in every fertile and pleasant spot; awing, or wheedling the rich and foolish out of their lands and possessions; and, at length, bursting out into the most bitter quarrels amongst themselves, became like so many rabid dogs before the public eye; and hastened, in no small degree, the downfall of the church which had set them up for its own support. They, as well as the secular clergy, were forbidden to marry; and hence flowed a torrent of corruption throughout the world. In the third century they formed, says Mosheim, connexions with those women who had made vows of chastity; and it was an ordinary thing for an ecclesiastic to admit one of these fair saints to his bed, but still under the most solemn declarations that nothing passed contrary to the rules of chastity and virtue! These holy concubines were called *Mulieres Subintroductæ*.

> Yet more,—round many a Convent's blazing fire
> Unhallowed threads of revelry are spun;
> There Venus sits disguised like a Nun,—
> While Bacchus, clothed in semblance of a Friar,
> Pours out his choicest beverage high and higher
> Sparkling, until it cannot choose but run
> Over the bowl, whose silver lip hath won
> An instant kiss of masterful desire—
> To stay the precious waste: through every brain
> The domination of the sprightly juice
> Spreads high conceits, to madding Fancy dear,
> Till the arched roof, with resolute abuse
> Of its grave echoes, swells a choral strain,
> Whose votive burden is—" OUR KINGDOM'S HERE!"
> WORDSWORTH.

These fellows too, especially the Mendicants, wandering over Europe, were the most active venders of relics, and propagators of every superstitious notion and rite. Their licentiousness, so early as the fifth century, was become proverbial; and they are said to have excited thus early, in various places, the most dreadful tumults and seditions. In the next century they multiplied so prodigiously in the east, that whole armies might have been raised of them without any sensible diminution of their numbers. In the western provinces also they were held in the highest veneration, and both monks and nuns swarmed. In Great

Britain, an abbot, Cougal, persuaded an innumerable number of persons to abandon the affairs, duties, and obligations of life, and to shut themselves up in idleness, or to wander about in holy mischief. In the seventh century, the contagion spread still more enormously. Heads of families, striving to surpass each other's zeal for the advancement of monkery, shut up their children in convents, and devoted them to a solitary life as the highest felicity. Abandoned profligates, terrified by their guilty consciences, were comforted with the delusive hopes of pardon, by leaving their fortune to monastic societies. Multitudes deprived their children of their rich lands and patrimonies, to confer them on the monks, whose prayers were to render the Deity propitious. In the following century the mania had reached such a height, that emperors and kings conferred whole provinces, cities, and titles of honour on these creatures. In the succeeding ages, so much did their licentiousness and ignorance increase, that in the tenth century few of the monks knew the rules of their own orders which they had sworn to obey, but lived in the most luxurious and prodigal magnificence with their concubines. The fourteenth century was distracted with the contentions of the various orders of the monks, who had grown so full of wealth, luxury, pride and all evil passions, that they not only turned their wrath against each other, but against the popes themselves. Their bitter and presumptuous bickerings filled this century with the most strange and hateful scenes.

We must pass over an infinite quantity of the monkish history, and content ourselves with a few remarks of Mosheim, on their state in the sixteenth century, at the time when their crimes and excesses were bringing on them the Reformation. The prodigious swarms of monks, says this historian, that overran Europe, were justly considered as burdens to society; and, nevertheless, such was the genius of the age, an age that was just emerging from the thickest gloom of ignorance, and was suspended, as it were, in a dubious situation between darkness and light, that these monastic drones would have remained undisturbed, had they taken the least pains to preserve any remains even of the external air of decency and religion, which distinguished them in former times. But the Benedictine, and other monkish fraternities, who were invested with the privilege of possessing certain lands and revenues, broke through all restraint, and made the worst possible use of their opulence; and, forgetful of the gravity of their character, and of the laws of their order, rushed headlong into the shameless practice of vice, in all its various kinds and degrees. On the other hand, the Mendicant orders, and especially the Dominicans and Franciscans, lost their credit in a different way: for their rustic impudence, their ridiculous superstitions, their ignorance, cruelty, and brutish manners, tended to alienate from them the minds of the people. They had the most barbarous aversion to the arts and sciences, and expressed a like abhorrence of certain learned men, who being eagerly desirous of enlightening the age, attacked their barbarism in both their discourse and their writings;—this was the case with Reuchlerius, Erasmus, and others.

The Dominicans possessed the greatest power and credit of all monks;—they presided in church and state; were confessors to the great, and judges of the horrible Inquisition—circumstances which put most of the European princes under their control; but, not content with these means of influence, they resorted to the most infamous frauds, to enslave the ignorance of the age. One of the most singular instances of this sort, is that recorded by Reuchat, in his Histoire de la Reformation en Suisse; by Hottinger, and by Bishop Burnett, in his Travels on the Continent. So remarkable is it, that I must give it as compendiously as I can.

"The stratagem was in consequence of a rivalry between the Dominicans and Franciscans, and more especially of their controversy concerning the immaculate conception of the Virgin Mary. The latter maintained that she was born without the blemish of original sin: the former asserted the contrary. The doctrine of the Franciscans, in an age of superstition, could not but be popular; and hence the Dominicans lost ground daily. To obviate this they resolved, at a Chapter held at Vimpsen in 1504, to have recourse to fictitious visions, in which the people at that time had an easy faith; and they determined to make Bern the scene of their operations. A lay-brother of the name of Jetzer, an extremely simple fellow, was fixed on as the instrument of these delusions. One of the four Dominicans who had undertaken the management of this plot, conveyed himself secretly into Jetzer's cell, and about midnight appeared to him in a horrid figure, surrounded with howling dogs, and seeming to blow fire from his nostrils by means of a box of combustibles which he held near his mouth. He approached Jetzer's bed, and told him he was the ghost of a Dominican who had been killed at Paris, as a judgment of heaven for laying aside his monastic habit; that he was condemned to purgatory for this crime, and could only be rescued from his horrible torments by his means. This story, accompanied with horrid cries and howlings, frightened poor Jetzer out of what little wits he had, and engaged him to do all in his power to rescue the Dominican from his torment. The impostor then told him that nothing but the discipline of the whip applied for eight days by the whole monastery, and Jetzer's lying prostrate on the chapel floor in the form of a cross during mass, could effect this. He added, these mortifications would secure Jetzer the peculiar favour of the Blessed Virgin; and told him he would appear to him again, with two other spirits.

Morning was no sooner come, than Jetzer related these particulars to the whole convent; who enjoined him to undergo all that he was commanded, and promised to bear their part. The deluded simpleton obeyed, and was admired as a saint by the multitude who crowded about the convent; while the four friars who managed the imposture, magnified, in the most pompous manner, the miracle of this apparition in their sermons and conversations. Night after night the apparition was renewed, with the addition of two other impostors, dressed like devils; and Jetzer's faith was augmented, by hearing from the spectre all the secret of his own life and thoughts, which the impostors had got from his confessor. In this and subsequent scenes, whose enormities we must pass over, the impostor talked much to Jetzer of the Dominican order; which, he said, was peculiarly dear to the Blessed Virgin; that the Blessed Virgin knew herself to be born in original sin; that the doctors who taught the contrary, were in purgatory; that she abhorred the Franciscans for making her equal to her Son; and that the town of Bern would be destroyed for harbouring such plagues within it.

In one of these apparitions, Jetzer, silly as he was, discovered the similarity of the spectre's voice to that of the prior—who it actually was—yet he did not suspect the fraud. The prior appeared in various disguises; sometimes as St. Barbaro, sometimes as

St. Bernard, and, at length, as the Virgin herself, clothed in the habit which adorned her statue at festivals. The little images that on these days are set on the altar, were used for angels, which being tied to a cord which passed through a pully over Jetzer's head, rose up and down, and danced about the pretended virgin, to increase the delusion. The virgin addressed a long discourse to Jetzer; gave him a marvellous wafer,—a *host* which turned, in a moment, from white to red; and, after various visits, in which the greatest enormities were acted, the virgin-prior told Jetzer she would give him the most undoubted proof of her Son's love, by imprinting on him the five wounds that pierced Jesus on the cross, as she had done before to St. Lucia and St. Catherine. Accordingly she took his hand, and thrust a large nail through it, which threw the poor dupe into the greatest torment. The next night, this masculine virgin brought, as she pretended, some of the linen in which Christ had been buried, to soften the wound; and gave Jetzer a soporific draught, composed of the blood of an unbaptized child, some incense, consecrated salt, quicksilver, the hairs of a child's eye-brows, with some poisonous and stupifying ingredients, mingled by the prior with magic ceremonies, and a solemn dedication of himself to the devil, in hope of his aid. This draught threw the poor wretch into a lethargy, during which the other four wounds were imprinted on his body. When he awoke and discovered them, he fell into unspeakable joy, and believed himself a representation of Christ in the various parts of his passion. He was, in this state, exposed to the admiring multitude on the principal altar of the convent, to the great mortification of the Franciscans. The Dominicans gave him some other draughts, and threw him into convulsions, which were followed by a voice conveyed through a pipe into the mouths of two images, one of Mary, the other of the child Jesus; the former of which had tears painted upon its cheeks in a lively manner. The little Jesus asked his mother why she wept; she answered, for the impious manner in which the Franciscans attributed to *her* the honour that was due to him.

The apparitions, false prodigies, and abominable stratagems were repeated every night: and were, at length, so grossly overacted, that even the simple Jetzer saw through them, and almost killed the priest. Lest this discovery should spoil all, they thought it best to own the whole to Jetzer, and prevail on him to join in the imposture; engaging him, by the most seducing promises of opulence and glory, to carry on the delusion. Jetzer appeared to be persuaded, but lest he should not be faithful and secret, they attempted to poison him; and it was alone owing to the vigour of his constitution that they did not succeed. Once they gave him a rich spiced loaf, which, growing green in a day or two, he threw a piece to a wolf's whelps, kept in the monastery, and it killed them immediately. Again they poisoned the host, or consecrated wafer; but he vomited it up. In short, the most detestable means to destroy him and his evidence were employed; but he succeeded in getting out of the convent, and throwing himself into the hands of the magistrates. The whole thus came to be sifted out; commissioners were sent from Rome to examine the affair; and the four friars were solemnly degraded, and burnt alive on the last day of May, 1509. Jetzer died soon after. Had he been destroyed before this exposure, this execrable plot would have been handed down to posterity as a stupendous miracle."

Rome could hasten to punish such vile frauds when they were made public, but she was not the less ready to practise them herself in the most daring manner, as I shall proceed to shew: but before leaving this strange case of Jetzer it may be remarked, that audacious and even incredible as it may appear to many, it rests upon too good authority to be doubted. Hundreds, indeed, of similar instances might be brought, for the whole history of the Romish church is that of fraud and delusion: but we need not go out of our own country for similar transactions. Who does not call to mind the affair of the Maid of Kent, enacted in the reign of Henry the Eighth at the very moment he was aiming a death-blow at popery, and in the face of a people whose eyes were opening to the acts and impostures of the papal sorceress? The case may be seen at large in Hume. The substance of it is this: some monks, and one Masters, the vicar of Aldington, in Kent, got hold of a girl of the name of Elizabeth Barton, who was subject to convulsive fits, and induced her to enter into a system of deception on the public mind. They gave out that she was inspired, and in these fits delivered the words of the Virgin Mary. Having once imposed, not merely on the common people, but engaged the Archbishop of Canterbury and other dignitaries of the church in the affair, they proceeded to promulgate heavenly messages against the reforming principles, and even threatened destruction to the king if he proceeded in them. The friars, throughout the country, countenanced the delusion, and propagated it with all their zeal and might. But they had a man to deal with very inauspicious for their purpose. He arrested the holy maid and her accomplices, brought them before the Star Chamber, and soon terrified them into a full confession of their imposture. A most scandalous scene was laid open. Her principal accomplices, Masters the vicar, and Dr. Bocking, a canon of Canterbury, were found to have a private entrance to her chamber, and to have led a most licentious life with her. The girl and six of her coadjutors were executed; and the Bishop of Rochester and others were condemned for misprision of treason, because they had not revealed her criminal speeches, and were thrown into prison. This was in England in the sixteenth century, and is a good specimen of the spirit of monkery: but another of a more menacing kind was soon given. Their "Diana of the Ephesians" was in danger; the king threatened not only to destroy popery, but to root out the monasteries; and it was not in the nature of priests and monks to resign their ill-gotten booty without a struggle. They set up the standard of rebellion. A monk, the Prior of Barlings in Lincolnshire, was at the head of it. He marched with 20,000 men at his heels, till he fell into the king's hands. But another army from the north was not so easily scattered. This, which consisted of 40,000 men, called its enterprise the *Pilgrimage of Grace*. Some priests marched before in the habits of their order, carrying crosses in their hands; in their banners was woven a crucifix, with the representation of the chalice, and the five wounds of Christ. They wore on their sleeve an emblem of the five wounds, with the name of Jesus wrought in the middle: and all took an oath that they had no motive but *love to God, care of the king's person* and issue; and a *desire to purify the nobility*, drive base-born persons from about the king, and restore the church, and suppress heresy. With those pretensions they marched from place to place; took Hull, York, and other towns; excited great disturbance and clamour, and were not dispersed but with great difficulty. This was a trial of force where fraud could not succeed of itself, according to the established papal policy; but FRAUD was alone one of its most successful means of acquiring power, and in order to contemplate this instrument more clearly we must go back again to an earlier age.

To advance their power the popes did not shrink from the most audacious FORGERY. Such was that of the notorious DECRETALS of ISIDORE; documents purporting to be written by the early pontiffs, and containing grants of the Holy See from Constantine; of the supremacy of the pope, and other privileges; all proved by the clearest evidence to be the most barefaced inventions.

FRAUDS were multiplied abundantly to besot and blind the popular spirit. Monks, bishops, warriors, and men of the worst characters, nay of neither character nor real existence, as St. George and his dragon, were canonized, made into saints, and their lives written in a manner most calculated to beguile the ignorance of the times. Shrines were set up, and churches dedicated to them, where people might pray for their aid. Dreams and miracles were pretended to throw light on the places of their burial; solemn processions were set on foot to discover and take them up; and the most miraculous powers attributed to them. Bones were buried, and afterwards pretended to be found, and declared by heaven to belong to saints and martyrs: and bits of bone, hairs, fragments of filthy rags, and other vile things; chips of the true cross, etc., were sold at enormous prices, as capable of working cures and effecting blessings of all kinds. The milk of the Virgin, and the blood of St. Januarius, which liquified on the day of his festival, were particularly famous in Italy. In England, at the dissolution of the monasteries, many very curious ones were found. The parings of St. Edmond's toes; some of the coals that roasted St. Lawrence; the girdle of the Virgin, shewn in eleven several places; the belt of St. Thomas of Lancaster, an infallible cure for the headach; part of St. Thomas of Canterbury's shirt; but chief of all, the blood of Christ brought from Jerusalem, and shewn for many ages at Hales in Gloucestershire. This sacred blood was not visible to any one in mortal sin; but in doing sufficient good work, *i. e.*, paying money enough, it revealed itself. It was preserved in a phial, one side of which was transparent, the other opaque. Into this the monks every week put a fresh supply of the blood of a duck; and, on any pilgrim arriving, the dark side was shewn him, which threw him into such consternation for his sinful state, that he generally purchased masses and made offerings, till his money or fortune began to fail; when the charitable monks turned the clear side towards him; he beheld the blood, and went away happy in his regenerate condition.

Rumours were spread of prodigies to be seen in certain places; robbers were converted into martyrs; tombs falsely given out to be those of saints; and many monks travelled from place to place, not only selling, with matchless impudence, their fictitious relics, but deluding the eyes of the people with ludicrous combats with spirits and genii. Ambrose, in his disputes with the Arians, produced men possessed with devils, who, upon the approach of the relics of Gervasius and Protatius, were obliged to cry out that the doctrine of the Council of Nice on the Trinity was true, and that of the Arians false. One of the precious maxims of the fourth century was, " that it was an act of virtue to deceive and lie when it could promote the interest of the church."—a maxim never afterwards forgotten. PILGRIMAGES to distant holy places were hit upon as a strong means to employ the minds and enslave the affections of numbers; houses, as that of the Virgin at Loretto, were even said to descend from heaven to receive the sacred enthusiasm of men; and CRUSADES, those preposterous and tremendous wars, whose details are filled with the most exquisite miseries, and most abhorrent crimes and licentiousness, were promoted, as potent means of employing the power and exhausting the treasures of kings. In those crusades, millions of miserable wretches, men, women, and children—the low, the ignorant, the idle, the dissolute—after wandering from kingdom to kingdom, the wonder and horror of the inhabitants, were consumed; and from those crusades in return, loads of relics were poured out of Syria over all Europe.

All kinds of CEREMONIES and FESTIVALS were imported from paganism for the same end. AURICULAR CONFESSION was invented, by which the clergy became the keepers of the consciences of the whole world; and the spiritual tyrants, not merely of the weak and the wicked, but of every one capable of a sense of shame or of fear. INDULGENCES were granted for the commission of crimes, and past sins pardoned for money and gifts of lands:—and PURGATORY! that most subtle and profitable invention of priestcraft, was contrived, to give the church power over both living and dead. Thus was the religion of Christ completely disfigured by pagan ceremonies, and made to sanction all wickedness for the sake of gain. The very CELEBRATION OF WORSHIP was ordered to be in LATIN; an unknown tongue to the great mass of those who heard it, so that they were reduced not only to feed on the chaff and garbage of priestly fables, but in the very temple of God himself to fill themselves with mere wind and empty sounds. The bread was taken from the children and given to the dogs. MASS was invented—that splendid piece of mummery, which, filling the eyes while it enlightened not the mind, was at once an instrument of keeping the people in ignorance; of fixing them fast by the imagination to the hollow trunk of formality; and of filling the pockets of the priests, by whom it was never performed without a fee;—for the souls of the dead paid more or less according to the imagined need. For many a great sinner masses were established for ever; and whole lordships were given to the church, to support chapels and chantries for the peace of souls that were already beyond rescue, or need of redemption. Every prayer and paternoster had its price. Thus was heaven, earth, and all therein turned into a source of beastly gain. The rage for dominion in the popes, says Mosheim, was accompanied by a most insatiable avarice. All the provinces of Europe were drained to enrich those spiritual tyrants, who were perpetually gaping after new accessions of wealth.

Another mode of influence was, constituting churches ASYLUMS for robbers and murderers; another, that dark one of EXCOMMUNICATION; another, the borrowing of ORDEALS from the pagans; another, the right of PATRONAGE; and, lastly, the terrors of the INQUISITION.

Such were the multiplied means employed for the monopoly of all the wealth, power, and honour of the universe by this infamous race of vampyres; and we have but too many instances of their determination to quench and keep down knowledge in their treatment of Bacon, Petre d'Abano, Arnold of Villa Nuova, and Galileo; to say nothing of the reformers, whom they regarded as their natural enemies, and destroyed without mercy. Mankind owes to the Roman church an everlasting reward of indignation for its attempts to crush into imbecility the human mind, and to insult it in its weakness with the most pitiful baubles and puerilities.

And for what end were all these outrages on humanity,—these mockeries of every thing great,—these blasphemies of every thing holy, perpetrated? That they might wallow, undisturbed, in the deepest mire of vice and sensuality, and heap upon those they had deluded and stripped of property, of liberty and of mind, insult and derision. Let every man who hesitates to set his hand to the destruction of state religions, look on this picture of all enormities that can disgrace our nature, and reflect that such is the inevitable tendency of all priestcraft. Is it said we see nothing so bad now? And why? Because man has got the upper hand of his tyrant, and keeps him in awe,—not because the nature of priestcraft is altered; and yet, let us turn but our eyes to Catholic countries, Spain, Portugal, Italy, and the scene is lamentable; and even in our own country, where free institutions check presumption, and the press terrifies many a monster from the light of day,—we behold things which make our hearts throb with indignation.

I had intended to give some specimens of papal lust, gluttony, and other infamous habits, but I turn from them in disgust; for those who seek them, ecclesiastical history is full. I shall only devote a few pages to Romish arrogance and atrocities, and then dismiss this Harlot of the Seven Hills.

## CHAPTER XIII.

POPISH ARROGANCE AND ATROCITIES.

---

Unless to Peter's Chair the viewless wind
Must come and ask permission where to blow,
What further empire would it have?—for now
A ghostly Domination, unconfined
As that by dreaming bards to love assigned,
Sits there in sober truth—to raise the low,
Perplex the wise, the strong to overthrow—
Through earth and heaven to bind and to unbind!
Resist—the thunder quails thee!—crouch—rebuff
Shall be thy recompense! from land to land
The ancient thrones of Christendom are stuff
For occupation of a magic wand,
And 't is the Pope that wields it;—whether rough
Or smooth his front, our world is in his hand!
WORDSWORTH.

---

WE have seen, in the progress of this volume, that arrogance and atrocity are prominent and imperishable features in the priestly character; and it might be imagined that instances had been given in various ages and nations which could not be surpassed: but if we consider the fierce and audacious exhibition of those qualities in the Romish priests; the greatness and extent of the kingdoms over which they exercised them; and the mild and unassuming nature of the religion they professed to be the teachers of, it must be confessed that the world has no similar examples to present. The papal church seemed actuated by a perfect furor and madness of intolerance, haughty dictation, and insolent cruelty. In the 12th century the pope proclaimed himself LORD OF THE UNIVERSE; and that neither prince nor bishop possessed any power but what was derived from him; in the 14th he, on one occasion, at a great dinner, ordered Dandolo, the Venetian ambassador, to be chained under the table like a dog. In 1155 the pope insisted on the celebrated emperor, Frederick Barbarossa, holding his stirrup, at the emperor's own coronation; a proposal at first rejected with disdain, and which led to contests of a most momentous nature. Some writers affirm that his successor, having compelled the emperor to submit, trod upon his neck, and obliged him to kiss his foot while the proud prelate repeated, from Psalm xci.—" Thou shalt tread upon the lion and the adder; the young lion and the dragon shalt thou trample under foot." Our great poet receives it as fact.

> Black Demons hovering o'er his mitred head,
> To Cæsar's successor the pontiff spake;
> " Ere I absolve thee, stoop! that on thy neck
> Levelled with earth this foot of mine may tread."
> Then he who to the altar had been led,
> He, whose strong arm the Orient could not check,
> He who had held the Soldan at his beck,
> Stooped, of all glory disinherited,
> And even the common dignity of man!
> Amazement strikes the crowd.
>
> WORDSWORTH.

In the eighth century the humiliating ceremony of kissing the pope's toe was introduced. In 1077 the famous pope, Gregory VII., compelled the emperor, Henry IV., to do penance for his resistance to his monstrous claims. The unhappy monarch passed the Alps in a severe winter; waited on the pontiff at Canusium, where, unmindful of his dignity, he stood three days at the entrance of the fortress (within which the detestable pope was feasting with his mistress, the Countess Matilda), with his head and feet bare, and no other raiment than a wretched piece of woollen cloth. On the fourth day he was admitted to the pontiff, who scarcely deigned to grant him the absolution he sought, and absolutely refused to restore him to his throne till after further delay and further indignities. The humiliation of holding the stirrup was also forced on the emperor Louis II.; and every reader is familiar with the arrogant spectacle of pope Alexander riding into the French camp, with the French monarch on the one side, and the English on the other, walking at his stirrup. We have already seen the boundless assumption and insolence of the popes in the thirteenth, fourteenth and fifteenth centuries; how they thundered their anathemas against kings and emperors, dethroned and beheaded as they pleased; made bloody wars on them to wrest from them their power, and even set up new kingdoms.

Their clergy naturally caught the same spirit, and carried into every region and every house the same intolerable haughtiness. The papal legates came to the courts of the greatest princes, with an odious arrogance that fully represented that of their master. From the history of the European nations, we might select the most astonishing instances of legates, cardinals, and bishops, before whom both monarch and people trembled; but I shall only select one or two from our own annals. Who can ever forget the notorious Thomas à Becket, Archbishop of Canterbury? one of the most perfect personifications of priestly insolence and audacity. This wretch, who had been raised to his high dignity by his royal master, and loaded with every honour, having once gained all that his ambition could hope from the indulgent monarch, became one of the most captious and troublesome villains that ever disturbed, with priestly pride, the peace of kingdoms. Henry, by an act of the Council of Clarendon, endeavoured to bring into some tolerable degree of restraint, the power and license of the clergy. Becket most arrogantly refused all obedience to the king's wishes; and backed by Alexander III., the same pope who had so humiliated Frederick Barbarossa, commenced a course of annoyance to the mild-spirited king, which, even at this distance of time, makes one's blood boil with indignation to read. The monarch, aroused by it, compelled Becket to retire to France. Hereupon the pope and the French king interposed; and endeavoured so far to pacify the offended sovereign, as to allow Becket to return to England, and resume his office. But who that knows any thing of priests could hope that he would be touched with any sense of shame, or gratitude towards his forgiving prince? He became only more inveterately rebellious, and carried his insolence so far, that four gentlemen who witnessed with indignation the vexations heaped on their sovereign, hastened to Canterbury, and inflicted on the haughty and sanctimonious wretch, deserved and exemplary death.

But if Becket was dead, the haughty pope was alive, and soon compelled poor Henry to the most humiliating degradations;—to go, bare-headed and bare-footed, on pilgrimage to Canterbury, and do penance at the canonized shrine of the now sainted Becket!

A similar fate was that of poor king John,—the weak and wicked Lack-land. He ventured to oppose the pope's power, who had proceeded to set aside the election of John de Grey to the see of Canterbury, and to appoint, spite of the king and the nation,

Stephen Langton, primate of England. John assumed a high tone; and threatened to extinguish the papal power in England. What was the consequence? Innocent laid John's kingdom under the BANN. A stop was put to divine worship; the churches were shut in every parish; all the sacraments, except baptism, were superseded; the dead were buried in the high ways, without any sacred rites. Several, however, of the better and more learned clergy, indignantly refused obedience to this detestable interdict; and the pope accordingly proceeded to further measures. In 1209, he excommunicated John; and two years afterwards, issued a bull, absolving all his subjects from their allegiance, and ordering all persons to avoid him. The next year, the enraged pope assembled a council of cardinals and bishops, deposed John, declared the throne of England vacant; and ordered the king of France to take it, and add it to his own. The French king was ready enough to do this; he assembled an army;—John assembled another to oppose him; and had he been a monarch of an enlightened mind and steady fortitude, England would have been rescued from popish thraldom, and the reformation accelerated by some ages. But Pandolph, the pope's legate, arriving in England, so succeeded by his artful representations of the power of France, and the defection of John's own subjects, that his courage broke down, and he submitted to the most abject humiliations. He promised, among other things, that he would submit himself entirely to the judgment of the pope; that he would acknowledge Langton for primate; that he would restore all the exiled clergy and laity who had been banished on account of the contest; make them full restitution of their goods, and compensation for all damages, and instantly consign eight thousand pounds in part of payment; and that any one outlawed, or imprisoned for his adherence to the pope, should be instantly received to grace and favour. He did homage to the pope; resigned his crown to him; and again received it from him as a gift; and bound himself to pay seven hundred marks annually for England, and three hundred for Ireland: and consented that any of his successors who refused to pay it, should forfeit all right to the throne. All this was transacted in a public assembly in the house of the Templars at Dover,—for the popish priests always took care that refractory kings should suffer the most public and excruciating degradations; and the legate, after having kept the crown and sceptre five whole days, returned them, as by special favour of the pope. John, however, presented a sum of money in token of his dependence, which the proud prelate trod under his feet.

In reviewing these things, one is ready to exclaim, can it really be England in which such scenes have been exhibited, and suffered by Englishmen? Thanks to the progress of knowledge, which has crushed the hydra-head of such monstrous priestcraft!

The ATROCITIES of POPERY were on a par with its arrogance. In every age it has been ready with the fire and the fagot; and every one who dared to dissent from its opinions, was put to death with the cruellest brutality. We have already adverted to its treatment of learned men, whose discoveries tended to shake its power over the public mind. Galileo's forced renunciation of what he knew to be the truth—the verity of the Copernican system—has been a popular theme in every age.

>           They bore
> His chained limbs to a dreary tower,
> In the midst of a city vast and wide.
> For he, they said, from his mind had bent

> Against their gods keen blasphemy,
> For which, though his soul must roasted be
> In hell's red lakes immortally,
> Yet even on earth must he abide
> The vengeance of their slaves! a trial
> I think men call it.
>
> SHELLEY.

He succumbed in the trial—he recanted the truth openly; yet as he rose from his knees before his stupid judges, he whispered to a friend—*e pur si muove!* it does move though! Yes! it moved!—the world moved, and that in more respects than one; and popery is become a wreck and a scorn, and man and knowledge have triumphed.

> Fear not, that the tyrants shall rule for ever,
> Or the priests of the bloody faith:
> They stand on the brink of that mighty river,
> Whose waves they have tainted with death.
> It is fed from the depths of a thousand dells,
> Around them it foams, and rages, and swells,
> And their swords and their sceptres I floating see,
> Like wrecks in the surge of eternity.
>
> SHELLEY.

The reformers became their victims in most instances; and if Wycliffe escaped, his remains received the implacable resentment of the sacerdotal spirit. They were dug up; burnt, and scattered, on the waters of the neighbouring river, whence they floated to the ocean, and became the seeds of life and resistance to papal despotism in myriads of minds in all regions. A list of all the victims who have perished by papal cruelty would amount to some millions. Even in England, in the reign of Queen Mary, when this horrid religion was restored for a short space, two hundred and seventy persons were brought to the stake, besides those who were punished by fines, imprisonments, and confiscations. Amongst those who suffered by fire were five bishops, twenty-one clergymen, eight lay gentlemen, eighty-four tradesmen, one hundred husbandmen, servants and labourers, fifty-five women, and four children. This persevering cruelty appears astonishing, yet is much inferior to what has been practised in other countries. A great author, Father Paul, computes that in the Netherlands alone, from the time that the edict of Charles V. was promulgated against the reformers, there had been fifty thousand persons hanged, beheaded, buried alive, or burnt on account of religion; and in France a great number.

The Massacre of St. Bartholomew will remain to the end of time in characters of infamy on the history of France. This horrid carnage, which was an attempt to exterminate the protestants, commenced at Paris on the 24th of August, 1572, by the secret orders of Charles IX, at the instigation of the Queen Dowager of Medici. The Queen of Navarre was poisoned by order of the court. About daybreak, says Thuanus, upon the toll of the great bell of the church of St. Germain, the butchery began. Coligni, admiral of France, was basely murdered in his own house; and then thrown out of the windows, to gratify the malice of the Duke of Guise. His head was cut off, and sent to the king and queen-mother; and his body, after a thousand indignities offered to it, hung up by the feet on a gibbet. After this the murderers ravaged the whole city, and butchered, in three days, 10,000 lords, gentlemen, and people of all ranks. A horrible scene, when the very streets and passages resounded with the noise of those who met together for murder and plunder; the groans of the dying, the shrieks of those about to be butchered, were everywhere heard. The bodies of the slain were thrown out of the windows; the courts and chambers filled with them: the dead bodies of others dragged along the streets; their blood running in torrents down the channels to the river: an innumerable multitude of men, women, and children involved in one common destruction; and the gates of the king's palace besmeared with their blood.

From Paris, the massacre spread through the provinces, throughout nearly the whole kingdom. In Meaux they threw above two hundred into gaol; ill-treated and then killed a great number of women; plundered the houses of the protestants, and then exercised their fury on their prisoners; calling them out, one by one, and butchering them as sheep for the market. The bodies of some were flung into the Maine, and others into ditches. The same cruelties were practised at Orleans, Angers, Troyes, Bourges, La Charité, and especially Lyons, where they inhumanly destroyed above eight hundred protestants; children, hanging on their parents' necks; parents embracing their children; putting ropes round the necks of some, dragging them through the streets, and flinging them half dead into the river. The soldiers and very executioners refused, says a detailed account of this transaction, in the first volume of the Harleian Miscellany, to partake in this hellish carnage, and the butchers, and lowest populace were admitted to the prisons, where they chopped off the hands, feet, and noses of the captives, and derided their agonies, as they mangled them.

When the news arrived at Rome, where the letters of the pope's legate, read in assembly of the cardinals, gave assurance that all this was done by command of the king, the joy was excessive; and it was instantly decreed that the pope and cardinals should march to the church of St. Mark in solemn procession, and return God thanks for so great a blessing conferred on the see of Rome and the

Christian world! That high mass should be celebrated, the pope and all his cardinals attending; a jubilee should be published throughout the Christian world. The cannon of St. Angelo were fired, and the city illuminated as for a most splendid victory.

But even this was exceeded by the unrestrained vengeance of the great Roman Anti-Christ against the poor Vaudois, a simple people of Piedmont, who from the Apostolic age had preserved the purity of the faith, and refused to bow to the swollen pride and worse than pagan idolatry of Rome. These primitive people were, from age to age, persecuted with fire and sword; their own prince was stirred up and compelled to become against them, the butcher of the Roman pontiff. They were hunted from their houses; suffocated in caves with flaming straw by hundreds; their wives and children massacred without mercy:—but in vain! They continued through all; and still continue, as may be seen by Mr. Gillies' most interesting account of his visit to them; and their sufferings have been immortalized in the fiery burst of Milton's indignation.

> Avenge, O Lord, thy slaughtered saints, whose bones
> Lie bleaching on the Alpine mountains cold;
> Even them who kept thy truth so pure of old,
> When all our fathers worshipped stocks and stones,
> Forget not; in thy book record their groans
> Who were thy sheep, and in their ancient fold
> Slain by the bloody Piedmontese, who rolled
> Mother with infant down the rocks. Their moans
> The vales redoubled to the hills, and they
> To Heaven. Their martyred blood and ashes sow
> O'er all the Italian fields where still doth sway
> The triple tyrant; that from these may grow
> A hundred fold, who having learned thy way,
> Early may fly the Babylonian woe.

Milton did not content himself with thus venting his indignation; he made such representations to

Cromwell of the situation of these suffering people that the Protector zealously interceded for them with the Duke of Savoy; but with too little effect.

In the same spirit the papal tyrant quenched the literature of the Troubadours, which exerted a faint, but pleasant twilight gleam in the 13th century; and was highly influential in the revival of poetry, by exciting the spirit of Petrarch, and through him of Chaucer, and the following English poets. This light, Rome put out by exterminating the Provencal people in a war, so singular and expressive of the nature of priestcraft, when full grown, that I shall give a brief account of it, principally from Sismondi's Literature of the South of Europe, with a few particulars from Milner's venerable History of the Church of Christ.

The excessive corruption of the clergy had furnished a subject for the satirical powers of the Troubadours. The cupidity, the dissimulation, and the baseness of that body, had rendered them odious both to the nobility and the people. The priests and the monks incessantly employed themselves in despoiling the sick, the widowed, and the fatherless, and indeed all whom age, or weakness, or misfortune placed within their grasp; while they squandered in debauchery and drunkenness, the money which they extorted by the most shameful artifices. If God, said Raymond de Castelnaú, will the black monks to be unrivalled in their good eating and their amours, and the white monks in their lying bulls, and the Templars and Hospitallers in pride, and the canons in usury, I hold St. Peter and St. Andrew to have been egregious fools for suffering so much for the sake of God, since all these people also are to be saved. The gentry had imbibed such contempt for the clergy, that they would not educate their children to the priesthood, but gave their livings to their servants and bailiffs. The persecutions of Theodora in 845, and of Basil in 867 and 886, after having effected the destruction of more than a hundred thousand victims, compelled the remainder to seek refuge, some amongst the Musselmans, and others amongst the Bulgarians. Once out of the pale of persecution, their faith, of a purer and simpler kind, made rapid progress. In Languedoc and Lombardy the name of Paterins was given them, on account of the sufferings to which they were exposed wherever the papal power extended; and they afterwards received the name of Albigenses, from the numbers that inhabited the diocese of Alby.

Missionaries were dispatched into Higher Languedoc in 1147 and 1181, to convert these heretics; but with little success. Every day the reformed opinions gained ground, and Bertrand de Saissac, the tutor of the young Viscount of Beziers, himself adopted them. At length Innocent III. resolving to destroy these sectaries, whom he had exterminated in Italy, sent, in 1198, two Cistercian monks with the authority of legates *à latere*, to discover and bring them to justice. The monks, ambitious of extending their already unprecedented powers, not contented with merely attacking the heretics, quarrelled with all the regular clergy, who had attempted to soften their proceedings. They suspended the Archbishop of Narbonne, and the Bishop of Beziers; and degraded the Bishops of Toulouse and of Veviers. Pierre de Castelnau, the most eager of the legates, accused Raymond of Toulouse of protecting the heretics, because that prince, being of a mild disposition, refused to lend himself to the destruction of his subjects. The anger of the priest, at length led him to excommunicate the count, and place his estates under interdict: and he proceeded to such irritating insolence, that one of the count's followers, in his indignation, pursued him to the banks of the Rhone, and killed him. This crowned the misfortunes of Languedoc. It gave Innocent a pretext to proceed to bloodshed, and he took instant advantage of it. He addressed a letter to the king of France; to all the princes and most powerful barons, as well as to the metropolitan bishops, exhorting them to vengeance, and to the extirpation of heresy. All the indulgences and pardons, which were usually granted to the crusaders, were promised to those who exterminated these unbelievers. Three hundred thousand pilgrims, induced by the united motives of avarice and superstition, filled the country of the Albigenses with carnage and confusion for a number of years. The reader who is not versed in history of this kind, can scarcely conceive the scenes of baseness, perfidy, barbarity, indecency, and hypocrisy, over which Innocent presided; and which were conducted partly by his legates, and partly by the infamous Simon de Montford. Raymond VI. terrified at this storm, submitted to every thing required of him; but Raymond Roger, Viscount of Beziers, indignantly refused to give up the cause of his subjects. He encouraged them to resist; shut himself up in Carcassone, and gave Beziers to the care of his lieutenants. Beziers was taken by assault in July, 1209, and fifteen thousand inhabitants, according to the Cistercian monk, or sixty thousand according to others, were put to the sword. This Cistercian monk was asked before the city was taken, how he could separate the heretics from the catholics? he replied, "*Kill all; God will know his own!*"

The brave young Viscount of Beziers did not shrink; he still defended Carcassone. Peter II. of Arragon attempted to make terms for him with his monkish besiegers, but all that they would grant was, to allow thirteen of the inhabitants, including the count, to leave the city; the remainder were reserved for a butchery like that of Beziers. The viscount declared he would be flayed alive rather than submit to such terms. He was, at length, betrayed; poisoned in prison; four hundred of his people burnt, and fifty hanged. Simon de Montford, the most ferocious monster of all the crusaders, received from the legate, the viscount's title; and devastated the whole of the south of France with the most frightful wars. They who escaped from the sacking of the town were sacrificed by the fagot. From 1209 to 1229, nothing was seen but massacres and tortures. Religion was overthrown; knowledge extinguished; and humanity trodden under foot. In the midst of these horrors, the ancient house of Toulouse became extinct.

Connected with this melancholy history, is one of the last horrid instruments of Papal tyranny which remains to be mentioned—THE INQUISITION. These monks, Arnold Ranier and Pierre Castelnau, were followed by the notorious Spaniard, Dominic, and others, who, proceeding to seek out and execute heretics, gained the name of INQUISITORS. On their return from this infernal expedition, the Popes were so sensible of their services, that they established similar tribunals in different places. In time, Italy, Spain, and other countries, were cursed with these hellish institutions; and their history is one of the most awful horror that can affright the human soul. But these, and the Jesuits, demand a separate notice.

## CHAPTER XIV.

#### JESUITS AND INQUISITORS.

---

The land in which I lived, by a fell bane
Was withered up. Tyrants dwelt side by side,
And stabled in our homes—until the chain
Stifled the captive's cry, and to abide
That blasting curse, men had no shame—all vied
In evil, slave and despot; fear with lust,
Strange fellowship through mutual hate had tied,
Like two dark serpents tangled in the dust,
Which on the paths of men their mingling poison thrust.
             REVOLT OF ISLAM.

But onward moved the melancholy train
   In their false creeds, in fiery pangs to die.
This was the solemn sacrifice of Spain—
   Heaven's offering from the land of chivalry!
             THE FOREST SANCTUARY.

---

WE have passed rapidly through strange scenes of priestly wickedness and bloodshed,—but of all the agents of the devil which were ever spawned in the black dens of that earthly pandemonium, the Papal Church, none can compare with the Jesuits and Inquisitors.

The Jesuits arose in the latter days of popery. Their doctrines were those of popery grown to thorough ripeness. They seemed created to shew to what lengths that system could be carried, and to crown it, in conjunction with their fellow demons of the Inquisition, with that full measure of popular indignation which should hasten its great " immedicable wound" from the hand of Luther. The Jesuits took up the favourite dogmas of the Papal Church: that the end sanctifies the means—that evil may be done that good may come of it—and pushed them to that degree which causes the good and the simple to stand in astonishment at the daring acts and adroit casuistry of " bold bad men." All oaths, all obligations, all morality, all religion, according to their creed, were to be adopted or set aside, just as it suited the object they had in view. They might cheat and lie, steal and kill, all for righteousness' sake. They embodied in practice the pithy maxims of Hudibras.

> That saints may claim a dispensation
> To swear and forswear on occasion,
> I doubt not but it will appear
> With pregnant light: the point is clear.
> Oaths are but words, and words but wind;
> Too feeble instruments to bind.
> But saints whom oaths and vows oblige,
> Know little of their privilege.
> For if the devil, to serve his turn,
> Can tell truth; why the saints should scorn
> When it serves theirs to swear and lie,
> I think there's little reason why.
> Else he has a greater power than they,
> Which 'twere impiety to say.

They thought with him,

> The Public Faith, which every one
> Is bound to observe, is kept by none.
> And if that go for nothing, why
> Should Private Faith have such a tie?
> Oaths were not purposed more than law,
> To keep the good and just in awe,
> But to confine the bad and sinful,
> Like mortal cattle in a pinfold.

> Then why should we ourselves abridge
> And curtail our own privilege?
> Quakers that, like dark lanterns bear
> Their light within them, will not swear.
> Their gospel is an accidence
> By which they construe conscience.
> And hold no sin so deeply red
> As that of breaking Priscian's head—
> The head and founder of their order,
> That stirring hats held worse than murder.
> These thinking they're obliged to troth
> In swearing, will not take an oath:
> Like mules, who if they've not their will
> To keep their own pace, stand stock still,
> But they are weak, and little know
> What freeborn consciences may do.
>
> 'T is the temptation of the devil
> That makes all human actions evil.
> For saints may do the same things by
> The spirit in sincerity,
> Which other men are tempted to,
> And at the devil's instance do.
> And yet the actions be contrary,
> Just as the saints and wicked vary.
> For as on land there is no beast
> But in some fish at sea's expressed,
> So in the wicked there's no vice
> Of which the saints have not a spice:
> And yet that thing that's pious in
> The one, in 't other is a sin.
> Is 't not ridiculous and nonsense
> A saint should be a slave to conscience!

These were their precious tenets—the quintessence of the wisdom of this world, to which that of the children of light is unprofitable foolishness. Their founder, Ignatius Loyala, a Spaniard—an ominous name when connected with religion,—was a most acute and happy genius in his way. He saw the advantages which the Popes had derived from their accommodating ecclesiastical logic, and he conceived the felicitous idea of creating a sort of second series of

Popes, taught and enlightened by the old series. He adopted their facile code of morals, and he even outwent them in the exquisite finesse of his policy. The head of this system was to take the name of General of the Order; his emissaries were to go forth into all kingdoms; to insinuate themselves into all cities, houses, and secret hearts of the people. They were to adopt all shapes, to follow all circumstances; to wear an outside of peculiar mildness, and an inner-man of subtle observance; to have the exterior of the dove—the interior of the serpent. With all this sequacity, flexibility and disguise, they succeeded wonderfully. What, indeed, could resist them, when they came in all shapes, and with all pretences;—at the first glimpse of discovery of their real designs, or of popular indignation, ready to eat up their words, and swear that they were anything but what they really were? But when they found themselves in any degree of strength,—when they were desirous of carrying some point that compliance and duplicity could not carry,—who so dogged and insolent as they? They bearded people, magistrates, kings,—the pope himself, with the most immoveable assurance. The popes, who regarded them as active maintainers of ignorance and obedience, were desirous to tolerate them as much as possible. But they often found it a severe task for their patience. They were in the condition of a man who has tamed a serpent or a lion; they might soothe the beast by coaxing, perhaps, but were every moment in danger of rousing its ferocity, and even of falling before its rage. When struck at, they stood and hissed, and fought with true snaky pertinacity; but if they saw actual destruction coming, they suddenly disappeared, only to raise their hydra heads in a thousand other places. Expelled from states in their own character of Jesuits, they came back in all sorts of disguises; and, instead of open enemies, the people and their governors had to encounter the secret influence of their poison, and their stings which struck in the dark. They insinuated themselves into colleges and schools under false colours, till they could seize upon them and convert them into engines of their designs. They became confessors, especially of women, that they might learn all the secrets of their husbands; of kings and ministers, to learn those of states: all the intelligence thus gathered was regularly transmitted to the General from every kingdom, so that he and his counsellors knew the condition and intentions of all nations; and, at a moment's notice, his creatures were ready to seize upon universities, churches, governments, or whatever they desired. They entered into trade, and were scattered all over the world, wearing no outward appearance but that of merchants; yet keeping up a secret correspondence with one another, and with their General, and transmitting intelligence and wealth from all quarters of the globe. They were not satisfied with exercising their arts over the Christian world; they proceeded into all pagan countries as missionaries, and sought to bring the savages of Asia, Africa, and America under their dominion. They evidently had formed the bold design of acquiring the spiritual and political sovereignty of the world: but, with all their subtlety—their ambition and their unprincipled grasping at power so alarmed and disgusted all people, that their history is a continual alternation of their growing into numbers and strength, and of their expulsion from almost every kingdom that can be named. England, France, Spain, Germany, Poland, Bohemia, Italy, the East and the West Indies, America, North and

South, in all these countries their arts were repeatedly tried, and they were as repeatedly expelled with ignominy and vengeance.

The rapidity with which they spread themselves, is shewn by the following statement from the memorial presented by the University of Paris to the king in 1724 :—" In 1540, when they presented their petitions to Paul III., they only appeared in the number of ten. In 1543 they were not more than twenty-four. In 1545 they had only ten houses; but, in 1549 they had two provinces: one in Spain, and the other in Portugal, and twenty-two houses; and at the death of Ignatius, in 1556, they had twelve large provinces. In 1608, Ribadeneira reckoned twenty-nine provinces, and two vice-provinces; twenty-one houses of profession; two hundred and ninety-three colleges; thirty-three houses of probation; ninety-three other residences, and ten thousand five hundred and eighty-one Jesuits. In the catalogue printed at Rome in 1629, are found thirty-five provinces, two vice-provinces, thirty-three houses of profession, five hundred and seventy-eight colleges, forty-eight houses of probation, eighty-eight seminaries, one hundred and sixty residences, one hundred and six missions, and, in all, seventeen thousand six hundred and fifty-five Jesuits, of whom seven thousand eight hundred and seventy were priests. At last, according to the calculation of Father Jouvency, they had, in 1710, twenty-four houses of profession, fifty-nine houses of probation, three hundred and forty residences, six hundred and twelve colleges, of which above eighty were in France, two hundred missions, one hundred and fifty-seven seminaries and boarding-houses, and nineteen thousand nine hundred and ninety-eight Jesuits.

On their mercantile concerns, M. Martin, governor

of Pondicherry, observes, " It is certain that, next to the Dutch, the Jesuits carry on the greatest and most productive commerce in India. Their trade surpasses even that of the English, as well as that of the Portuguese, who established them in India. There may possibly, indeed, be some Jesuits who go there from pure religious motives; but they are very few, and it is not such as those who know the grand secret of the company. Some among them are Jesuits secularized, who do not appear to be such, because they never wear the habit; which is the reason why at Surat, Agra, Goa, and every where else, they are taken for real merchants of the countries whose names they bear: for it is certain that there are some of all nations, even of America and Turkey, and of every other which can be useful and necessary to the society. These disguised Jesuits are intriguing everywhere: The secret intercourse which is preserved among them instructs them mutually in the merchandize which they ought to buy and sell, and with what nation they can most advantageously trade; so that these masked Jesuits make an immense profit of the society, to which they are alone responsible, through the medium of those Jesuits who traverse the world in the habit of St. Ignatius, and enjoy the confidence, know the secrets, and act under the orders of the heads of Europe. These Jesuits, disguised and dispersed over the whole earth, and who know each other by signs, like the Freemasons, invariably act upon one system. They send merchandize to other disguised Jesuits, who, having it thus at first hand, make a considerable profit of it for the society. This traffic is, however, very injurious to France. I have often written respecting it to the East India Company trading here; and I have received express orders from it (under Louis XIV.) to concede and advance to these fathers whatever they might require of me. The Jesuit Tachard alone owes that company, at this moment, above four hundred and fifty thousand livres. Those Jesuits who, like Tachard, pass and repass between this quarter and Europe, are ambulatory directors and receivers of the bank and of the trade."

"In the Antilles," says Coudrette, "Lavalette, the Jesuit, has half the worth of the property for whose conveyance to France he undertakes. In Portugal the Jesuits had vessels employed exclusively in their service, which facts are established by the process of Cardinal Saldanha. All the accounts of travellers in the East Indies speak in the same way, with astonishment, of the extent of their commerce. In Europe, and even in France, they have banks in the most commercial cities, such as Marseilles, Paris, Genoa, and Rome. In addition to this, they publicly sell drugs in their houses; and, in order to their sanction in this, they procured from Pope Gregory XIII. the privilege of exercising the art of medicine. Even in Rome, in spite of the opposition of the tradesmen, and the prohibitions of the Pope, they carry on trade in baking, grocery, etc. Let us imagine twenty thousand traders, dispersed over the world, from Japan to Brazil, from the Cape of Good Hope to the north, all correspondents of each other, all blindly subjected to one individual, and working for him alone; conducting two hundred missions, which are so many factories; six hundred and twelve colleges, and four hundred and twenty-three houses of professors, noviciates, and residents, which are so many entrepôts; and then let us form an idea, if we can, of the produce of so vast an extent."

There have not been wanting advocates for these persevering, intriguing priests; who have represented them as merely labouring to promote religion amongst the civilized, and civilization amongst the savage nations. But what says all history? What says the indignation of every realm which has ever harboured them? That wherever they were, whatever they undertook, whether the education of youth in Europe, or that of the natives of savage lands, all their plans turned to one object—absolute dominion over the minds and bodies of their disciples. They seem to have taken a particular pleasure in breaking in upon the labours and in persecuting all other missionaries; —and by their detestable and ambitious acts, Christianity has been expelled from various regions where it was taking root. This was the case in Japan and China. Here they first thwarted the measures of other missionaries, then got all power into their hands, and finally were driven out with wrath by the natives. In China their suppression was connected with circumstances of peculiar aggravation. The Bishop of Nankin names two to the Pope whose vices had become public. " But the crime of Father Anthony Joseph, the superior of the mission, is yet more scandalous. This man has remained there eight years past, continually plunged in the abominable practice of sinning with women at the time they come to confess, and even in the place where he confessed them; after which he gave them absolution, and administered the Sacrament to them! He told them that these actions need not give them any concern, since all their Fathers, the Bishops, and the Pope himself, observed the same practice!

" All this was known to Christians and to Heathens. Some persons represented these crimes to the superiors of the Jesuits; but the commissary whom they sent for the purpose, declared him innocent—I know not upon what pretence. While I was considering the best means of punishing this man, the mandarins caused him to be arrested, suddenly, with two of his brethren, and about one hundred Christians. What occasioned still greater scandal, the mandarins, who had been some time acquainted with part of the facts, collected correct depositions to establish his crimes, and announced them at full length in their sentence, which they made public. He was condemned to death, with the other Jesuit, on the 22d of September, 1748, and they were both strangled in prison. Of the hundred persons who were arrested with him, there was not one who did not renounce Christianity, and the Chinese missionary was the first to do so.

For more than two hundred years they maintained a system of opposition and vexation to the bishops and missionaries of India, in the very face of the Pope's commands to the contrary. Of their attempt to establish an independent kingdom in Paraguay, every one has heard. Under pretence of preserving the Indians free from the vices of the Europeans, they forbade them to learn their language; under pretence of protecting them from the oppressions of the Europeans, they regularly disciplined large bodies of them in arms. For them these simple creatures toiled, and their minds they moulded entirely to subserviency to them. They refused all Europeans, except their own confederates, entrance to the province; and actually, on the authorities marching into it in the name of the Kings of Portugal and Spain, rose against them and attempted to expel them by force of arms. They hesitated not to send emissaries over to Europe to blow the flames of sedition there, and even attempted the life of the King of Portugal, in order to divert the efforts of their rightful monarchs from them; but finally they were themselves subdued, and driven out of the country, to the total dissipation of their grand scheme of rebellion and empire. For those who have patience to read the scandalous and bloody squabbles of priests, there are copious details of these matters in the second volume of Southey's History of Brazil; and especially of their contests with Cardenas, the bishop.

In Europe they signalized themselves by perpetual attempts against the peace of states, and the lives of monarchs. In Venice, in 1560, they excited great commotion, and were very near being driven away. They shewed great anxiety to confess the wives of the senators, for the purpose, it was believed, of acquiring the secrets of the republic. Trevisani, the Patriarch of Venice, says Sacchini, satisfied himself of the charge, and made other discoveries of still greater importance. In the Netherlands, in Portugal and Spain, they were busy in similar schemes, and with similar results. In Poland, they had the fortune to get a man of their order, Sigismund, upon the throne. He desired to introduce them into Sweden, where his uncle, Duke Charles, was his lieutenant. Charles remonstrated, in vain, that the people of Sweden would not endure the Jesuits: the king persisted, and the people took arms against him. He was beaten both by sea and land; taken prisoner; and only released on condition that he would assemble his states, and act in conjunction with them. He then escaped from Sweden, and strove to arm the Poles against the Swedes; but they refused the alliance, and in the mean time his uncle seized upon his towns.

With the continual attempts of these pertinacious wretches against the liberties of England, and the lives of Elizabeth and James I., every English reader is familiar: the names of Crichton, Garnett, Parry, Cullen, Gerard, and Tesmond, successively engaged in the design of assassinating the protestant queen, or in the attempt to blow up our English Solomon and all his parliament, will for ever perpetuate their abhorrence in England; and in Ireland the general massacre of the protestants in 1641, which they were principally concerned in exciting, and similar proceedings in that country, will keep alive their remembrance there. But of all their atrocities there are none which more affect one with indignation, than their persecutions and murder of Henry III. and Henry IV. of France. In 1563, according to Mezerai, the famous catholic league took its rise, whose object was to extirpate the protestants in France. The jesuits became the soul of this infamous federation. Henry III. assembled the states at Blois in 1579, for the purpose of dissolving this conspiracy; and from that time, was marked for destruction. Sammier, a jesuit, traversed Germany, Italy, and Spain, to excite the princes of those countries against him. Mattheiu, another, styled the courier of the league, made several journeys to the pope, to obtain a bull against him; and though the pope hesitated at this, he delivered his opinion, that the person of Henry should be secured, and his cities seized. Commolet and Rouillet were the trumpets of sedition. In the college of the Rue St. Jaques, the jesuits met and conspired the murder of the king. It was there Baniere came to be stirred up by the doctrines of Varade,—and that Guinard composed the writings, for which he was hung. It was there that the Sixteen signed an absolute cession of the kingdom to Philip of Spain; and that Chastel acquired the lesson of parricide he afterwards acted upon. There Clement, animated by such horrible instructions, formed the resolve which he fulfilled on the 1st of August, 1589, the assassination of Henry III.

Henry IV., a generous spirited and noble monarch, was educated in protestantism;—this was enough to arouse their murderous and unappeasable hatred. It was almost by miracle that he escaped, then a youth, from the massacre of St. Bartholomew. On his coming to the throne, he was pursued by them with such continual animosity, that to allay their fury, he consented to embrace catholicism. This produced no effect—he was a man of liberal opinions; and such a man they could not tolerate. They made his life miserable; and at length nearly effected his murder by the knife of Baniere, at Melun, in August 1593. On the 27th of December, 1594, his life was again attempted by Chastel, another jesuit. He struck at him with a knife, but missed his aim, and instead of killing him, only cut his lip, and struck out a tooth. This circumstance, and the ferment of infernal fanaticism, which induced the papists and jesuits to continually seek the destruction of the king, caused the banishment of the whole order. This, however, did not mend the matter, as it regarded the king;—he had only the same enemies in disguise, and, if possible, ten times more embittered. With that good nature which characterized him, he at length consented to allow them to return. It was in vain that Sully, his minister, represented to him that no kindness could soften such foes;—he recalled them, and fell a victim to their instigations, being stabbed by Ravaillac, on May 14th, 1610.

Many books had been written of late by the jesuits, vindicating and commending the killing of kings, particularly the work of Mariana,—De Rege et Regis Institutione, in which the killing of a king was termed a "laudable, glorious, and heroic action." It was by such writings that this assassin was spurred on to his diabolical act. Aubigny, his confessor, a jesuit, when confronted with the murderer, and charged with being privy to the design, at first denied knowing the man at all; but when driven from that assertion, he declared that "God had given to some the gift of tongues, to others the gift of prophecy, and to him the gift of forgetting confessions."

Such were the abominable principles which led them to these abominable actions. For a full account of this assassination, the reader may consult the fourth volume of Sully's Memoirs. So generally was the conspiracy known amongst the catholic subjects of this unfortunate monarch, that many people declared, on the day when the murder took place, that the king was then dying, though they were in distant places. An astrologer had foretold the very day and hour to the king, the manner of the act, and that it would take place in a coach. So much impressed was the king with his approaching fate, that he was frequently in great agony of mind, and would fain have put off the queen's coronation, which was about to take place at the time predicted. He had terrible dreams, and so also had the queen, waking in horror, and crying out the king was stabbed. All these things which the common mind loves to believe supernatural intimations, only shew to the more reflecting one, the audacity of these bloody wretches, who were so confident in their power of doing evil, that they spoke of it till it became a universal impression.

From the terrible Jesuit there is but one step further in horror, and that is to the Inquisitor! And, in fact, it can scarcely be called a step at all, for both characters are frequently combined in the same individual. Jesuits, it will be seen in all the histories of the inquisition, are as active as the Dominicans themselves, who claim the peculiar honour, or more properly infamy, of possessing, from the head of their order, the office of inquisitors; that is, fiends incarnate. In speaking of the extermination of the Troubadours, we have already noticed the rise of the Inquisition. It was an institution so congenial to the nature of popery, that its HOLY OFFICES—its OFFICES OF MERCY, as they were called in that spirit of devilish abuse of Christianity in which they were conceived, were speedily to be found in various countries of Europe, Asia, and America, but distinguished most fearfully in Spain. Their horrors have been made familiar to the public mind by the writers of romance, especially by Mrs. Ratcliffe; but all the powers of romance have not been able to overcolour the reality. Spain has always claimed and gloried in the supremacy of her inquisition. She has strenuously contended with the pope for it; and has deemed it so national an honour, as to parade the auto-da-fé as one of her most fascinating spectacles. Her kings, her queens, her princes, and nobles, have assembled with enthusiasm to witness them. So great a treat did the Spaniards formerly consider them, that Llorente states that on February 25th, 1560, one was celebrated by the inquisitors of Toledo, in which several persons were burnt, with some effigies, and a great number subjected to penances; and this was performed to *entertain* the new queen Elizabeth, daughter of Henry II. of France, a girl of thirteen years of age, accustomed in her own country to brilliant festivals suitable to her rank and age. So completely may priestcraft brutalize a nation, and so completely has this devilish institution stamped the Spanish character, naturally ardent and chivalric, with gloomy horror, that both Llorente and Limborch represent ladies witnessing the agonizing tortures of men and women expiring in flames, with transports of delight. By means of this infernal machine, the

Spanish kings have contrived to crush the mind of the country; to check the growth of literature; to nourish a spirit of ferocity; and to produce a race of people the slaves of the worst government, and the most ignorant and bigoted priests. To this cause in fact, Spain owes its present misery and degradation. Llorente, whose work is founded on official documents, drawn from the archives of the inquisition itself, when he was secretary to it, gives a long list of the learned and ingenious Spaniards whom it has persecuted and condemned. The ostensible object of its early exertions, was to extirpate the Jews, Moors and Morescoes; and so successful were its efforts, that Llorente calculates that in one hundred and nineteen years it deprived Spain of three millions of inhabitants. Mariana says 170,000 families of Jews were banished, and the rest sold for slaves. They entered Portugal, but were again commanded by the Portuguese king to quit that realm also. The Moors were suffered to depart; but as the Jews were preparing to do so, the king commanded that all those who were not more than fourteen years old, should be taken from their parents and educated in the Christian religion. It was a most afflicting thing, to see children snatched from the embraces of their mothers; and fathers embracing their children, torn from them, and even beaten with clubs; to hear the dreadful cries they made, and every place filled with the lamentations and yells of women. Many through indignation, threw their sons into pits, and others killed them with their own hands. Thus prevented on the one hand from embarking, and on the other oppressed and persecuted, many feigned conversion, to escape from their miseries. The cruelties practised on these people, to compel them to embrace a religion which was thus represented as only fit for devils, make one's blood boil to read them. The Reformation appeared, and found these monsters fresh employment. The doctrines of Luther appear to have made so rapid a progress scarcely in any country as in Spain. Numbers of the highest ranks, of the most intelligent ladies, of ecclesiastics, embraced the principles of the reformer; and, had it not been for the inquisition, that country might now have figured in the front of Europe with a more glorious aspect, as a great and enlightened state, than it did under Charles V. The inquisition had the satisfaction of extinguishing the revived flame of Christianity, and of reducing Spain to its present deplorable condition. All the fury and strength of that great engine of hell was brought to bear upon it: its auto-da-fé were crowded with Lutheran heretics; its fires consumed them; its secret cells devoured them—men, women, children were swept into its unfathomable gulph of destruction. Priestly malice triumphed over truth and virtue.

To such gigantic stature of power did this dismal institution attain, that no one was safe from its fangs. The confiscation of the goods of its victims whetted the appetite of priestly avarice so keenly, that a man to be guilty of heresy had only to be rich. Llorente gives several cases of English merchants, who were pounced upon by it in defiance of the law of nations. On one occasion Oliver Cromwell had to intercede for an English consul, whom they had got into their dens. The king replied, he had no power over the inquisition. "Then," added Cromwell, in a second message, "if you have no power over the inquisition, I will declare war against it." The threat was effectual. So little power had the Spanish kings over it, indeed, that it did not hesitate to accuse them; and Llorente's lists are full of nobles, privy councillors, knights, magistrates, military commanders, and ladies of the highest birth, on whom these daring priests laid their hands, and loaded them with chains and infamy. It seemed a peculiar delight to them to insult and degrade those who had moved in the most distinguished spheres. In Portugal, says Limborch, all the prisoners, men and women, without any regard to birth or dignity, are shaved the first or second day of their imprisonment. Each prisoner has two pots of water every day: one to wash, and the other to drink; a besom to cleanse his cell, and a mat of rushes to lie upon.

The same historian gives, in a few passages, a vivid summary of the operations of this odious institution. "In countries where the inquisition has existed, the bare idea of its progress damped the most ardent mind. Formidable and ferocious as the rapacious tiger, who from the gloomy thicket surveys his unsuspecting prey, until the favoured moment arrives in which he may plunge forward and consummate its destruction, the inquisition meditates in secret and in silence its horrific projects. In the deepest seclusion the calumniator propounds his charge; with anxious vigilance the creatures of its power regard its unhappy victim. Not a whisper is heard, or the least hint of insecurity given, until at the dead of night a band of savage monsters surround the dwelling; they demand an entrance:—upon the inquiry, by whom is this required? the answer is, "the holy office." In an instant all the ties of nature appear as if dissolved, and either through the complete dominion of superstition, or the conviction that resistance would be vain, the master, parent, husband is resigned. From the bosom of his family, and bereft of all domestic comforts, he enters the inquisition house; its ponderous doors are closed, and hope excluded—perhaps for ever. Immured in a noisome vault, surrounded by impenetrable walls, he is left alone; a prey to all the sad reflections of a miserable outcast. If he venture to inquire the reason of his fate, he is told, that silence and secresy are here inviolable. Accustomed to the conveniences of social life, and perhaps of a superior station, he is now reduced to the most miserable expedients. The most menial offices now devolve upon him; while the cruel reflection obtrudes itself upon his mind, that his family may, ere long, be reduced to indigence by an act of inquisitorial confiscation." And with such fiendish ingenuity is the punishment of confiscation aggravated, that it is followed as of necessary consequence, by the person being rendered for ever infamous,—that is, he is incapable of holding office of any kind; his children are disinherited, and made infamous, or incapable to the second generation by the father's side, and first by the mother's. All his relations are liberated from their obligations to him, or connexion with him; his children are freed from his control; his wife is liberated from her marriage vows; his servants or vassals are freed from their servitude; he is compelled to answer inquiries of others on any affair, but no one need answer him. He has no protection from the laws, and no remedy against oppression or injustice. His very children, brothers and sisters, ought to abandon him; and the only way of a son escaping the infamy of his father, is by being the first to accuse him to the tribunal of the inquisition.

Then come the secret examinations, the accusations from unknown sources, the intimidations,—the torture! The torture has five degrees:—first, being threatened to be tortured: secondly, being carried to the place of torture: thirdly, by stripping and binding: fourthly, the being hoisted on the rack: fifthly, squassation.

The stripping is performed without regard to humanity or honour, not only to men, but to women and virgins. As to squassation, it is thus performed: the prisoner has his hands tied behind his back, and weights tied to his feet, and then he is drawn up on high, till his head reaches the very pulley. He is kept hanging in this manner for some time, that by the greatness of the weight hanging at his feet, all his joints and limbs may be dreadfully stretched, and on a sudden he is let down with a jerk, by slackening the rope, but kept from coming quite to the ground; by which terrible shake his arms and legs are all disjointed, whereby he is put to the most exquisite pain; the shock which he receives by the sudden stop put to his fall, and the weight at his feet, stretching his whole body more intensely and cruelly. According to the orders of the inquisition, this squassation is repeated once, twice, or three times in the space of an hour.

Another mode of torture is, by covering the mouth and nostrils with a thin cloth, so that the victim is scarcely able to breathe through them; then, letting fall from on high water, drop by drop, on his mouth, which so easily sinks through the cloth to the bottom of his throat, so that it is impossible for him to breathe, his mouth being filled with water, his nostrils with the cloth; so that the poor wretch is in the agony of death. When this cloth is pulled out of his mouth, as it often is, to answer questions, it is all over water and blood, and is like pulling his bowels through his mouth. All this time he is lying in what is called the wooden-horse; that is, a trough across which a bar is placed, on which the man's back rests, instead of on the bottom, while his arms, shins, and thighs are tied round with small cords, drawn tight by screws, till they cut to the very bones.

The physician Orobio, a Jew, gave a most lively account of the torture practised upon him after he had lain in his dungeon three years. He was brought to the place of torture. It was towards evening. It was a large underground room, arched, and the walls covered with black hangings. The candlesticks were fastened to the wall, and the whole enlightened with candles placed in them. At one end there was an enclosed place, like a closet, where the inquisitor and notary sate at a table: so that the place seemed to him the very mansion of death, everything appearing so terrible and so awful. After some preliminary torments, such as tying his thumbs with small cords till the blood spouted out from beneath the nails; they fastened him with small cords, by means of little iron pulleys, to a wall as he sate upon a bench; then drawing the cords which fastened his fingers and toes with great violence, they drew the bench from under him, and left him suspended in the strings, till he seemed to be dissolving in flame, such was his agony. Then they brought a sort of ladder and struck it against his shins, giving five violent strokes at once; under the exquisite pain of which he fainted away. They then screwed up his cords with fresh violence, and tied others so near that they slid into the gashes the first had made, and produced such an effusion of blood that they supposed him dying. On finding, however, that he was not, they repeated the torture once more, and then remanded him to his cell!" To imagine men practising these cruelties on men, and that in the outraged name of Christ, the fountain of love and mercy, is revolting enough; but to read of them mangling, dislocating, and dashing to pieces the delicate frames of young and lovely women, of which Llorente gives various instances, puts the climax to our abhorrent indignation. Such, in particular, were the treatment of Jane Bohorques, and her attendant, a young Lutheran girl, afterwards burnt at the auto-da-fé.*

A word on these auto-da-fé, and we will escape from these horrors. Dr. Geddes' account of the manner of celebrating them, as quoted in Limborch, is one of the best and most condensed. " In the morning of the day the prisoners are all brought into a great hall, where they have the habits put on they are to wear in the procession, which begins to come out of the inquisition about nine o'clock in the morning.

"The first in the procession are the Dominicans, who carry the standard of the inquisition, which on the one side hath their founder Dominic's picture, and on the other side the cross between an olive tree and a sword, with this motto, ' Justitia et Miserecordia.' Next after the Dominicans come the penitents, some with benitoes and some without, according to the nature of their crimes. They are all in black coats without sleeves, and barefooted, with a wax candle in their hands. Next come the penitents who have narrowly escaped being burnt, who, over their black coat have flames painted with their points turned downwards, to signify their

---

* The methods of torture are not merely such as I have here given—they are infinitely varied, and too dreadful to be borne even in the recital. With them it is, indeed, a matter of science; and is treated of in a volume to be found in the libraries of this country—THE ART OF TORTURE—in which the most ingenious modes of producing physical agony are detailed with the coolest accuracy. I recollect the horror with which a friend of mine opened this book, in the library of the Earl of Shrewsbury at Alton.

having been saved, but so as by fire. Next come the negative and relapsed that are to be burnt, with flames upon their habit, pointing upward; and next come those who profess doctrines contrary to those of the church of Rome, and who, besides flames on their habit pointing upward, have their picture, which is drawn two or three days before, upon their breasts, with dogs, serpents, and devils, all with open mouths, painted about it.

"Pegna, a famous Spanish inquisitor, calls this procession 'Horrendum ac tremendum spectaculum;' and so it is, in truth, there being something in the looks of all the prisoners, besides those that are to be burnt, that is ghastly and disconsolate beyond what can be imagined; and in the eyes and countenances of those that are to be burnt, there is something that looks fierce and eager.

"The prisoners that are to be burnt alive, besides a familiar which all the rest have, have a jesuit on each hand of them, who is continually preaching to them to abjure their heresies; but if they offer to speak any thing in defence of the doctrines for which they are going to suffer death, they are immediately gagged. This I saw done to a prisoner presently after he came out of the gates of the inquisition, upon his having looked up at the sun, which he had not seen for several years, and cried out in a rapture—'How is it possible for people that behold that glorious body, to worship any being but Him that created it!' After the prisoners, comes a troop of familiars on horseback, and after them the inquisitors and other officers of the court upon mules; and last of all comes the inquisitor-general, upon a white horse led by two men, with a black hat and green hat-band, and attended by all the nobles that are not employed as familiars in the procession.

"At the place of execution, which at Lisbon is the Ribera, there are so many stakes set up as there are prisoners to be burnt, with a good quantity of dry furze about them. The stakes of the professed, as the inquisitors call them, may be about four yards high, and have a small board whereon the prisoner is to be seated, within half a yard of the top. The negative and relapsed being first strangled and burnt, the professed go up a ladder betwixt the two jesuits, who spend about a quarter of an hour in exhorting them to be reconciled to the church of Rome; which, if they refuse, the jesuits descend, the executioner ascends and secures them to the stake. The jesuits then go up a second time, and at parting tell them— 'they leave them to the devil, who stands at their elbow to receive their souls, and carry them into the flames of hell-fire.' Upon this a great shout is raised, 'Let the dogs' beards be made!' which is done by thrusting flaming furzes, fastened to long poles, against their faces. And this inhumanity is commonly continued until their faces are burnt to a coal, and is always acompanied by such loud acclamations of joy as are not to be heard on any other occasion; a bull-feast or a fair being dull entertainments to this.

"The professeds' beards having been thus made, or trimmed, as they call it in jollity, fire is set to the furze which are at the bottom of the stake, and above which the professed are chained so high that the top of the flame seldom reaches higher than the seat they sit on; and if there happen to be a wind, to which that place is much exposed, it seldom reaches so high as their knees. If it be calm they may be dead in half an hour, but if windy they are not dead in an hour and a half or two hours, and are really roasted, not burnt to death. But though, out of hell, there cannot possibly be a more lamentable spectacle than this, being joined with the sufferers' continual cry of, '*Miserecordia por amor de Dios,*' Mercy for the love of God! yet it is beheld by people of both sexes, and all ages, with such transports of joy and satisfaction, as are not witnessed on any other occasion."

Mr. Wilcox, afterwards Bishop of Gloucester, wrote to Bishop Burnet, that he witnessed at Lisbon in 1706, Hector Dias and Maria Pinteyra burnt alive. The woman was alive in the flames half an hour; the man about an hour. The king and his brother were seated at a window so near as to be addressed for a considerable time in very moving terms by the man as he was burning. All he asked was a few more fagots, yet he could not obtain them. The wind being a little fresh, the man's hinder parts were perfectly roasted; and as he turned himself round, his ribs opened before he left speaking, the fire being recruited as it wasted, to keep him just in the same degree of heat; but all his entreaties could not procure him a larger allowance of wood, to despatch him more speedily.

The victims who have suffered death or ruin from this diabolical institution in various quarters of the world, are estimated at some millions. Llorente gives, from actual examination of its own records, the following statement of the victims of the Spanish Inquisition alone.

| | |
|---|---:|
| Number of persons who were condemned and perished in the flames | 31,912 |
| Effigies burnt | 17,659 |
| Condemned to severe penances | 291,450 |
| | 341,021 |

And these things the choicest agents of the devil,

have dared to act in the name of Christ, and men have believed them! Amid all the crimes of Napoleon, let it be for ever remembered that he annihilated this earthly hell with a word,—but Englishmen restored Ferdinand to the throne of Spain, and Ferdinand restored the inquisition. We fought to give Spaniards freedom, and we gave them the most blasting despotism which ever walked the earth—the despotism of priestcraft; with fire in one hand, and eternal darkness and degradation in the other. Cromwell had a different spirit—he menaced war on the inquisition—and the menace was heard to the lowest depths of its infernal dens. If the arm of cruelty be shortened, it is neither owing to the priests nor their creature Ferdinand, but to the light which has entered Spain during its political concussions.

Another subject connected with this history might also form a separate chapter—the state of those European countries which yet retain popery. It would be an interesting inquiry, and would amply bear out the character already drawn of priestcraft; but the consideration of our own state-religion draws me on, and I must refer my readers to the abundant works of our modern travellers for those matters—if indeed it be not enough to lift our eyes, and, at a cursory view, see the mark of the beast stamped on the bosom of every nation where it prevails—in characters of slavery, ignorance, calamity, and blood. France, roused by the united oppressions of kingcraft and priestcraft, rushed into a premature struggle with them, in which religion and liberty were both wrecked, and such horrors perpetrated as turn the sickening eyes of the beholder away, blinded with burning tears. France, thirsting for civil and religious freedom, yet unprepared in its popular heart for its secure enjoyment, arose like a giant in wrath, and smarting with the accumulated inflictions of popery and civil despotism, crushed together its wrongs and its hopes. France, starting from the extreme slumber of papal slavery—a state in which its population received passively all dogmas and all ordinances, a state without inquiry—plunged at once into the opposite extreme of restless scrutiny after the true principles of government and religion; and like a man issuing at full speed from darkness to the glare of noonday, has seen nothing but indistinct and overpowering images of things—felt nothing but the wild frenzy of suddenly-acquired freedom; and has consequently floundered on through changes, revolutions, and reeling instability, that have been more fatal to the progress of true liberty than all the assaults of its determined enemies. On the other hand, Spain and Portugal, with a certain portion of intelligent and philosophical inhabitants, groan under the dead weight of their old papal institutions and trains of priests, and wound themselves to death in the vain endeavour to throw them off, before the people are sufficiently regenerated with the inbreakings of knowledge to give vigour to the contest. In them we see the full consequences of the establishment of inquisitions, by which the public mind acquires a habit of fear, and an incapacity for daring development of mental energy, even where the cause of real fear is no more. Were the people of these countries once educated, they would throw off monks, priests, and wicked kings, with the ease that Sampson threw off his writhes—but where shall this begin, where knowledge has long been treated as damnable, and has been punished with death? Such is the state of ignorance, which it is the interest and has always been the practice of popery to maintain in those countries, that Lord Byron, speaking of the ladies, **says,** they are beautiful, but the countess is no better informed than the commonest peasant girl. Italy too lies prostrate beneath the double tyranny of the altar and the throne of the foreign barbarian,— and the end of those things it is not easy to see. Eternal are the thanks, the gratitude, and the honours due to Huss, to Jerome of Prague, to Oldcastle, to Wycliffe, and other martyrs and reformers, who attempted, and to Luther and his contemporaries, who finally succeeded in breaking down this mightiest of spiritual despotisms, and freeing part of mankind from the nightmare of a thousand years; leaving *us* in the bright day-beams of knowledge and freedom, not to suffer, but to sigh over the miseries which the bloodiest of priesthoods has inflicted for centuries on the world; —and not to sigh only, but to exert ourselves to spread still wider the impulse of good which they have given. Who shall tell what effects on the continental nations the regeneration of the religious institutions of this mighty and illustrious nation shall yet produce?

## CHAPTER XV.

### THE ENGLISH CHURCH.

Where one particular priesthood has rank in the state, others are not free; and where they all have, the people are not free. So far as the ceremonies of one particular faith are connected with filling any particular occupation, entering into the relations, or enjoying any of the advantages of civil life, there is not religious liberty. It is a fallacious distinction which has sometimes been drawn, that a state may patronize, though it should not punish. A government cannot patronize one particular religion without punishing others. A state has no wealth but the people's wealth; if it pay some, it impoverishes others. A state is no fountain of honour. If it declare one class free, it thereby declares others slaves. If it declare some noble, it thereby declares others ignoble. Whenever bestowed with partiality, its generosity is injustice, and its favour is oppression.
W. J. Fox's Sermons on the Mission, Character, and Doctrine of Christ.

One would have imagined that when the horrors and enormities of that long reign of spiritual slavery which I have been detailing—that of the infamous papal hierarchy—had roused a great part of Europe to scotch the old serpent of Rome; to burst asunder the vile and envenomed folds which she had wrapped round the soul, the life, and liberties of man,—that the reformed churches would have been careful so to organize themselves as to prevent temporal power again enslaving religion. But, in the first place, it is no easy matter to escape the grasp of regal and political dominion; and in the next, it is rarely the case that men are prepared, after a long sufferance of slavery, to enjoy and secure freedom. To expect this, is to expect that he whose body has been cramped by chains, and wasted by vigils in the dark dungeons of power for years, should at once, on coming out, stretch forth his limbs, acquire in a moment the vigour and elasticity of his muscles, and bound over the hills with the breathing buoyancy of the youthful hunter, to whom every day brings exercise, and with exercise, force and adroitness. It is to expect that the issuer from the dungeon shall bear at once the light of day with an eagle's glance, and regard every thing around him with the perspicuous familiarity of those who have daily walked about in the eye of heaven. Besides, in the exultation of conquest over an old despotism, the populace are always, for the moment, too credulously trusting to the professions of those who pretend to rejoice with them in order to enslave them anew. In a while they wake from their dream of good nature, but it is too late,—they are again clasped in bonds, and environed with bars that nothing but the oppressions of ages can corrode, and some far-off out-breaking of popular indignation can dash asunder.

Such has been the fate, more or less, of all the reformed churches of Europe; but their fortunes we cannot follow, we must confine ourselves to the Church of England;—the least reformed, the most enslaved of all. The reformation in England was commenced and continued, and so far as it went, under unfortunate circumstances. It was not the result of such a ripened and irrestrainable enthusiasm of the popular mind as must have thrown down all before it; but it was brought about by the arbitrary passions of that monster, Henry VIII.—one of the most libidinous and bloody wretches that ever disgraced a throne. At one moment it was his will, because it suited his pleasure, to be the advocate of the pope; at another, because it was necessary to the gratification of his indomitable desires,—his most desperate antagonist. For this he threw off the papal yoke—but not to give the church freedom—nothing could be farther from his intentions: it was only to make it his servant and his slave. He declared himself the head of the church of Christ in these kingdoms. What a head for such a church! The despotism of opinion was only changed in name; and it appears to have been the effect of the merest accident that it was changed at all. Everything was on the point of being amicably settled between the British and the Italian tyrant, when it was rumoured at the papal court, that Henry had witnessed a dramatic representation in which that court was ridiculed. In a moment of impolitic passion, the "triple tyrant" thundered against Henry his bull of denunciation, and the breach was made immortal. Heavily and long did the pontiff curse the moment in which he forgot, in his passion, the priest's proper cunning; but his regret was unavailing—England was lost for ever.

Edward VI. was a truly pious youth, and was unquestionably desirous of doing what was right; but he was a feeble invalid, and was in the hands of priests, who did with him as they pleased. By authority exercised in his name, a liturgy was framed for the church; which Elizabeth afterwards revised by her bishops, and brought to that state in which it substantially remains to this day. It was not in the nature of that man in petticoats,—that

Henry VIII. in a female mask,— to consult the inclinations of the people so much as her own high will, in which glowed all the dominance and all the spirit of the Tudors. Instead of being willing, say Heylin and Strype, to strip religion of the ceremonies which remained in it, she was rather inclined to bring the public worship still nearer to the Roman ritual; and had a great propensity to several usages in the church of Rome which were justly looked upon as superstitious. She thanked publicly one of her chaplains who had preached in defence of the *real presence;* she was fond of images, and retained some in her chapel; and would undoubtedly have forbidden the marriage of the clergy, if Cecil, her secretary, had not interposed. Having appointed a committee of divines to revise king Edward's liturgy, she gave them an order to strike out all offensive passages against the pope, and make people easy about the corporal presence of Christ in the sacrament.

That an imperious woman, who, not finding it accordant with the love of undivided power to marry, was jealous of all who did; who even imprisoned her relatives and maids of honour who presumed to marry, should attempt to prevent the clergy marrying, was not very wonderful: but she did not stop here. Those of her subjects who were desirous of a purer, simpler, more apostolic, and less worldly system of worship; who had fled to the continent from the fire and chains of her sister Mary, and had returned, hoping better things at her hands, she ordered to submit to her royal will; and passed the famous act of *Uniformity*, by which all her subjects were commanded to observe the rules her bishops had framed, and to take up with such a reformation of the church as she had pleased to give them, with herself as the visible head of the church upon earth. The puritans—for so they were called, for desiring a purer worship—refused their assent to these proceedings; pleaded the dictates of their consciences in behalf of their refusal; and complained heavily, that the gross superstitions of popery, which they had looked upon as abrogated and abolished, were now revived, and even imposed by authority. But they pleaded and complained in vain. What were their consciences to this she tyrant? the indulgence of whose self-will was of more precious value in her eyes than the rights and consciences of millions of people. She not only commanded and exacted; but following the example of popery, she set up the fire and fagot, and stopped all objections with those powerful arguments. It is a singular fact, that no state religion, pagan or Christian, from the foundation of the world, as this history will shew, but is stained with blood. Henry VIII., Edward VI., and Elizabeth, all resorted to it, and while professing to reform religion, they gave the death-blow to liberty of conscience, and reacted all the horrors of Roman persecution. Edward, indeed, in the tenderness of youth, had a better sense of the nature of Christianity, and earnestly and with many tears endeavoured to avoid the bloody work of persecution put upon him by the priests about him, and especially by Cranmer, who afterwards received the fit retribution of dying in that fire he had so zealously kindled for others.

What could be expected of a church thus born in the throes of the most evil passions, cradled in arbitrary power, and baptized in blood?—Nothing but a melancholy death of all those high and glorious hopes which the Reformation awoke, and had it been permitted, unshackled by regal and priestly power, to take its course, would naturally have realized. Elizabeth proceeded, with that rigorous and strong hand which made her civil government respected, but was most unhallowedly and calamitously thrust into the sacred tabernacle of conscience, to establish a court of high commission to enforce those popish rites, doctrines, and ceremonies which she had compelled the English church to adopt. For the particulars of the tyrannies exercised by this Inquisition over those who asserted the rights of conscience, in the face of this strangely reformed church, let the reader consult Rapin, Hume, and Neale's History of the Puritans. It took its rise from a remarkable clause in the Act of Supremacy, by which the queen and her successors were empowered to choose persons " to exercise under her all manner of jurisdiction, privileges, and pre-eminences, touching any spiritual or ecclesiastical jurisdiction in England and Ireland; as also to visit, reform, redress, order, correct, and amend all errors, heresies, schisms, abuses, contempts, offences, and enormities whatever; provided that they have no power to determine anything to be heresy but what has been adjudged by the authority of the canonical scriptures, or four first general councils, or any of them, or shall be so declared by parliament with consent of the clergy in convocation." These commissioners were empowered to make inquiry, not only by legal methods, but also by all other means which they could devise, that is by rack, torture, inquisition and imprisonment. They had authority to examine all persons that they suspected, or feigned to suspect, by an oath, not allowed by their commission, and therefore called *ex-officio*, who were obliged to answer all questions, and thus to criminate themselves and friends. The fines they imposed were discretionary; the imprisonment to which they doomed was limited by no rule but their own pleasure; they imposed as they pleased new articles of faith on the clergy, and practised all the cruelties and iniquities of a real inquisition.

Thus, indeed, was the inquisition as fully and completely set up in England, by a *soi-disant* reforming queen and reformed church, as in Italy, Spain, or any of the old priest-ridden countries of popery; and how its powers were exercised may be seen in too fearful colours on the broad page of English history; in the more full relations of the non-conformists and dissenters. Clergymen who could not thus mould their consciences at the will of the state, were ejected without mercy from their livings, and they and their families exposed to all the horrors of poverty, contempt, and persecution. So far as the regular clergy, however, were concerned, the grievance was not great; for these principally consisted of Catholics, who had got in during Mary's reign, and having a clear perception that they were well off, and that there was little hope of another Romish prince succeeding very speedily, they acted according to the dictates of the priestly cunning, accommodated their consciences to their comfortable condition, and came over in a body to the new state of things. The bishops, Hume says, having the eye of the world more particularly on them, made it a point of honour, and having, by a sickly season, been reduced to fourteen, all these, except the Bishop of Landaffe, refused compliance, and were degraded: but out of the 10,000 parishes of England, only eighty vicars and rectors, fifty prebendaries, fifteen heads of colleges, twelve archdeacons, and as many deans, sacrificed their livings to their religious principles; a fact rendered more striking to us by a future one,—that of the Presbyterian clergy, who had obtained livings during the Commonwealth, and who, on the passing of the Act of Uniformity again, on the restoration of

Charles II., resigned, to the number of 2000, in one day, to the astonishment of even their enemies, who had no notion of the existence of such high principle, especially as they had not failed to tempt the most able of these clergy with offers of deaneries and other preferments, and to Baxter, Calamy, and Reynolds bishoprics,—the last of whom only was weak enough to accept it. It was chiefly, therefore, on the dissenters, and on the more conscientious clergy who had been ejected from their livings in Mary's reign, that the weight of persecution from the Ecclesiastical Court fell. These were harassed with every possible vexation. They were fined, imprisoned, and destroyed without mercy. This state of things did not cease, excepting during the short interval of the Commonwealth, till the Act of Toleration, in the reign of William III. put an end to it, and gave to conscience some degree of liberty. The Stuarts, who succeeded Elizabeth, with far less talent than the Tudors, had all their love of tyrannical power: and so incorrigible was this principle in them, that it soon brought one of them to the block; made his son a fugitive for the greater part of his life; and, finally, notwithstanding the good-natured relentings of the people, who had restored his line to the throne, made them rise once more, and drive the hopelessly despotic family from the throne for ever.

But, before we quit Elizabeth, we must give some clearer idea of her notion of a reformed church establishment. She insisted that the simpler forms and doctrines of the church of Geneva should be avoided; and that a splendid hierarchy should be maintained of archbishops, bishops, archdeacons, deans, canons, and other officials; declared that the church of Rome was a true church, and adopted most of its relics and ceremonies. Its festivals and holidays in honour of saints were to be kept; the sign of the cross was to be used in baptism; kneeling at the sacrament of the Lord's supper; bowing at the name of Jesus; giving the ring in matrimony; confirmation of children by episcopalian hands; forbidding marriage at certain seasons of the year; and many other popish appendages were retained. The doctrine of the absolution of sins, and the damnatory creed of Athanasius were held fast; so that to many—except as to the marriage of the clergy, auricular confession, and a less pompous and ornate form of worship—little difference between popery and the English church could be discerned; and, to make the case still more intolerable, matters of indifference, such as were neither commanded nor forbidden by Scripture—as the external rites of worship, the vests of the clergy, religious festivals—were put under the authority of the civil magistracy; and those who refused to conform to them were thus made rebels to the state, and punishable accordingly. It was impossible to conceive a more thorough extinction of the rights of the subject in affairs of conscience—not in popery itself! The bishops having thus got power into their hands, speedily proceeded to exercise it,—to shew the old priestly spirit. In 1588, Bancroft, archbishop of Canterbury, declared that the episcopal order were, by express appointment of God, superior to the presbyters, and that all priests not ordained by bishops were spurious. This, says Mosheim, was the form of religion established in England, which laid the foundation for perpetual dissensions and feuds in that otherwise happy and prosperous nation.

Such was the formation of the church of England! such it remains to the present hour! After such an origin, can any one wonder that it needs reform, thorough reform, not merely of its abuses, which are, as might naturally be expected from so absurd and despotic a constitution, become monstrous, but reform and entire remodelling of its canons? While all around it has been progressing in knowledge and better understanding of the rights of conscience, and the true nature of Christianity, here has this eldest daughter of popery been standing still in body, covered with all her deformities, with the mark of the beast blazing on her forehead, and the filthy rags of cast-off popery fluttering about her; and while every clearer eye has been regarding this patchwork progeny of priestcraft and barbarism with mingled wonder, ridicule, and abhorrence, she has been hugging herself in the fond idea, that she was the queen of beauty, and the perfection of holiness! While the civilized world has been moving about her, casting off the mind, the manners, and the harsh tenets of feudal rudeness, she has lain coiled up in the bright face of advancing day, like some huge slimy dragon cast up by the sea of ages, in the midst of a stirring and refined city; and has only exhibited signs of life by waving her huge scaled tail in menace of her foes, and by stretching out her ten-talented paws to devour a tenth of the land. Can such a monster longer encumber the soil of England? As soon might we expect St. George to come leading his dragon into London, or Dunstan present the devil, pincered in his fiery tongs, at the door of Lambeth palace.

Dissent was forced on the nation by the bigotry of the rulers and the priests; it was fanned into inextinguishable flame by continual jealousies and persecutions under every reign, till that of William and Mary; and in our own time, has, by the lukewarmness of the established clergy, led to its extension tenfold in the new schism of the Methodists.* The history of the Society of Friends is full of the most singular persecutions on the part of the clergy, and the magistracy incited by them. At one time, according to Sewell, their historian, almost every adult of this persuasion was in prison. At a very early period of their association, two thousand four hundred of them were incarcerated. From the time of their rise to the very day of the passing of the Act of Toleration, they were harassed and abused in all possible manners. Their property was seized; their meetings forcibly scattered with rude soldiers and the scum of the people; they were confined in the most loathsome prisons, where many perished, from hardships and severities of winter, and of men more wintry than the elements. To escape from this state of shameful and intolerable oppression, William Penn, one of the greatest and most illustrious men which this country ever produced, led out his persecuted brethren to America, and there founded one of the states of that noble country, which has now risen to a pitch of prosperity which is the natural fruit of

* The sagacious mind of Milton, saw in his day the advantages of that system which Wesley in ours has put so successfully into operation. " Thus taught, once for all, and thus now and then visited and confirmed in the most destitute and poorest places of the land, under the government of their own elders, performing all ministerial offices amongst them, they may be trusted to meet and edify one another, whether in church or chapel, or to save them the trudging of many miles thither, nearer home, though in a house or barn. For, notwithstanding the gaudy superstition of some still ignorantly devoted to temples, we may be well assured, that he who did not disdain to be laid in a manger, disdains not to be preached in a barn; and that, by such meetings as these, being, indeed, most apostolical and primitive, they will, in a short time, advance more in Christian knowledge and reformation of life, than by many years preaching of such an incumbent, I may say such an incumbrance oft-times, as will be merely hired to abide long in such places."

liberty; and stands an every-day opprobrium of priestcraft, and a monument not merely of the uselessness, but the impolicy and nuisance of establishments. In the new, but great cities of that vast empire—in the depths of its eternal forests, and on its mountains and its plains, that scorn to bear the scorching foot of despotism, millions of free men, who have escaped from the temporal and spiritual outrages of Europe, lift up their voices and their hearts in thanksgivings to Him who has given them a land wide as human wishes, and as free as the air that envelopes it. They have gone out from us to escape our cruelties and indignities, and are become our practical teachers in the philosophy of religion and government.

The English church, which has been so lauded by its interested supporters, as a model of all that is pure, dignified, holy, and compact, has not only thus compelled dissent by its tyranny; but by the consent of all historians, has, from its commencement, been composed like Nebuchadnezzar's image, of most ill agreeing materials, mingled brass and clay; and has consequently been continually rent with differing factions. The Tudors established popish rites, and Edward IV. introduced Calvinistic doctrines; and these, retained by Elizabeth and James I., Charles I. by a singular inconsistency sanctioned, at the same moment that, under the management of his domineering Archbishop Laud, he was carrying the claims of episcopal power to the highest pitch, and would not only force them upon the English, but on the Scotch. This prelate, as complete a papist in spirit as any that ever exercised despotism in the bosom of that arbitrary church, has been much eulogised by good men of the present day, who, themselves most amiable in their own private circles, exhibit in their writings too much of the harshness and the bigotry of the middle ages to be agreeable in this. The opinion of Hume has been often quoted in his favour; let us therefore see what Hume does say of him. "This man was virtuous, if severity of manners alone, and abstinence of pleasure, could deserve that name. He was learned, if polemical knowledge could entitle him to that praise. He was disinterested; but with unceasing industry he studied to exalt the priestly and prelatical character, which was his own. His zeal was unrelenting in the cause of religion; that is, by imposing, by rigorous measures, his own tenets and pious ceremonies on the obstinate puritans, who had profanely dared to oppose him. In prosecution of his holy purposes, he overlooked every human consideration; or, in other words, the heat and indiscretion of his temper made him neglect the views of prudence, and rules of good manners. He was in this respect happy, (how exactly the character of some eminent men of this day!)—that all his enemies were also imagined by him the declared enemies of loyalty and true piety; and that every exercise of his anger, by that means, became in his eyes, a merit and a virtue. This was the man who acquired so great an ascendant over Charles, and who led him by the facility of his temper, with a conduct which proved so fatal to himself and to his kingdom." He adds, that, " in return for Charles's indulgence towards the church, Laud, and his followers took care to magnify, on every occasion, the regal authority, and to treat with the utmost disdain or detestation, all puritanical pretensions to a free and independent constitution." At the same time, he continues, that " while these prelates exalted the kingly power, they took care to set the priestly still higher, and endeavoured to render it independent of the sovereign. They declared it sacred and indefeasible; all right to private judgment in spiritual matters was denied to laymen; bishops held spiritual courts without any notice taken of the king's authority; and in short, rapid strides were made, not only towards the haughty despotism of popery, but towards its superstitious acrimoniousness. Laud, in spite of public opinion and private remonstrance, introduced pictures into the churches, shifted the altar back to its old papal standing, set up again the crucifix, and advised that the discipline and worship of the church should be imposed in all the colonies, and in all the regiments and trading companies abroad, and that no intimacy should be maintained with the reformed churches of the continent. All his measures, in fact, tended to a most popish state of ceremonies in worship, and tyranny and intolerance in behaviour; and if any one, after reading the following account of his consecration of St. Catherine's church, given by the same historian on the authority of Wellwood, Rushworth, and Franklin, can see any difference between him and a most thorough-going papist, he has better eyes than I.

" ' On the bishop's approach to the west door of the church, a loud voice cried, ' Open, open, ye everlasting doors, that the king of glory may enter in.' Immediately the doors of the church flew open, and the bishop entered. Falling on his knees, with eyes elevated, and arms expanded, he uttered these words: ' This place is holy; the ground is holy; in the name of the Father, the Son, and the Holy Ghost, I pronounce it holy.

" ' Going towards the chancel, he several times took up from the floor some of the dust, and threw it in the air. When he approached, with his attendants, near to the communion table, he bowed frequently towards it; and on their return, they went round the church, repeating as they marched along, some of the Psalms, and said a form of prayer, which concluded in these words—'We consecrate this church, and separate it unto Thee, as holy ground, not to be profaned any more to common uses.'

"'After this, the bishop standing near the communion table, solemnly pronounced many imprecations upon such as should afterwards pollute that holy place by musters of soldiers, or keeping in it profane law courts, or carrying burdens through it. On the conclusion of every curse, he bowed towards the east, and said—'Let all the people say, Amen.'

"'The imprecations being also piously finished, there were poured out a number of blessings on all such as had any hand in building and forming that sacred and beautiful edifice; and on such as had given, or should hereafter give to it, any chalices, plate, ornaments, or utensils. At every benediction he in like manner bowed towards the east, and cried—'Let all the people say, Amen.'

"'The sermon followed: after which the bishop consecrated and administered the sacrament in the following manner. As he approached the communion table he made many lowly reverences; and, coming up to that part of the table where the bread and wine lay, he bowed seven times. After the reading of many prayers, he approached the sacramental elements, and gently lifted up the napkin in which the bread was placed. When he beheld the bread, he suddenly let fall the napkin, flew back a step or two, bowed three several times towards the bread, then he drew nigh again, opened the napkin, and bowed as before.

"'Next he laid his hand on the cup, which had a cover upon it, and was filled with wine. He let go the cup, fell back, and bowed thrice towards it. He approached again, and lifting up the cover, peeped in. Seeing the wine, he let fall the cover, started back, and bowed as before. Then he received the sacrament, and gave it to others; and, many prayers being said, the solemnity of the consecration ended. The walls and floor and roof of the fabric were then supposed to be sufficiently holy."

The consequence of these ridiculous ceremonies on the one hand, and severities on the other,—for the English Inquisition, in the form of the High Commission Court, and the Star Chamber, was in full exercise, and many cruelties and iniquities were continually practised in them on those who dared to have an opinion of their own,—was, that Laud was brought to the block,\* and his sovereign was left in that calamitous course of unsuccessful despotism which actually brought him there, and deluged the whole nation in blood, and tossed it in years of anarchy and crime. By these circumstances, however, the church received, what Lord Chatham so expressly designated in Parliament—a Popish Liturgy—a Calvinistic Creed, and an Armenian Clergy.

The heterogeneous materials of the church shewed conspicuously in the famous assembly of divines at Westminster during part of Charles's reign and part

\* It is pity that an archbishop like Laud should be brought to such an end; because there are so much cheaper ways, and more economical of human suffering than the real murder of political enemies in the manner of Vane and Ney. But considerations of this kind should hinder no man from discerning, how entirely all that constitutes public and private freedom, happiness, and honour, has been obtained by the conquest and beating down, and is, in fact, the spoil of war carried off by the subjection and trampling under foot of that political and ecclesiastical party who have just received another mighty bruise; and of whom it has been truly said, that but for their successive defeats, England would at this moment have been Spain, Portugal, or Turkey.—*Westminster Review, No. XXXIV.*

of the Commonwealth, in which the Geneva form of worship was admitted by some of the most celebrated bishops, amongst them Tillotson and Selden. By the accession of William another rent was made: part of the hierarchy adhering to the Stuart line, refusing to swear allegiance to the new dynasty, and thus acquiring the name of Non-jurors,—splitting the church into High-church and Low-church,—two parties whose feuds and heart-burnings continued till late years, when the sect of the Evangelicals has appeared, to bear prolonged evidence to the internal destitution of the principles of cohesion in the Establishment. These lean towards the Calvinistic creed, which they justly assert is the strict, literal creed of the church according to the Thirty-nine Articles; and advocate a reform in the manners, and a renewed zeal in the spirit of the clergy. When we add to this that whereas in other countries the church is under the government of one deliberative body, and is in this split into two houses of convocation, we have before us a picture of unconnectedness that is perfectly amazing.

This is but a melancholy sketch of the history of this celebrated church; but it is one so broadly, copiously, and overwhelmingly delineated in the annals of the nation at large, that it cannot be controverted;—a history, as that of every state religion must be, of power usurping the throne of conscience; thrusting the spirit of the people from free address to, and communion with their God; and in refusal of obedience—an obedience more deadly and shameful than the most outrageous resistance could possibly be—following them with the fire and sword of extermination; or if that were not allowed, with the sneers and taunts of contempt. Alas! that such should be the miserable results of that reformation which at first promised such glorious fruits; that the blood of martyrs, and the fervid prayers and mighty exertions of the noblest intellects, and holiest men, should be spent so much in vain.

But such ever has been, and ever will be the result of that great fundamental error, of linking in unnatural union church and state; of making the church of Christ, who has himself declared that " his kingdom is not of this world," a tool of ambitious kings and rulers.

The nature of the Christian religion is essentially free; the voice of Christ proclaims to men—" the truth shall make you free!" The spirit of Christianity is so delicate in its sensibility, that it shrinks from the touch of the iron and blood-stained hand of political rule; it is so boundless in its aspirations, and expansive in its energies, that it must stand on the broad champaign of civil and intellectual liberty, ere it can stretch its wings effectively for that flight which is destined to encompass the earth, and end only in eternity. And what has been the consequence of attempting to chain this free spirit to the car of state? Why, that in its days of earlier union, arbitrary power sought to quench in its own sacred name, its own very life!—pursued with fire, sword, fetters, dungeons, and death, its primest advocates. The history of dissent is full of these horrors: and Ireland, in which the same system was pursued; and Scotland, that sooner than submit to it, rose, and stood to the death in many a mountain pass and bloody valley, can testify to the same odious policy. The oppressions and splendid resistance of the Scottish Covenanters,—the bloody havoc made amongst them by the soldiery of reformed kings and a reformed church; and their undaunted and most picturesque celebration of their own simple worship, lifting up their voices amid the rocks and desarts whither they were driven for their adherence to their religion, are well told by their own historians, but have been made of immortal interest by Sir Walter Scott. From the first to the last—from the accession of James I. to the throne of England, to the expulsion of James II. from that throne, a period of upwards of eighty years, the Stuarts persisted in the most tyrannical endeavours to force on their native country of Scotland the episcopal church; and, in consequence, deluged that high-spirited and beautiful country with blood. Many a solitary heath, many a scene of savage rocks in that land, where the peasant now passes by and only wonders at its wild silence, are yet loud in the ear of heaven in eternal complaints of the bloody and domineering deeds of the English church, wrought by its advice and by the hireling murderers of its royal head; many a name—as Kilsythe, Killicranky, and Bothwell Bridge—will rise up for ever in the souls of man against her. Does she stand before us and call herself holy and meek, and beneficent, with all these crimes, all these lives, all this blood and misery on her head? Well would it have been for Ireland, well for England, well for the Episcopalian Church itself, if some Jenny Geddes had been found, as in Edinburgh, to launch her three-legged stool at the head of the clergyman when he began to deal out a state liturgy; and had been followed by the simultaneous efforts of the whole people, to teach kings and priests to respect the inalienable rights of conscience: but in default of this, what has been the consequence? While power was left to the church, it persecuted, and would have continued to persecute. The act of William III. put an end to this; and we must henceforth look for the spirit of priestcraft in a different shape. The whole course of this volume has shewn that this wily spirit has conformed itself to circumstances. Where unlimited power was within its grasp, it seized it without hesitation, and exercised it without mercy. Egypt, India, all ancient Asia, and all feudal Europe, are witnesses of this. Where it could not act so freely, it submitted to the spirit of the people; and worked more quietly, more unseen, but equally effectually as in Greece and Pagan Rome. England, after William III., afforded no further scope for imprisonment, the martyr's flaming pile, or the bloody axe of the public executioner. It was rapidly careering in a course of knowledge and civilization, which made men acquainted with their rights, and has eventually lifted this nation to the proudest position ever occupied by any people in the whole history of the world. The established clergy, therefore, had nothing to do but to secure the full enjoyment of their revenues, and that parochial influence with which they were invested; and the consequence is that, in the noblest nation of the earth, they have become the richest body of priests and the most apathetic towards the people, from whom their wealth is drawn. The clergy, from these circumstances, have been long gradually diverging into two classes,—one, sunk into the slumberous bed of enormous wealth and gross luxury; the other, into the miserable slough of interminable toil and poverty. If we look at the dignitaries of the church, and at the description of the dignitaries of the papal church in its later days of universal influence, can we avoid being struck with the coincidence of character? " They pass their days amidst the pleasures and cabals of courts; and appear rather the slaves of princes, than the sèrvants of Him whose kingdom is not of this world. They court glory: they aspire after riches; while very few employ their time and labour in edifying the people, or in promoting among them the vital spirit of religion; and, what is more deplorable, those bishops who, sensible of the sanctity of their character, and the duties of their office, distinguish themselves by zeal in the cause of virtue, are frequently exposed to the malicious efforts of envy, often loaded with false accusations, and involved in perplexities of various kinds."

But it is not the bishops alone to whom this applies. These are the features of the establishment, at least, as they appear in the eyes of the people at large;—

A clergy, in part, overpaid, and inactive; in part, overworked, and ill paid.

Loaded, in part, with opulent sinecures and shameful pluralities; the greater part doing the duty of the lazy and the absent—on a paltry pittance.

Lukewarm in their duties; and proudly cold in their intercourse with the poor of their flocks.

A clergy, doggedly adhesive to the establishment as it is, in spite of the progress of the public mind; adhering to its most absurd, and most impolitic institutions, rites, and dogmas.

## CHAPTER XVI.

### THE ENGLISH CHURCH.

Thrice happy days! thrice blest the man who saw
Their dawn! The Church and State, that long had held
Unholy intercourse, were now divorced!
*Pollok's Course of Time, B. 4.*

Forced consecrations out of another man's estate are no better than forced vows, hateful to God, " who loves a cheerful giver;" but much more hateful wrung out of men's purses to maintain a disapproved ministry against their consciences.
*Milton on Hirelings.* \*

So intolerable has the state of the church, described in the conclusion of the last chapter, become, that the public is, at this moment, loud in demanding its reform; and the clergy themselves, sensible that reform is inevitable, with a wise policy, bend in some degree to the popular opinion. Already the ministers of a reformed government have published their plan of reform for the church of Ireland, that monstrous excrescence, where a revenue of 800,000*l.* according to the last clerical returns to Parliament, but according to other calculations, little short of 2,000,000*l.* is appropriated to a population of 500,000 protestants; while 8,000,000 of catholics not only help to support their establishment, but their

\* A spirited publisher, who should at this crisis reprint this most excellent pamphlet, would do a service to the public, and most likely to himself.

own priests. The proposed reform consists principally in reducing the archbishoprics and bishoprics from twenty-two to twelve; in reducing the incomes of the remaining ones; in laying on a tax of fifteen per cent. on the general income of the clergy; in taking off the church cess, or rate, from the people; and in selling off the lands of the extinguished bishoprics as they fall out of lease. The Irish members of parliament have received this announcement with ecstasies of delight. It is part of the Irish character to fly into sudden raptures; but cool reflection will come yet; and then—what will satisfy them? Why, nothing short of the utter abrogation of protestant episcopacy as a state religion. If it were necessary that a religion should be established, as it is called, it ought here to be the catholic. The opinions of the majority of a nation ought surely to command some respect; ought surely to be the guide in such matters. If a *nation* is to patronize and support one religion in preference to another, it ought surely to be the *religion of the nation*. The religion of Ireland is catholic,—the religion of Scotland is presbyterian,—why should Scotland be permitted to have a church of her own, and Ireland be refused one? Why should the majority in the other parts of the empire decide the establishment of their party, and in Ireland an *insignificant sect* be thrust upon the people as the NATIONAL RELIGION; and be bolstered up with tithes, glebes, and wealth enormous? These are plain questions, and suggest a plain answer.

One circumstance connected with Irish church reform is characteristic of its real nature and extent, as proposed by the present ministers, and ought to have opened the eyes of all men. The bishopric of Derry, the most enormously endowed in Ireland, was vacant at the very moment of the organization of this plan of reform. If a number of bishoprics were to be reduced, why should not this have been one? Or if it were not thought desirable to extinguish it, why should not the incumbent of one of those sees which were to be withdrawn, be translated to this, and thus one at least have been instantly removed? The surprise which the appointment of a bishop to this see, under these circumstances created, was at once dissipated; and gave place, in the public mind, to a higher surprise and a feeling of indignation, by the discovery that the bishop thus installed, was Dr. Poynton, *the brother-in-law of Earl Grey!* This was an assurance sufficiently intelligible. Will a man set himself heartily to cut down a tree in whose topmost branches he has placed his brother? Will a man assay to sink a vessel in which he has embarked his own family? Will a general proceed cordially to blow up a fortress in which his near relative is commandant? Then, will Earl Grey set himself heartily to work, to reform efficiently the Irish church!

The abolition of this bishopric would have been a thing of the highest importance. Its revenue, according to the present return, is 13,000*l.*; and it is proposed to reduce it to 8,000*l.* But what is the estimate of Mr. Wakefield of the value of this see?— a most competent authority. He calculates that the whole of its property, over and above the tenth part of the gross produce of the land, cannot be much short of 3,000,000*l.*; and that the bishop's land, at a fair rate of rent, would produce an income of 130,000*l.* a year. This, then, is the birth into which Earl Grey, in the face of a reformed parliament—of his own professions of real reform—of suffering England, and starving Ireland, has comfortably put his brother-in-law, and proposes to satisfy the country by the abatement of 5,000*l.* a year out of this immense property. By the extinction of this bishopric alone, a saving to the country would have been made at once of 3,000,000*l.*!—for the question in this case is, not what the bishop actually derives from the land, but what it is worth to the nation.

But the whole of this extraordinary establishment of state religion is of a piece. For the government of the whole church of England, twenty-six Archbishops and Bishops exist—for 500,000 Irish protestants there are twenty-two! According to former returns, there are 1,238 parochial benefices; according to the present, 1,401, in which are 860 resident clergymen. To provide for these archbishops and bishops, who superintend about as many people as one bishop in England would very well manage, it is calculated that out of 14,603,473 statute acres under cultivation, 13,603,473 are tithed. The glebe of the parochial clergy varies from 300 to 40,000 acres. The glebe in the diocese of Derry alone, amounts to more than 17,000 acres. The glebes, indeed, it is calculated in Derry and Kilmore would, if equally divided, give twenty acres to every parish in Ireland. Mr. Wakefield estimates that the property of six of the bishops, when out of lease, would produce 580,000*l.* a year;—a sum which would give an income of 500*l.* a year for each of the clergy, and a fund for the establishment of a school in every parish in Ireland. But if the property of six bishops amount to 580,000*l.* a year, what becomes of the clerical calculation which makes the whole income of the Irish church but 800,000*l.*?—leaving to the whole body of parochial clergy and sixteen bishops little more than 200,000*l.*?

The following is an extract from the returns to the House of Commons in February, 1824.

| Sees. | Acres. | Sees. | Acres. |
|---|---|---|---|
| Derry | 94,836 | Tuam | 49,281 |
| Armagh | 63,470 | Elphin | 31,017 |
| Kilmore | 51,350 | Clogher | 32,817 |
| Dublin | 28,784 | Cork and Ross | 22,755 |
| Meath | 18,374 | Cashel | 12,800 |
| Ossory | 13,391 | Killaloe | 11,081 |

Total, 439,953 acres; which at 20s. per acre, give a rental of 439,953l.

If we estimate the remaining ten bishoprics at one-third of the amount, there is 146,651,—a rental of diocesan lands of 586,604l.

If we estimate the glebes at 100,000 acres, which is, probably, far too little, when the glebe of Derry alone exceeds 17,000 acres, and the parochial glebes vary from 300 to 40,000 acres, at 20s., here is 100,000l.

The tithe of upwards of 13,000,000 acres, at only 2s., a tithe of the rental, not of the gross produce, would be 1,300,000l.—making a total of income for the Irish church, of 1,986,604l.

As women's fortunes are said to be paid in sixpences, so when the incomes of the clergy are returned to government, they seem to be calculated in farthings, or something less. Tithe and glebe seem suddenly to lose their natural value, surplice fees and fines shrink into insignificance. Yet these fines are pretty things, though they do not always amount to so much as the present Bishop of Durham is stated, on the authority of Mr. Beverly, to have received of Mrs. Beaumont, for the renewal of the lease of her lead mines—72,000l.!

Now admitting, that owing to the low rate of clerical leases, to waste land, to lay impropriation, and to the popular inability or repugnance to pay tithes, the income of the church falls far below this estimate, the question, so far as the country is concerned, is the same. Here is a monstrous amount of property appropriated to a certain purpose, and what good is done? What good, indeed, as it regards Ireland?—A prodigious waste of property (for in addition to all the rest, it appears that, at different times since the Union, about *half a million* has been voted to augment poor livings) only to render the name of protestant hateful to that nation, by the laziness, non-residence, and tithe-exactions of the clergy of a church, which the Edinburgh Review, some years ago, happily compared to an Irish regiment of volunteers, which consisted of sixteen lieutenant-colonels, two drummers, and one private! The same able journal has well remarked, that " whatever may be the supposed effects of a richly endowed church in maintaining a particular creed, it is evidently not the machine for the conversion of a people."

The justice and intelligence of the British people cannot long, therefore, be satisfied with lopping off a few enormities from such a system; they will demand its total extinction. Religion, and the best objects of all human government, demand it! For, if protestantism is to prosper in Ireland, it must not come before the people in the shape of a corporation, chartered in opposition to the predominant feelings of the country, and endowed with a vast portion of the people's wealth; it must not come in the shape of two and twenty archbishops and bishops to superintend some few hundred clergymen, on incomes of 10,000*l*. a year; in the shape of tithe-fed clergymen without parishes, parishes without churches, and churches without people; in the shape of men who profess to be teachers of Christian meekness and love, but are seen only as zealous collectors of tithes; in the shape of tithe-proctors, with troops of soldiery at their heels; in the shape of noon-day exaction and midnight retaliation and revenge; in short, of wealth and violence on the one hand, and destitution and despair on the other;—but if it come really to prosper and to bless, it must come as Christ himself came,—as a free personification of disinterested kindness; zealous love for the souls of men, rather than their purses; active endeavour to soothe the irritation and enlighten the minds of the poor; it must be offered to men's hearts, but not thrust upon their shoulders; it must stand before the public eye as a thing to be chosen, or refused; as a thing which invites observation, and can bear it; as a thing which obviously has no interest but what is blended with the whole happiness of man;—whose nobility is so striking, and its beauty so attractive, that hearts are drawn to its embraces, not crushed beneath its tread. The system of compulsion and lavish endowment has been tried long enough; long enough has state religion, to use Burke's sophistical metaphor, " reared its mitred front in courts and parliaments," its effects are before the public in characters of fire and blood! Instead of peace, we have horrible anarchy—instead of the milk of human kindness, deadly exasperation and relentless murder—in God's name let us see what the system of the apostles will now do!—a free offer,—an open hand,—and a zealous heart!—a system less of the bag and scrip, than of virtues and arguments that address themselves to the wants, the understanding, and the generosity of a generous nation.

To come now to England. The dissenters, now a great and important body of people—a people alive to their civil and religious rights, must be relieved from church-rates. Ministers have acknowledged the justice of this demand, by already proposing to abolish them in Ireland—the principle in both cases is the same. The Irish cess, it appears, produces only about 94,000*l*. What the dissenters pay in the shape of church-rates, Easter offerings, etc., I do not know—the sum must be enormous; but I do know that the Society of Friends, a comparatively small body, suffers the violence and vexation of distraint of their goods, for such things, to the amount of about 14,000*l*. a-year; and these people maintain their own religion, and their own poor.

That English dissenters should be compelled to contribute to the support of an established church, is a moral and political absurdity. By the Act of Toleration of King William, the rights of conscience are recognised: but by this compulsion all the rights of conscience are violated. In the words of the able writer from whom I have taken the motto at the head of the last chapter—" A government cannot patronize one particular religion without punishing others. A state has no wealth but the people's wealth. If it pay some, it impoverishes others." To tell us that we may all enjoy our own opinions, and celebrate our own worship in perfect freedom; and yet to compel us to support another mode of religion, and another set of opinions, in our eyes erroneous and unchristian, is at once an oppression and a bitter mockery. It is not so much the sum of actual money that we pay which constitutes the grievance,—that might be borne; but the *gravamen* lies here,—that by supporting an establishment, we support what, in the abstract, both religiously and politically, we believe ought not to exist. We believe it is the duty of a government, and especially of a Christian government, which acknowledges the sacred rites of conscience, to protect every modification of the Christian religion; but not to support one in preference to, and at the expense of the rest. This is not to patronize religion, but a party. That an establishment, unjust and impolitic in itself, never can, and never has, promoted true religion, is shewn abundantly by this volume; it is testified equally by the apathy of the established church, and the activity of the dissenters. Is it not a source of continual complaints and bitterness amongst clerical writers, that the dissenters are for ever intruding themselves into their parishes; and, with what they are pleased to term their fiery fanaticism, continually turn the heads of their parishioners, and seduce them to the conventicle? Now whether this zeal be healthful or not, whether it be pure or alloyed, refined or coarse, rational or fanatic, it matters not to our present question,—it is zeal,—and the vital question is, whence does it arise? how is it maintained? Not, certainly, from a state establishment!—not by charters and endowments. It springs from the soul of the people, and asks no breath of life but their approbation. Here, then, is an acknowledged principle of religious propagation, more efficacious than all the boasted influence of canonicals and mitres; of cathedral piles and sounding orchestras; of all the political machinery of tithes, and glebes, and church-rates, and forced payments, called by the sarcastic name of *gifts* and *offerings*, as if the imposition were not enough, but we must suffer the mockery of being placed in the light of free donors and bowing offerers of gifts at a shrine that we inwardly abhor. Here is a confessed power to keep alive the popular zeal for religion;—if that zeal wants better guidance, it becomes every good man to lend his hand to its due direction,—but the principle itself is indisputably manifested, and sets the seal for ever to the nonnecessity, and therefore to the political oppression, of a state religion. Nothing could justify a state religious establishment but the total and proven impossibility of keeping alive Christianity without it; but here it is seen that religious zeal rather takes any other form than that stamped upon it by legal enactments. Like the acanthus, pressed under the tile, it rises up with unquenchable vitality all around, and not only buries the dead tile of policy under its vigorous vegetation, but gives origin to new orders of Christian architecture. While the zeal of the established clerical order languishes under the weight of good things which its friends have cast upon it; while bishoprics, and deaneries, and prebends cannot stimulate it to the vital point of proselytism; while tithes, and glebes, and fines, and parochial fees cannot enliven it, the free breath of popular societies can blow it into a flame that spreads far and wide, and even scorches the canonical skirts of the state clergy. Who, after this, shall dare to repeat the stale sophism that Christianity needs the arm of human legislation to support her,—that she must be perched on cathedral pinnacles to be fairly seen; that she must be wrapped in alb or surplice, and crowned with shovel-hat or mitre to be reverenced, and seated on the episcopal throne to be adored? Who shall dare to turn his eye on the United States of America, where there is no state religion, yet where Christianity flourishes not less than amongst us, and then attempt to palm upon us the canting and selfish falsehood, that religion is bound up in the bundle of life with an Act of Parliament?

By compelling us to support an established religion, we are compelled to support and propagate all its errors, its injustice, and its absurdities, however great, and numerous, and pernicious they may be.

Every sect in England at present, in contributing to the establishment, contributes to that which it abhors. The denouncer of episcopacy is made to maintain a whole hierarchy of bishops; the Catholic, what he declares to be pestilent heresies of the most damnable sort; the Calvinist maintains Arminianism; the Arminian, Calvinism; for, in the church are combined " a Calvinistic creed, and an Arminian clergy." The Friend, who believes all hierarchies antichristian, who holds that all ministers should speak from the immediate influence of the Holy Spirit, and abominates hireling ministers, written sermons, a cut-and-dried liturgy, and half the doctrines of the church to boot, is forced, by distraint of his goods, to feed and uphold all these enormities: every man is made to maintain the doctrine of priestly absolution, for the church maintains it; and every man is made most heartily to damn himself, for the Athanasian creed, which is one of the creeds of the church, does declare every man to be damned who doubts it.

Such a preposterous abuse of power never can be much longer tolerated in this country. The church-rates must be abolished, and with them tithes. The removal of this last burden is now so universally deemed necessary, that I shall not say many words upon it. Tithes are politically condemned, and will disappear for ever. A more ingenious method could not have been devised for the support of a minister of religion, had it been the object of the deviser to place an eternal object of hatred, heart-burning, and dispute between him and his flock; to place him in the position of a harpy over the table of every one of his hearers; and to thus render abortive all his religious endeavours. A more iniquitous one never was conceived,—for it taxes not simply a man's land, but his capital, his genius, his skill, and industry; so that the priest reaps not merely a tithe of the fruits of the earth, but of the fruits of every man's heart and mind who ventures to till the earth. But they are condemned: and let them go, with this one observation of Milton's—" As well under the Gospel as under the law—say our English divines, *and they only of all Protestants* —is Tithes. That the law of tithes is in force under the Gospel, all other Protestant divines, though equally concerned, yet constantly deny. When any one of our's has attempted, in Latin, to maintain this argument,—though a man would think they might suffer him, without opposition, in a point equally tending to the advantage of all ministers—yet they cease not to oppose him, as in a doctrine not fit to pass unopposed under the gospel; which shews the modesty, the contentedness of those foreign pastors with the maintainance given them; their sincerity also in truth, though less gainful, and the avarice of ours, who, through the love of their old papistical tithes, consider not the weak arguments, or rather conjectures and surmises which they bring to defend them." What a striking fact is this! and what a singular feature it presents of the English church—the only one that has advocated and suffered itself to be fed by this iniquitous system of tithes! If we add to this the following paragraph, which appeared in the Essex Independent, and the principle of which, whatever the calculations may be, is notoriously correct, what an image of clerical rapacity and want of conscience we have before us! " The church ought to relinquish the property of the poor. The original tripartite division of tithes is acknowledged—one-third portion of the revenue of the church being the undoubted property of the poor. The entire possessions of the church, in tithe and landed property, amount in value to the sum of 170,450,000*l.*; and the extensive leaseholds lately reverted to the bishopric of London, raise the amount to 180,000,000*l.* One-third of this, 60,000,000*l.*, is therefore the sum which the state is most equitably entitled to demand from the church." After reading this, who can prevent himself recalling the words of Christ—" The poor ye have always with you, but *me ye have not always!*"

In the next place, the church must be divorced from the state. This unnatural union, the device of artful politicians, is an injustice to the subject, and an indignity to the church itself. The natural effect upon a church in becoming a state religion is, that its freedom is instantly extinguished; every principle of progression and improvement is annihilated; and the generous spirit which would lead it to expand, and spread itself abroad on the kindred spirits of men, is frozen by the cold breath of worldly policy. Like metal molten in the furnace, it flows into the state as into a mould, receives its shape and stamp, and sets for ever. It may be dashed to pieces by the application of external force; but, last as long as it may, it will never be moved, remodelled, or purified from within. It becomes stationary for ever. However all around may be quickened with the moving spirit of knowledge, and excited to activity and fruitfulness, it stands silent and barren,—like a tree covered with the knots and burs of antiquated absurdities; its head, a chaos of rotten boughs amid the green vigour of the forest; and while it is insensibly falling to decay, it bears itself with a sturdy and sullen pride, and wears a ludicrous air of superiority in the very moment of its fall. That such is the situation of the establishment, who can deny?—Who that calls to mind its doctrine of absolution of sins; its Athanasian creed,—a thing so monstrous as to horrify and make ashamed the best minds of its own sons, and which compelled Tillotson long ago, to wish they were well rid of it; and, moreover, its Thirty-nine Articles, that precious medley of follies and contradictions,—a medley, however, which every one, owing to the inflexible nature of the church, is obliged to swallow before he can be ordained a minister; and which Paley, after acknowledging that it was a Gordian-knot, endeavoured to cut asunder, by declaring these articles *articles of peace;* as if it would enable men to escape the guilt of falsehood, by treating bitter and contradictory professions of faith as physic, and swallowing them as a necessity? These articles lie at the door of the church as a threshold of lying; and if perjury does not depend on a form of words, but on the inward denial of a solemn truth,—of perjury to every one of its ministers who is not wild enough to believe impossibilities; and in one university stand in the way of every student. The great Jeremy Bentham, one of the noblest, as well as most sagacious minds which ever blessed earth by its presence, has left on record what it cost him to subscribe them; and numberless are the conscientious spirits which have turned away from them in disgust. Yet there they stand at the church-door, in all their glorious contrariety, and would for ever stand while the church was a member of the state.

When a church stands on its own simple basis, it may renovate its constitution; it may explode worn-out creeds; abandon dogmas or rites that have become hideous in the increased light of universal knowledge, and preserve itself in keeping with the spirit of the age, and in consequent capacity for usefulness; but, make it a portion of the state, and it immediately becomes a species of high treason to attempt the least change in it. Make its ministers illustrious with dignities, and fat with good livings, and they will for ever cry "great is Diana of the Ephesians!" The church will be the best of churches,—immaculate and divine; and they will growl on any one who even dares to look curiously at it, as a jealous dog growls over his bone. Make it the road to political power and honour, and you make its highest ministers the most obsequious slaves of state; the most relentless enemies of freedom and mercy.* This has been too con-

* The bulk of the incidents in the history of priestcraft, are bloody and revolting; but there are a few that are the very fathers of merriment. When Tetzel was selling indulgences in Germany for all sins past, present, and to come, and had well filled his saddle-bags with the money of pious fools of that generation, and was about to depart, a nobleman called on him to procure one for a future crime. Tetzel inquired what it was. The nobleman replied, he could not tell—he had not yet quite decided; but the holy father could charge what he pleased, and leave that to him. Tetzel charged accordingly; and the next day as he was riding through a wood in order to leave the country, the nobleman met him, and seized on his saddle-bags. "This," said he, "is the sin I meant to commit!" Tetzel enraged at being thus outwitted, hastened back to the emperor full of wrath and complaints; but when the nobleman appeared, it was with the indulgence in his hand which sanctioned the deed.

Waller, in his life, gives a curious instance of prelatical obsequience, which most miraculously was well met, by a brilliant instance of prelatical wit and independence. At a dinner with James I., were Neal, bishop of London, and Andrews, bishop of Winchester—"Have not I a right," said James," to take money from the people, without all this ceremony of going to parliament? "Undoubtedly your majesty has a right," replied Neal—"you are the breath of our nostrils!" "But what says my lord of Winchester?" added James. "I say," returned the bishop, "that your majesty has a right to take brother Neal's; for he has given it you."

Bloody Mary sent a commissioner over to Ireland, with a royal commission to the lord lieutenant to burn, destroy, and confiscate the property of the protestants, and bring them to what is called, justice. The man lodging at a widow Edmonds', in Chester, was waited on by the mayor; to whom he boasted that he had that with him that would bring the Irish heretics to their senses, and opening a box, he shewed him the commission. The

spicuous in the house of peers. Lord Eldon said some years ago, in the house of lords, that he could not bring himself to believe the slave trade was irreconcileable with the Christian religion, as the bench of bishops had uniformly sanctioned by their votes, the various acts authorizing that trade. A biting sarcasm, which ever way intended!*

Let us now hear our noble Milton, on the effect of a state religion. "That the magistrate should take into his power the stipendiary maintainance of church ministers, as compelled by law, can stand neither with the people's thought, nor with Christian liberty, but would suspend the church wholly upon the state, and turn the ministers into state pensioners. For the magistrate to make the church his mere ward, as always in minority;—the church, to whom he ought, as a magistrate, 'to bow down his face towards the earth, and lick up the dust of her feet,'—her to subject to his political drifts, or conceived opinions, is neither just, nor pious; no honour done to the

widow, who had a brother in Ireland, a protestant, happened to hear this, and was alarmed. As the commissioner shewed the mayor down stairs, she adroitly withdrew the commission, and supplied its place with a sheet of paper, in which was wrapped a pack of cards, with the knave of clubs uppermost. The deception was undiscovered. On the commissioner's arrival at Dublin, he had an audience of the lord lieutenant, in the presence of a splendid assembly. He made a fine speech, and boasted much of his powers, when on going to produce his commission, behold, to the astonishment of himself and his hearers, nothing but the pack of cards, and the knave of clubs uppermost. "It *was* the queen's commission," said the crest-fallen delegate, "but how it is changed I know not." "Well," said the lord lieutenant, "you must return to England for fresh powers, and in the meantime we will shuffle the cards!" He returned; but he was too late—the queen was dead; and on the subject being related to Elizabeth, she was highly diverted by it, and settled on Mrs. Edmonds 40*l.* a year.

* *Morning Chronicle,* Oct. 31*st*, 1813.

church, but a plain dishonour: and upon her whose head is in heaven,—yea upon him who is the only head in effect; and what is most monstrous, a human on a heavenly, a carnal on a spiritual, a political head on an ecclesiastical body; which at length, by such hetrogeneal, such incestuous conjunction, transforms her ofttimes into a beast of many heads, and many horns."

Such a beast has the church become by this state commerce, even by the confession of her friends; and that commerce must be annihilated. Justice, impartial justice, to this great and Christian nation demands it; the growth of Christianity demands it; the prosperity of the church itself demands it as well. This is a measure called for on behalf of the nation; and there are numbers who will contend that, the church ceasing to be a state church, should restore its property to the nation whence it was drawn. That in strict justice all national property should revert to the nation when the object for which it was bestowed ceases, there can be no question; in strict justice to the other Christian communities of this country, this ought clearly to be the case,—since, admitting the rights of conscience, the nation ought not to enrich one body of Christians at the expense of the rest; and that parliament has a right to recall the loan of church property is clear as daylight. The present priesthood form a standing proof and precedent of it, since it was taken from the Catholics and given to them. For my part I am perfectly easy to leave these matters in the hands of parliament; so that its wealth undergo a further process of distribution; its enormous salaries be broken down; its pluralities exploded; its sinecures abolished; and its labouring multitude more efficiently remunerated.

## CHAPTER XVII.

### THE ENGLISH CHURCH.

---

Oh ! said the hind, how many sons have you
Who call you mother, whom you never knew?
But most of them who that relation plead
Are such ungracious youths as wish you dead ;
They gape at rich revenues which you hold,
And fain would nibble at your grandame gold.
*Hind and Panther.*

He is the true atheist, the practical enemy to religion, who can offer to defend the present condition of the Church of England.
*Westminster Review*, No. xxix.

---

HAVING in the last chapter touched on the subject of the church revenue, we must not leave it without adverting to one particular. Whenever the excess of clerical income is introduced, we are immediately attempted to be disarmed by a statement that were the whole revenue of the church equally divided, it would give but about 112*l.* per annum to each clergyman. The British or Clerical Magazine for March, 1832, admits, from the Parliamentary Returns, that it would be 200*l.* per annum.* Now did we admit this to be correct, what a shame is it that in a church so economically provided, so many individuals should be allowed to wallow in the wealth and idleness they manage to combine. Can the church answer it to

---

* The present Parliamentary Returns make it about 287*l.*

her conscience, if she have one, that in such a slenderly beneficed system, there should be many a parish priest who holds from 1 to 5,000*l.* a year, and that the scale of payment to its dignitaries should stand thus, according to their own shewing:—

| | |
|---|---|
| Archbishop of Canterbury | £27,000 a year. |
| ——————— York | 10,000 — |
| Bishop of Durham | 17,000 — |
| ——————London | 14,000 — |
| ——————Winchester | 14,000 — |
| ——————Ely | 12,000 — |
| Nine others on an average | 5,000 — |
| The rest on an average | 3,000 — |

I am afraid we never can prove the church to be poor, or to have been at any time indifferent to the doctrine, that "godliness is great gain." There is nothing in which the spirit of priestcraft has shewn itself so grossly in the English clergy, as in their appropriation of what is called Queen Anne's Bounty. The most shameful selfishness and disregard of every thing like common honesty, like feeling for their poorer brethren, or respect for the motives of the deluded queen, mark the whole affair. The Edinburgh Review, in an able article in No. LXXV., made a very salutary exposition of this wretched business. Let the reader take this condensed view of it:—

"It is well known that, by the statute of Henry VIII. chap. 3, the first-fruits and tenths of spiritual preferments (which had formerly been paid to the Pope, or some other spiritual persons) were given to the king. The first-fruits were the revenues and profits for one year, of every such preferment, and were to be satisfied, or compounded for, on good security, by each incumbent, before any actual or real possession, or meddling with the profits of a benefice.

The tenths were a yearly rent of a tenth part of all the revenues and emoluments of all preferments, to be paid by each incumbent at Christmas. These revenues were, as the statute phrases it, united and knit to the imperial crown for ever! By the same statute a provision was made for a commission to be issued by the king's highness, his heirs and successors, *from time to time*, to search for the *just* and *true* value of the said first-fruits and profits; and similar means were provided for ascertaining the value of tenths. In consequence of this statute, which was suspended during the papistical reign of Mary, but recovered by the 1st of Elizabeth, a valuation was made, which is supposed to have been at the time an accurate one, of the yearly profits of the ecclesiastical preferments: and, according to this valuation, the first-fruits and tenths were, as the 1st of Elizabeth has it, ' well and justly answered and paid, without grief and contradiction of the prelates and clergy of the realm, to the great aid, relief, and supportation of the inestimable charges of the crown,' which inestimable charges may then possibly have amounted to a two-hundredth part of the present yearly sum.

"Under this valuation, which in course of time became quite unequal to the real emoluments of the preferments, these charges continued to be paid till the second year of Queen Anne, 1703; when an act was passed reciting the queen's most religious and tender concern for the church of England, stating that a sufficient settled provision for the clergy in many parts of the realm had never yet been made; and giving to a corporation, which was to be erected for the augmentation of small livings, the whole of the first-fruits and tenths. *Her Majesty, however, in her religious and tender concern, was completely overreached by the clergy.* The professed object of the queen was to increase the provision of the *poor* clergy; the real and only immediate effect of it was to release the rich clergy from a charge to which, by law, they were liable. We have before maintained that a provision was made in the statute of Henry VIII, for revising, from time to time, the valuations under which the first-fruits and tenths were paid. It is not improbable that the clergy were apprehensive, as the nation was then engaged in an expensive war, that such a revision might be made; and in persuading the queen to renounce her hereditary revenue for the sake of her poor clergy, they contrived most effectually to secure themselves by an ingenious clause in the statute in question.

"If the real purpose of this act of Anne had been to augment the small livings, nothing could have been more reasonable than to do it by enforcing the legal claims for the first-fruits and tenths on the holders of the larger benefices. The scandalous poverty of some livings—for there were then 1071 which did not exceed 10$l.$ a year—would then have speedily disappeared: but, as the old and inefficient rate of payment was fixed and made perpetual, the most religious queen went to her grave without seeing any effect from her bounty; as, in consequence of the incumbrances on the fund, and the impossibility of increasing its produce, it was not till 1714 that the governors of the bounty were enabled to make their first grants.

"The cunning of the rich clergy in thus shifting from themselves the burden of contributing to the relief of their poorer brethren, is only to be matched in degree by the folly shewn in the application of the diminished revenue which this trick of theirs still left for the improvement of small livings. At the time when Queen Anne's Bounty Fund was established there was, according to the returns, which were not quite accurate, 5597 livings in England and Wales with incomes not exceeding 50*l*. They were thus classed:—

| | | | |
|---|---|---|---|
| Not exceeding | 10*l*. | . . . . . | 1071 |
| ,, ,, | 20*l*. | . . . . . | 1467 |
| ,, ,, | 30*l*. | . . . . . | 1126 |
| ,, ,, | 40*l*. | . . . . . | 1049 |
| ,, ,, | 50*l*. | . . . . . | 886 |

"The sum which the Governors of Queen Anne's Bounty had to apply to the augmentation of these livings, averaged about 13,000*l*. a year. Any rational being would suppose that, under such circumstances, the governors and the legislature, by whom the disposal of the money was directed and superintended, would have made some inquiry into the circumstances of the different livings. Some of these livings were of very small extent, and scarcely any population, and might therefore have been advantageously united with one another, or with other parishes. The specific evil which was to be remedied was set forth in the preamble to the statute of Anne in these words:—' That diverse mean and stipendiary preachers are, in many places, entertained to serve cures, and officiate there; who, depending for their necessary maintenance upon the good-will and liking of their hearers, have been, and are, thereby under temptation of too much complying, and suiting their doctrines and teaching to the humours, rather than the good of their hearers, which has been a great occasion of faction and schism.' Precious philosophy! At least, therefore, one would have thought that some distinction would have been made between places where there were many hearers, and where there were few or none. Some even, might have been so extravagant as to expect, that when a sum was bestowed on any particular living, some security would have been taken for the residence of the incumbent. All these notions were, however, very far from the minds of the persons who had the distribution of Queen Anne's Bounty. The governors of this fund proceeded upon the idea which is commonly entertained in England respecting the church establishment; especially by its own functionaries—that, provided a sufficient sum of money be laid out on the clergy, every other good will follow: that, how absurd soever the distribution may seem, it is not for human hands to destroy the latent harmony of casual proportions. Above all things did they eschew the idea, which the church abhors, that where the public confers an obligation, it has a right to exact the performance of a duty. Among the livings on which they had to scatter the money, several were large and populous parishes, where the tithes had been impropriated; and these, if the holders of the tithes were not, as is often the case, ecclesiastical sinecurists—or dignitaries as they are called—whose incomes were at the disposal of Parliament, would have been proper objects for augmentation,—always supposing, what is false in point of fact, that an increase in the emoluments of a living has any tendency to secure the performance of clerical duties. Others were rectories, of which some were endowed with the tithe of all the produce of their district, but which were so insignificant as neither to need a separate clergyman, nor to afford a separate maintenance for him. In the case of such livings, instead of attempting to swell the incomes of needless offices, the natural course would have been, to have consolidated their neighbouring benefices, and in no case have made any augmentation, except where the revenue arising from a district of extent and population sufficient to need the cares of a clergyman, should have been found insufficient to maintain him. But this would have violated the fundamental principles of the excellent Church; it would have insinuated a connexion between money expended and duty performed; it would have seemed like an adaptation of means to an end; it would have made some inquiry and consideration necessary.

"The governors of the Bounty proceeded bountifully; they distributed a part of their money in sums of 200*l.* on any poor livings to which any private person would give an equal sum. The rest, and far greater part of their money, shewing them no respecter of persons nor of circumstances, these representatives of the ecclesiastical wisdom of the nation, distributed *by lot*, letting each poor living take an equal chance for a prize, without any regard to the degree of urgency of its claim. After this, the story of Bridoye deciding suits at law by dice, after making up a fair pile of papers on each side, seems no longer an extravaganza. Up to January 1, 1815, the governors had made, in this way, 7323 augmentations of 200*l.*; but with benefices as with men, fortune is not proportioned to desert or necessity. Some of the least populous parishes had a wonderful run of luck. We are not sure that, taking a few of those which meet our eye in running over the returns, we have selected the most remarkable. In the diocese of Chichester, the rectory of Hardham, which in 1811 contained eighty-nine persons, has received six augmentations by lot, or 1200*l.* The vicarage of Sollington, with forty-eight people, has had six augmentations, 1200*l.* In the diocese of Salisbury, Brewilham drew a prize; it contained fourteen people. Rotwood drew another; it had twelve people. Calloes had 1000*l.* including a benefaction of 200*l.*; its population was in

1811, *nineteen*. In the diocese of Winchester, Saint Swithin, with twenty-four people, has received 800*l.* including a benefaction of 200*l.*; and 200*l.* has been expended on Ewhurst, which has seven people. In the diocese of York, Ruthewick, with sixty-two people, has had five prizes, 1000*l.*; while Armby, with 2941 people, and Allendale, with 3884, have gained only one each. In the diocese of Rochester, two livings, with twenty-eight and twenty-nine people, received separate augmentations. In the diocese of Oxford, Elford, or Yelford, with sixteen inhabitants, drew a prize. In Lincoln, Stowe, with the same number, and Haugh, received 800*l.* The number of all its inhabitants is eight. When it is considered too, that Haugh pays vicarial tithes, which amounted in the reign of Henry VIII, to 6*l.* 13*s.* 4*d.* of yearly value, it must be admitted that this important district has been guarded against the danger of schism, with a liberality worthy of a Protestant government. If the rest of the people of England were fortified in sound doctrine, at the same rate of expense, the proper establishment of religious teachers in England and Wales would cost about 1200 millions sterling, and 1,500,000 parochial clergy, who, as Dr. Cove allows each of them a family of nine, would form a considerable portion of the population. In the diocese of Landaff we find two places following each other in the returns, which illustrate the equity of *le sort des dez*. Usk, with 1339 people, has had an augmentation, though its value remains low. Wilcock, a rectory with twenty-eight people, has had *three*. In Hereford, Hopton-Cangeford has had 1000*l.* for thirty-five people. Monmouth, 200*l.* for 3503.

"Even in cities, where the scattered condition of the population could afford no pretext against the union of parishes, the same plan of augmentations has been pursued. In Winchester, separate augmentations have been given to seven parishes, the population of all which would, united, have amounted to 2376, and would consequently have formed a very manageable, and rather small town parish. In short, the whole of the returns printed by the house of commons in 1815, No. 115, teem with instances of the most foolish extravagance,—just such a result as the original conception of this clerical *little-go* would have led any rational being to anticipate. The conviction is irresistibly forced upon us, that nothing could have been further from the minds of those who superintended this plan, than to secure a competent provision for all the members of the church, and to remove the poverty of some of its members,—which is, by a strange manner of reasoning, made a defence for the needless profusion with which the public wealth is lavished upon others. Indeed, we are led to suspect, that 'the church, in her corporate capacity,' looks upon the poverty of some of her members as sturdy beggars look upon their sores; she is not seriously displeased with the naked and excoriated condition of her lower extremities, so long as it excites an ill-judged compassion for the whole body, and secures her impunity in idleness and rapacity.

"We are sometimes told that the poverty of a large body of the parochial clergy is such that it is out of the power of the higher clergy, even by the surrender of their whole revenues, to remedy it. The statement we have given shows most clearly that this poverty is to be attributed, in the first place, to the fraudulent subtraction of the higher clergy from the burden of contributing to the relief of their poorer brethren; and, in the second place, to the absurdity of the ecclesiastical division of the kingdom, which, on the slightest effort of the clergy, would have been remedied by the legislature. If the first-fruits and tenths had been paid subsequently to the gift of Anne, according to the rate which the law provided for, and as they had been paid, 'without grief or contradiction,' *i. e.* according to the real value of the benefices, instead of a million and half, at least 30 millions would have been raised from these taxes;—a sum not only quite sufficient to have removed the poverty of all the poor livings in the kingdom, but to have established schools in every parish of England, and to have left a large surplus for other useful purposes.

"In the course of these augmentations no security has been taken against non-residence, or plurality. The governors go on, therefore, increasing the incomes of two small livings, in order to make each of them capable of supporting a resident clergyman; while after, as well as before the augmentation, one incumbent may hold them together—reside on neither—and allow only a small part of the accumulated income to a curate, who performs the duty of both!"

This absurd system, which is at once an insult to the memory of Queen Anne, and to the whole British nation, has been continued to the present moment. By the returns made to the present parliament, the same shameful additions to rich livings of that which was intended to have gone to poor ones, are made apparent; the same shamelessly miserable payment of the curates, who do the actual work for which the money is received by the selfish and the idle, has been continued. It is not within the compass of this volume to go at great length into these details;—a sample will suffice. These cases were lately adduced by Lord King in the house of peers.

"Dean and Canon of Windsor, impropriator of the

following parishes, received from parliamentary grant and Queen Anne's Bounty:—Plymsted, 1811, 600*l*.; 1812, 400*l*.; 1815, 300*l*. Plympton, ——, 600*l*. St. German's, 1811, 800*l*.; 1814, 400*l*. Wembury, 1807, 200*l*.; 1816, 1400*l*. Northam, 1764, 200*l*.; 1812, 400*l*. South Moulton, 1813, 600*l*.

" Dean and Canon of Winchester, impropriators of tithes of two large parishes in Wales:—Holt, 1725, 200*l*.; 1733, 200*l*. Iscoyd, 1749, 200*l*.; 1757, 200*l*.; 1798, 200*l*.; 1818, 200*l*.

"Dean of Exeter, impropriator of tithe;—Landkey, 1775, 200*l*.; 1810, 200*l*.; 1815, 1400*l*. Swimbed, 1750, 200*l*.; 1811, 400*l*.

" Dean and Chapter of Carlisle, impropriators of valuable tithe:—Hesket, 1813, 600*l*.; 1815, 2000*l*. to purchase land; 1816, 300*l*.; 1817, 300*l*.

" Dean of Bangor, impropriator of tithe (curate paid 32*l*. 4*s*.):—Gyffin, 1767, 200*l*.; 1810, 200*l*.; 1816, 1400*l*.

" Bishop of Bangor, impropriator of valuable tithe (curate paid 30*l*. 12*s*.):—Llandegar, 1812, 200*l*.; 1815, 1600*l*.; ——, 300*l*.; ——, 300*l*.

" Bishop of Lichfield, impropriator of large tithes in Merionethshire (curate paid only 27*l*.):—Tallylyr, 1808, 200*l*.; 1816, 1400*l*. Penal, 1810, 200*l*."

Thus these returns proved, that for thirteen parishes these Rev. Gentlemen had drawn 14,500*l*. which ought to have been paid from their own pockets.

The Edinburgh Review, in the same able article above quoted, says—" Those who complain of the poverty of the clergy pretend to suppose that no security for residence is necessary; and, that as soon as the small livings are raised high enough, non-residence will disappear as a matter of course. For instance, Dr. Cove says, ' all the Church of England's sons are, with few exceptions, ever intent on their appropriate duties; and would be still more diligent were each of them possessed of *a more enlarged and comfortable independence*, and furnished with more suitable abodes.' This, unfortunately for the Doctor, is more capable of being brought to the test than the 'unrecorded revelation' to Adam in favour of tithes. We have returns of small livings, and we have returns of non-residence. In the diocese of Rochester there are only six livings under 150*l.* a year, and of those six not one is returned under 110*l.* Of the 107 benefices returned in that diocese, there were, in 1809, but 50 with resident incumbents—less than half the livings. In the diocese of Chester, where the livings under 150*l.* a year are numerous, 377 out of 592 being of that description, a considerably larger proportion of the benefices have residents than in Rochester—there are 327 residents. In other dioceses the number of poor livings bears no regular proportion to the number of non-residents. The fact is, that under the discipline of the church of England, where there are so many grounds of exemption or of license for non-residence, the only persons who may be expected to reside, are those whose narrow incomes make their residence in their own parsonages a matter of necessity or convenience.

I shall speedily have occasion to shew that in all countries where the incomes of the clergy are moderate, there the clergy themselves are at once the most attentive to their duties, and most respected and beloved by the people. For the present, the following statement from the *Carlisle Journal* will afford a striking confirmation of the justice of these remarks; and so impressive an example of the shameless pluralities of the higher clergy, and the miserable manner of their paying the poor labouring curates, as may render further selections superfluous.

## PLURALITIES, AND CURATES' STIPENDS.

Small as is the see of Carlisle, it affords some admirable specimens of the working of the church system, and of these we will now give a sample. And first of the pluralists, we have—

Hugh Percy, bishop of Carlisle, a prebend of St. Paul's, and a chancellor of Sarum.

R. Hodgson, dean of Carlisle, vicar of Burgh-on-Sands, rector of St. George's, Hanover-square, and vicar of Hillington.

E. Goodenough, prebend of Carlisle, Westminster, and York; vicar of Wath All Saints on Dearn, chaplain of Adwick, and chaplain of Brampton-Bierlow.

S. J. Goodenough, prebend of Carlisle, rector of Broughton Poges, vicar of Hampton, and deputy lord-lieutenant of Cumberland.

Wm. Goodenough, archdeacon of Carlisle, rector of Marcham-le-Fen, and rector of Great Salkeld.

W. Vansittart, D.D., prebend of Carlisle, master of Wigston's Hospital, Leicester, vicar of Waltham Abbas, and vicar of Shottesbrooke.

W. Fletcher, chancellor of the diocese of Carlisle, prebend of York, vicar of Bromfield, vicar of Dalston, and vicar of Lazenby.

It is not our intention, at present, to inquire into the incomes of these dignitaries; but as they are pretty considerable, it may be worth while just to contrast the salaries they award to those who really work, with the moneys they receive from the livings. The tithes received by the Dean and Chapter for

Hesket, amount to 1000*l*. or 1500*l*. a-year; they pay to the curate who does the duty 18*l*. 5*s*. a-year! —that is to say, 1*s*. a-day—being after the rate of the bricklayer's labourer's wages! In Wetheral and Warwick, the Dean and Chapter draw about 1000*l*. a-year from tithes, and 1000*l*. a-year from the church lands; and they pay the working minister (probably one of the most exemplary and beloved men in England in his station) the sum of 50*l*. a-year—the wages of a journeyman cabinet-maker! The tithes of the parishes of St. Cuthbert and St. Mary, amount at the least to 1500*l*. a-year. The two curates (who do the duty) receive each the sum of 2*l*. 13*s*. 4*d*. a-year!!! And then, to the minor canons, who do the cathedral duty (such as it is), they pay the sum of 6*s*. 8*d*. a-year each! The Dean and Chapter hold several other impropriate rectories, pay the curates a mere nominal sum for performing the duties, and pocket the tithes themselves—for doing nothing!"

*Carlisle Journal.*

The Rev. W. Pullen, rector of Little Gidding, Huntingdonshire, asserts in a pamphlet of his, that a late bishop held twelve places of preferment at the same time, and the greater number, parochial benefices!

With such things as these before our eyes,—and which way can we turn and not see them?—who can believe that the British public can much longer suffer the church to remain unregenerated? Look where we will, we behold the most gross instances of simony, pluralities, non-residence, and penurious remuneration of the working clergy. But of these matters in the next chapter:—two other ramifications of the establishment which require reform—Ecclesiastical Courts and the Universities, I must passingly notice, and then close this.

These two organs and auxiliaries must necessarily

come within the sweep of any reform which visits effectually the church;—they are vital parts of that great priestly system which has so long rested in ease and comfort on the shoulders of this much-enduring country. As their reform is a necessary consequence of that of the church, I shall say less of them; but they involve enormities of such a nature, as nothing but the apathy induced by long custom could have brought Englishmen to tolerate.

The universities, founded and endowed by kings and patriotic men, for the general benefit and encouragement of learning in the nation, are monopolized by the priests of the establishment. All offices in them are in their hands; no layman, much less a dissenter, can hold a post in them. The Thirty-nine Articles are set up like so many Giants Despair, to drive away with their clubs of intolerance all who will not kiss their feet. These chartered priests grasp the emoluments and the immunities of these ancient seats of learning, and triumphantly tell us of the great men which the establishment has produced. This is a little too much for the patience of any but an Englishman. Had the gates of these great schools been thrown open to the whole nation for whose benefit they were established, and to the popular spirit of improvement which has been busy in the world, they might have told us of thousands more as great, as good, and far wiser, inasmuch as they would have been educated in an atmosphere of a more liberal and genial character. As it is, they have lagged, like the establishment to which they are linked, behind the spirit of the age, to a degree which has disgusted the most illustrious even of their own sons. It never was my lot to make a practical acquaintance with the advantages or abuses of either of them; but, if the best authorities are to be trusted, the devil never found himself more in his element, since he descended from his position in the Tree of Knowledge, in the Garden of Eden, to mount those of Oxford and Cambridge.

To the two great popular journals of Edinburgh and Westminster, the country is indebted for several most able expositions of the abuses of both spiritual courts and universities; and the latter in No. XXIX. speaks thus—" The rents and fines arising from broad lands, amongst the most fair and fertile in the realm; from lordly manors and goodly farms; the profits of the advowsons of numerous and valuable benefices; tithes, and tolls, and every advantage that earth can yield; palaces, for such indeed are most of our colleges, for the habitation of the learned; noble churches, halls, libraries, and galleries, for their use and delight, with gardens, groves, and pleasure-grounds; plate, and pictures, and marbles; a countless store of hidden books and MSS., as well as a more vulgar wealth, accumulated in vast sums of money, yielding interest in the funds, or upon mortgage. How strange would the large opulence appear, were the inventory correctly taken, to the inhabitants of foreign universities, which nevertheless are accounted wealthy; and not less strange to its rightful owners, the people of England, to a brave, generous and loyal people, who have been ready in all ages to contribute largely from their store to works of learning and piety, but who have been ill-requited by their rulers.

" Astonishing is the wealth of our universities, greatly exceeding the sum of all the possessions of all the other learned bodies in the world; yet would it be an unfair and injurious statement to affirm, that not a single shilling of their enormous income is truly applied to the purposes for which it was designed? The accusation is still more grave; not only do these corporations neglect to furnish any direct encouragement to the studious, but they offer much positive discouragement. The sedulous youth who entered the walls of his college thirsting for honourable distinction, can best tell how his ardent curiosity was chilled by the oscitancy, the inertness, the narrow illiberality of those to whom he looked for assistance, excitement, and support. The favour that Locke found at Oxford is matter of history: Gibbon has recorded his contemptuous scorn for 'the monks of Magdalene.' It would be easy to name other children of genius, who have proved that the self-styled *alma mater* was a most unjust and cruel step-mother.

"Amongst the evils of ecclesiastical sway, there is a mischief which annuls our universities, and destroys their very existence for every purpose of utility; it arises out of their spiritual constitution, and converts establishments that ought to be schools of learning, into race-courses and amphitheatres, wherein competitors and gladiators, as worthless as our jockeys, or the Thracians of old, struggle, or collude, to get possession of livings. This is the grand, the sole object of academical existence; the pursuit of learning is the flimsy pretext—the real aim is to obtain preferment in the church. The cause of the evil must be instantly removed; we will speak briefly of its operation. An university ought to be, and at all other places except Oxford and Cambridge really is, *one* establishment, every part co-operating for the augmentation and communication of knowledge. Simony, in its most pernicious form, has destroyed at once the unity and utility of institutions which we would gladly venerate. Ancient schools, designed for the use of the whole body, still exist at Oxford, to attest the degradation of modern times; each of these is inscribed with the title of one of the liberal sciences, or of one of the faculties, but it is never applied to the use for which it was designed. Numerous professors are decorated with honourable titles, and receive salaries for giving various lectures, which are never delivered; or if, as sometimes happens, an obstinate statute, which cannot be neglected or evaded, compels him to discourse in public, the dishonest priest gives what are significantly called 'wall-lectures,' since he addresses himself to the walls alone; and it is generally understood that no one ought to stand between them and their teacher. Unless these abuses be speedily remedied, it is manifest that the march of mind, of which some now boast, is a retreat, a shameful flight; and if the schoolmaster be indeed abroad, as some affirm, it is because he is not at home: having robbed his scholars, the scoundrel has absconded.

" The university of Oxford has long ceased to exist, except for the purpose of electioneering; for some time it was doubtful whether it was creditable to represent its M. M. A. A. in parliament, but the dispute has been finally determined, and we may reasonably question, whether an unworthy abuse of almost unbounded patronage be not too high a price to pay for the credit, whatever it be, that arises from sitting for the sister university. Except for the purpose of vain pageants, designed to aucupate benefices, by cajoling the patrons, the university of Oxford has long ceased to exist; for the purposes of learning it has been annihilated, dissolved, and destroyed, by having been divided into many minute, insignificant, and worthless portions. There are about thirty colleges;—the system of education, if it deserve that name, is separate and distinct at each, and miserable in all: the greater part of the funds, and the best apartments of every college, are set apart for a priest who, under the name of master, provost, warden, principal, or the like, enjoys at the expense of the public, every luxury that the most sensual could desire; yet this person contributes as little to the instruction of the youth of his society, as the Chief of the Black Eunuchs in the Grand Sultan's seraglio, or the Jew who takes toll at one of the turnpikes near London. A stranger would suppose that, being thus pampered in idleness, and growing fat upon the appropriation of charitable funds, the reverend sinecurist, through a certain decorous shame, would be at least civil and unpresuming; we appeal to those who are experienced in the deportment of contumelious insolence, whether it be so.

" The residue of the funds of the college is wasted upon a long list of fellows, the greater part of whom are absentees, and are alike unwilling and incapable of earning their salaries. The lowest and least of these is usually the tutor;—with or without the assistance of a drudge, still more unworthy than himself, this poor hack endeavours, by a few wretched lectures, to conceal the total want of all sound and wholesome instruction, and the monstrous misapplication of the wealth of the nation. He is often a man of low birth, whom laziness or physical infirmity rendered unfit for the flail or the loom; and, having availed himself of some eleemosynary foundation, he has won his way to an office which ought to be accounted honourable, but, by the accumulation of the grossest abuses has been rendered servile. If the aspiring clown had elevated himself by a generous excellence, by a preeminence in liberal learning, his low birth far from being a stain, would shed a lustre upon his new station; but under the present unhappy constitution of our universities, these mushrooms are culled for deleterious, not for wholesome properties.

If his birth was low, his mind is commonly lower; he is not selected on account of his learning, but of his subserviency. When a teacher of gentle blood is taken, it may happen perchance, that although he was born a freeman, he has the soul of a slave. The fellowships in like manner, are for the most part conferred upon kinsmen, upon tools, upon all but those who are best entitled to hold them. It may be that, with much pomp and ceremony, and an ostentatious display of the favour shewn to letters, some little proficient in the course of elementary instruction, prescribed to keep up the shew of attention to education, is now and then put into possession of one of those valuable annuities; but the yawning sluggard, the dull sot, is generally deemed more eligible than the zealous scholar.

"Let us suppose, however, that all fellowships were fairly bestowed upon the young men who were most worthy to hold them, still would our universities fall far short of that utility which we have an unalienable right to insist upon reaping from our public domains. In the case we have supposed, all improvement would cease at the end of the first year of academical residence; after taking the first degree there would be no motive to advance further on the road to learning. Each college would be, as it now is, a clerical tontine; an abominable institution, alike hostile to learning and subversive of piety. Surely our sagacious, clear-headed fellow-countrymen are not aware that every one of the numerous colleges which they maintain at such an enormous cost, is merely a clerical tontine! The instant a young man is elected a fellow, he has but one object; to outlive his brethren,—and thus to receive, in succession, the valuable benefices attached to his college, which were designed to reward the most learned, but which are blindly and dishonestly handed over to the longest liver.

Now what is thus written in the present day, is exactly of the same stamp as what was uttered by Gibbon:—" The schools of Oxford and Cambridge were founded in a dark age of false and barbarous science; and they are still tainted with the vices of their origin. Their primitive discipline was adapted to the education of priests and monks; and their government is still in the hands of the clergy, an order of men whose manners are remote from the present world, and whose eyes are dazzled by the light of philosophy." Nay, it is exactly the same as what Milton wrote in his time. We hear those who have studied there continually declaring that the system of education pursued is infinitely behind that given by dissenters to their ministers, so far as it regards their real preparation for the office of Christian teachers. I have frequently heard young men declare that they had no need to study there. With a certain quantity of mathematics, or of Greek and Latin, they could take a degree, and that was enough. So it must have been in Milton's days. "They pretend that their education either at school or university hath been very chargeable, and therefore ought to be repaired in future by a plentiful maintainance; whereas it is well known that the better half of them are oft-times poor and pitiful boys, that having no merit, or promising hopes, that might entitle them to the public provision, but their poverty, and the unjust favour of friends; have had their breeding both at school and university at the public cost; which might engage them the rather to give freely, as they have freely received.

" Next it is a fond error, though too much believed among us, to think that the university makes a minister of the gospel. That it may conduce to other arts and sciences, I dispute not now, but that which makes fit a minister the Scriptures can best tell us to be only from above. *How shall they preach, unless they be sent?* By whom sent? By the university, or the magistrate, or their belly? No surely; but sent from God only, and that God who is not their belly. And whether he be sent from God, or from Simon Magus, the inward sense of his calling and spiritual ability will sufficiently tell him.

"But yet, they say, it is also requisite he should be trained up in other learning, which can be had no where better than at the universities. I answer, that what learning, either human or divine, can be necessary to a minister, may as easily and less chargeably be had in any private house. How deficient else, and to how little purpose are all those piles of sermons, notes, and comments on all parts of the Bible,—bodies and marrows of divinity, beside all other sciences in our English tongue; many of the same books which in Latin they read at the university? And the small necessity of going there to learn Divinity I prove first from the most part of themselves, who seldom continue there till they have well got through logick, their first rudiments. And those theological disputations there held by professors and graduates, are such as tend least of all to the edification or capacity of the people, but rather perplex and leaven pure doctrine with scholastical trash, than enable any minister to the better preaching of the gospel.'"  *Milton on Hirelings.*

When past and present authorities thus agree to describe the great universities of the nation, wo be to that nation if it do not break the slumbers of these clerical drones, throw wide the gates to the influx of real knowledge, and of all those who thirst for knowledge, that we may never more hear of such men as Locke being expelled for their love of freedom, or Wesley for their piety.

Of the continuance of ecclesiastical courts to this enlightened period, what shall we say,—but that Englishmen are a most patient race? A dark and mysterious assemblage as of bats and owls! A sort of Inquisition shorn of its power by public opinion, and suffered by public opinion to exist. Priests, allowed no longer to summon men to their hidden tribunals, and rack their persons, but permitted still to seize on their wills with rude hands, and rack their purses without mercy! Clerical peers and clerical legislators are anomalous enough; but clerical taxers of orphans, and clerical guardians of testamentary documents, are still more anomalous. Here is a popish institution existing in a protestant country, which even popish countries have abandoned, and conveyed its functions into the hands of laymen! Our wise Saxon ancestors suffered nothing of this kind amongst them: it is true they permitted bishops to take their seats in the civil courts to protect their own rights, but it remained for the Norman invader to concede to Rome this dangerous privilege of clerical courts. Time and knowledge have thrown into desuetude most of those powers by which they formerly harassed our forefathers. They no longer trouble themselves about the reformation of manners, the punishing of heresy; nor do churchwardens care to present scandalous livers to the bishop: but refuse to pay a fee, and they will speedily " curse thee to thy face." They are in fact a sort of obscure and dusty incorporations for collecting and enjoying good revenues, under the names of bishop, surrogates, proctors, registrers, deputy-registrers, and so forth, from fees on wills, consecrations, and various other sources and immunities. For the greediness of these clerical owls in past days, let any one consult Chaucer. The worthy Lyon-king-at-arms of Scotland, Sir David Lindsay of the Mount, also made merry with them in his days:

> Marry, I lent my gossip my mare to fetch home coals,
> And he her drowned in the quarry holes.
> And I ran to the consistorie, for to pleinze,
> And there I fell among a greedy meinze.
> They gave me first a thing they call *citandum;*
> Within eight days I got but *libellandum;*
> Within a month I got *ad apponendum;*
> In half a year I got *inter loquendum;*
> And then I got—how call ye it?—*ad replicandum;*
> But I could never a word yet understand 'em.
> And then they made me pull out many placks,
> And made me pay for four and twenty acts;
> But ere they came half way to *concludendum,*
> The devil a plack was left for to defend him.
> Thus they postponed me two years with their train;
> Then, *hodie ad octo,* bade me come again.
> And then, their rooks, they croaked wonderous fast;
> For sentence silver they cried at the last.
> Of *pronunciandum,* they made me wonder fain,
> But I never got my good grey mare again!

This is spoken in the character of a poor man; another character then adds,

> My Lords, we must reform these consistory laws,
> Whose great defame, above the heaven blows.
> I knew a man, in sueing for a cow,
> Ere he had done, he spent full half a bow.*
> So that the king's honour we may advance,
> We will conclude as they have done in France;
> Let spiritual matters pass to spiritualitie,
> And temporal matters unto temporalitie.
> *Satyre of Three Estaites.*

Whoever would see what troublesome and extortionate nuisances these courts are, has only to consult the voluminous returns made to parliament in 1829 on this subject. Amongst the lesser evils of the

* Half a fold of cows.

system are the consecration of burial grounds, and what are called surplice fees. Nothing is more illustrative of the spirit of priestcraft than that the church should have kept up the superstitious belief in the consecration of ground in the minds of the people to the present hour, and that, in spite of education, the poor and the rich should be ridden with the most preposterous notion that they cannot lie in peace except in ground over which the bishop has said his mummery, and for which he and his rooks, as Sir David Lindsay calls them, have pocketed the fees, and laughed in their sleeves at the gullible foolishness of the people. When will the day come when the webs of the clerical spider shall be torn not only from the limbs but the souls of men? Does the honest Quaker sleep less sound, or will he arise less cheerfully at the judgment-day from his grave, over which no prelatical jugglery has been practised, and for which neither prelate nor priest has pocketed a doit? Who has consecrated the sea, into which the British sailor in the cloud of battle-smoke descends, or who goes down, amidst the tears of his comrades, to depths to which no plummet but that of God's omnipresence ever reached? Who has consecrated the battle-field, which opens its pits for its thousands and tens of thousands; or the desart, where the weary traveller lies down to his eternal rest? Who has made holy the sleeping place of the solitary missionary, and of the settlers in new lands? Who but He whose hand has hallowed earth from end to end, and from surface to centre, for his pure and almighty fingers have moulded it! Who but He whose eye rests on it day and night, watching its myriads of moving children—the oppressors and the oppressed—the deceivers and the deceived—the hypocrites, and the poor whose souls are darkened with false knowledge and fettered with the bonds of daring selfishness? and on whatever innocent thing that eye rests, it is hallowed beyond the breath of bishops, and the fees of registrers. Who shall need to look for a consecrated spot of earth to lay his bones in, when the struggles and the sorrows, the prayers and the tears of our fellow men, from age to age, have consecrated every atom of this world's surface to the desire of a repose which no human hands can lead to, no human rites can secure? Who shall seek for a more hallowed bed than the bosom of that earth into which Christ himself descended, and in which the bodies of thousands of glorious patriots, and prophets, and martyrs, who were laid in gardens and beneath their paternal trees, and of heroes whose blood and sighs have flowed forth for their fellow men, have been left to peace and the blessings of grateful generations with no rites, no sounds but the silent falling of tears and the aspirations of speechless, but immortal thanks? From side to side, from end to end, the whole world is sanctified by these agencies, beyond the blessings or the curses of priests! God's sunshine flows over it, his providence surrounds it; it is rocked in his arms like the child of his eternal love; his faithful creatures live, and toil, and pray in it; and, in the name of heaven, who shall make it, or who can need it holier for his last resting couch! But the greediness of priests persists in cursing the poor with extortionate expenses, and calls them blessings. The poor man, who all his days goes groaning under the load of his ill-paid labours, cannot even escape from them into the grave except at a dismal charge to his family. His native earth is not allowed to receive him into her bosom till he has satisfied the priest and his satellites. With the exception of Jews, Quakers and some few other dissenters, every man is given up in England as a prey, in life and in death, to the parson, and his echo, and his disturber of bones.

The following, from the *Leeds Mercury*, is a fair example of the expense incurred for what is called consecration of the smallest addition to a burial-ground—and wretched must be the mental stupidity of a people who can believe that such fellows can add holiness to the parish earth.

To the churchwardens of Tadcaster was sent the following letter:—

(COPY.)

Gentlemen,—I send you enclosed the charges on the consecration of the additional churchyard at Tadcaster.

I am, Gentlemen, your obedient servant,
JOSEPH BUCKLE.

York, 26th March, 1829.

Fees on consecration of the additional Burial-ground at Tadcaster.

| 1828. | £. | s. | d. |
|---|---|---|---|
| Drawing and engrossing the petition to the Archbishop to consecrate | 1 | 5 | 0 |
| Drawing and engrossing the sentence of consecration | 2 | 2 | 0 |
| Drawing the Act | 0 | 13 | 6 |
| Registering the above instruments and the deed at length, and parchment | 2 | 2 | 0 |
| The Chancellor's fee | 5 | 0 | 0 |
| The principal Register's fee | 5 | 0 | 0 |
| The Secretary's fee | 5 | 0 | 0 |
| The Deputy Register's attendance and expenses | 3 | 15 | 6 |
| The Apparitor's fee | 1 | 1 | 0 |
| Fee on obtaining the seal | 1 | 1 | 0 |
| Carriage | 0 | 5 | 0 |
| | £27 | 5 | 0 |

For burying a poor man this is the common scale of charge in this town:—For the burial of even a pauper 7*s*. 6*d*.—for a child six months old, the same —if the child be not baptized, 1*s*.; for in that state it is, by clerical logic, deemed not a human being, but a thing, until their mummery has ennobled it—

a thing beneath God's notice—it is therefore thrust into any hole by the sexton. In the principal churchyard, a man who wishes to choose the place of burial must pay 10*l.* for the size of a grave; and for opening such a grave, about 2*l.* 15*s.* 6*d*. For opening a vault, even in village churchyards, 5*l.* is commonly demanded; in the church 10*l.*; and what is worst, after all, it has been proved by more than one legal decision, no man's family vault is sacred and inviolable. The church and churchyard are the parson's freehold. In them, during his life, he can work his own will, but he cannot sell a right of vault beyond his own life. There are numbers of families who flattered themselves they had a place of family sepulture into which no stranger could intrude; but let them excite the wrath of some clerical parish tyrant, and he can shew them that not only can he refuse to permit the opening of their vault to receive their dead till his demands, however exorbitant, are satisfied, but that he can refuse to have it opened at all; and moreover, can thrust in, at his pleasure, the carcasses of the vilest wretches in the parish. Thus, by dealing with priests, the people are served as they always have been—juggled out of their money for "that which is nought;" and thrown into the absolute power of a most mercenary order of men. They are suffered to buy that which cannot be really sold; and when they look for a freehold, they find only a trap for clerical fees. From root to branch the whole system is rotten;—GIVE! GIVE! GIVE! is written on every wall and gate of the church: and though a man quit it and its communion altogether, he must still pay, in life and in death, to it. Nay, by a recent case in the diocese of Salisbury, it is shewn by the bishop that a man once having taken orders can never lay them down again. A Mr. Tiptaft having resigned his living from conscientious motives, began to preach as a dissenter; but the bishop attempted to stop his mouth with menacing the thunders of the church; and, on his astonished declaration that he was no longer a son of the church, the prelate let him know that he was, and must be—for clerical orders, like Coleridge's infernal fire—must

   Cling to him everlastingly.

To this church, which empties the pockets of the poor, and stops the mouth of the conscientious dissenter, let every Englishman do his duty.

## CHAPTER XVIII.

### THE ENGLISH CHURCH.

The Church of England is unpopular. It is connected with the crown and the aristocracy, but is not regarded with affection by the mass of the people; and this circumstance greatly lessens its utility, and has powerfully contributed to multiply the number of dissenters.  *Edinburgh Review*, No. lxxxviii.

We are overdone with standing armies. We have an army of lawyers with tough parchments and interminable words to confound honesty and common sense; an army of paper to fight gold; an army of soldiers to fight the French; an army of doctors to fight death; and an army of parsons to fight the devil—of whom he standeth not in awe!
*The late William Fox of Nottingham.*

---

But while the nation demands those alterations just enumerated, the internal prosperity, nay the very existence of the episcopal church, as a vital and fruitful Christian community, demands others. And first of all, that it should be delivered from the curse of patronage,—the source of a thousand evils,—the cause of lamentable moral lethargy and paralysis. While every Christian society around it enjoys the just privilege of choosing its own ministers, will it be long endured by this church that it should be kept in a condition of everlasting tutelage; that its members, however wise, enlightened, and capable of managing all their affairs for themselves; who would hold it as the highest insult that the state should appoint overseers to choose for their children schoolmasters, and for themselves stewards, attorneys, or physicians—will it be endured long that some state favourite who never saw them, or their place; or some neighbouring fox-hunting squire, whose intellect, if it exhibit itself any where, is in his boot-heels,—that some horse-jockey, or gambler, some fellow whose life is a continual crime, his conversation a continual pestilence; who, if he were a poor man, would have been long since hanged, but being a rich one, he is at once the choicest son and purveyor of Satan, and the hereditary selector of the minister of God,—will it be endured that such a man shall put in over the heads of a respectable, pious, and well-informed community, a spiritual guide and teacher?—put him in, in spite of their abhorrence and remonstrances? and that once in, neither patron nor people shall get him out, though he be dull as the clod of his own glebe, and vicious as the veriest scum of his parish, who prefers the pot-house to his polluted house of prayer? From this source has flowed the most fatal results to the church; nay, it may be safely asserted, nine-tenths of the evils which afflict it. By this means it has been filled with every species of unworthy character;—men who look upon it as a prey; who come to it with coldness and contempt; who gather its fruits, while other and better men toil for them; and squander them in modes scandalous not merely to a church but to human society. By this means it has been made the heritage of the rich man's children, while the poor and unpatronized man of worth and talent has plodded on in its labours, and despaired. By this means so worldly a character has grown upon its ministers, that they have become blind to the vilest enormities of the system, and now look on simony as a matter of course. Whoever doubts this—and yet who does doubt it?—let him look into the British, or Clerical Magazine,

and he will find the reverend correspondents asking with the utmost simplicity—how can the bishops help men selling advowsons? It never seems once to occur to them, that if there were no clerical buyers there would be no sellers. In the same journal for June, 1832, p. 357, is also the following statement;—
" Of the whole number of benefices in England, very nearly 8000, that is, more than two-thirds of the whole, are in private patronage. Of the clergy, a very considerable number have purchased the livings which they hold; and of the remainder, most have been brought up to the church, and educated with a view to some particular piece of preferment in the gift of their family and relations. Whether this be right or wrong, it is an effect almost necessarily following from so large a portion of the property of the church being private property; a state of things not to be altered, and which they who wish to abolish pluralities do not talk of altering."

Now here in one sentence, written by a clergyman, and published in a clerical magazine, we have the root and ground of three-fourths of the evils and enormities of the establishment. We have a statement, that out of 10,000 livings in England, nearly 8,000 are in the hands of private people; that is, in the hands each of a man who, whatever be his life or his qualifications for judging, can and does put in a clergyman over the heads of his neighbours, to serve his own views, which are commonly to establish some rake or blockhead of a son or nephew, or to make what money he can out of a stranger, if he has no children; that is, not to seek the most pious man, but the highest bidder. And consequently the next assertion is, that a very considerable number have purchased these livings;—thus, not the pious man, but the highest bidder, the boldest dealer in simony has had the livings. Oh! poor people who are doomed to sit under such pastors, and vainly hope to grow in heavenly knowledge! The remainder, says this most logical writer, have been brought up with a view to some particular piece of preferment from their friends and relations. Yes, younger sons—no matter what their heads or their hearts are made of—doomed to deal out God's threats and promises to the people. Desperate handlers of God's sacred things—who rush fearlessly into his temple, not because he has called them, but because their relations have the key of the doors. And all this, this clerical writer puts forth with the most innocent face imaginable. While he enumerates causes enough to have made St. Paul's hair stand on end; when he tells us that simony is common as daylight; that the bulk of the livings in England are not open to the pious and the worthy, but are the heritage of certain men who may be neither—he is so far from seeing any thing amiss, that he goes on to point out the advantage of such a state of things. He declares *it cannot be altered;* and this is one of his reasons why the church should not be reformed. He does not at all perceive that no church with so scandalous and preposterous a foundation, can possibly stand many years in the midst of a country where the spirit of man is busily at work to pry into the nature of all things, and where any monopoly, but especially of religious patronage, must assuredly arouse an indignation that will overturn it. Miserably dark must be the moral atmosphere of a church where its members come forward with a mental obtuseness like this, to advocate its abominations as if they were virtues, while the very people gape round them with astonishment, and they perceive it not. But there are no labourers in the demolition of a bad institution like its own friends.

They are like insects in a rotten tree; roused by external alarm to activity, they bustle about and scatter the trunk, which holds them, into dust. Such men put a patch of new arguments into the old garment of corruption, and the rent is made worse.

To proceed.—By these means the church has been filled with pride and apathy; and it is notorious, that of all Christian ministers, the ministers of the establishment are the least interested in their flocks,—cultivate and enjoy the least sympathy with them. I accidentally, the other day, took up Sir Arthur Brooke Faulkner's Tour in Germany, and immediately fell on this passage, which coming from a man fresh from the observation of the continental churches, is worthy of attention. " Nowhere else in Europe are clergymen, and no wonder, less respected among the multitude than in the British dominions." He proceeds to account for this by their apathy, their pluralities, their exorbitant revenues, maintenance by tithes, and acting as legislators. He adds—" If the statement which has already been alluded to may be credited, the clergy of the United Kingdoms are paid more than the clergy of all the rest of Christendom besides by a million sterling and upwards, the full amount of their annual revenue being 8,852,000$l$. In primitive times, and in the different countries at the present time which I have visited, the remuneration of their labour is, as we have seen, in many cases, chiefly voluntary. In these countries it needs no prelacy strutting in lawn sleeves, and ' raising their mitred fronts in courts and parliaments,' to clothe it with respect."

This, in contradiction of the many assertions of the advocates of our English establishment, who contend that without dignities and large revenues the clergy would sink into contempt, is borne out by the experience of all the world. The dignities and large revenues of the papal church did not embalm its clergy in public estimation; and to whatever country we turn, we find that wherever the clergy are but moderately endowed, there they are diligent, and there they are esteemed. What is the opinion of Milton, of the preferments which have been so much vaunted as stimulants to activity and talent in the church? That they are but " lures or loubells, by which the worldly-minded priest may be tolled, from parish to parish, all the country over." The Scotch clergy are but slenderly incomed, and what is the testimony of their countrymen, the Edinburgh Reviewers, concerning them? " In Scotland there are 950 parish clergymen, whose incomes may average 275*l.* a-year each; and the Scottish clergy are not inferior in point of attainments to any in Europe: no complaints have ever been made of the manner in which they perform their duty; but, on the contrary, their exemplary conduct is the theme of well-merited and constant eulogy."

Let us now turn again to Sir A. B. Faulkner's account of the German clergy.—" The Hessean clergy are exemplary in the discharge of their multifarious duties. A clergyman, no matter what his grade, deems it in no respect derogatory from his dignity to prove his faith by his works. The spiritual and temporal comfort of their flocks, and their nurture in all sound impressions of religion, is their unceasing care; while they hold out, in their own respectable and uncompromising conduct, both in public and private, the fairest patterns to enforce the precepts which they teach. However this may appear to our church of Englanders, it is fact. The average of a

Hessean clergyman's stipend, is about forty dollars a-year—the dollar three shillings stirling—to which there is added a house and garden, or little farm."

"The clergy at Marberg," he says, "are, in the strictest sense, a working clergy. They are perpetually among their flocks, correcting and training, and guiding; and in such unremitting labours of love, earn a reputation not the less likely to abide by them for being the capital on which they must chiefly rely for most of their comforts and happiness. And it surely is most fitting there should exist this reciprocity of feeling and good offices between the pastor and his flock. The protestant and the catholic are on the best possible footing with each other; and share equally in the offices of government." Wherever he mentions the clergy, it always is in similar terms. It is only necessary for us always to remember that this is a clergy very moderately paid, and we then see the exact value of the arguments for high salaries.

Sorry should I be to see our noble ecclesiastical piles deserted and falling to decay, because the national funds were withdrawn; but I should like to see them filled with ministers of zeal, and overflowing congregations. Sorry should I be to see, in my Sunday rambles into the country, the picturesque village church deserted by its accustomed minister, and occupied by some ignorant and clamorous fanatic; but I should rejoice when I entered, to find there, not a mere journeyman hireling, but the worthy pastor,—not a man standing like a statue, and reading in monotonous tones, a discourse cold as his own looks; but one full of overflowing love, and a lively though rational zeal, that made his hearers warm at once to him, towards each other, and towards God; and when we went forth I should be glad to see, not what I too often see, a stately person who smiles sunnily, shakes hands heartily, talks merrily with the few wealthy of his fold; gives to those of a lower grade a frigid nod of recognition; to the poor a contemptuous forgetfulness of their presence, and stalks away in sullen stateliness to his well-endowed parsonage. Whatever be chargeable on the catholic priests, it cannot be denied that they excite a strong and lasting attachment in their followers. They are more affable, more humble in manner, kind and condolent in spirit, and are found diligently at the bedside of the sick, and at the councils of the poor man beset with difficulties. But he who enters on his living as his birth-right, who looks on himself as a gentleman, and his hearers as clowns, what can arouse his zeal? He who has no fear of censure, or removal, whence spring his circumspection and activity? "My father," said the natural son of a nobleman, "said to me—it is time you should choose a profession. You must not be a tradesman, or you cannot sit at my table; you have not shrewdness enough for a lawyer; you would forget, or poison your patients through carelessness were you a physician;—I must make a parson, or some devil of a thing of you;—and he made a parson of me;—and I hate the church and every thing belonging to it!" From such ministers what can be expected? and such ministers are supplied to the church in legions by this odious system of private patronage. The ambition of maintaining the character of gentlemen has made clergymen cold, unimpassioned, insipid and useless. It was the same in the latter days of popery. Chaucer sketches us a priest.

> That hie on horse willith to ride
> In glitterande golde of grete arraie,
> Painted and portrid all in pride,
> No common knight maie go so gaie;

> Chaunge of clothing every daie,
> With goldin girdils grete and small,
> As boistrous as is bere at baie,
> All soche falshede mote nedis fall.

Now we don't want a set of fine gentlemen; we want a race of zealous, well-informed, kind and diligent parish priests. If we must have gentlemen, let us have them of the school of the carpenter's son, whom honest Decker, the tragic poet, declares was

> A soft, meek, patient, humble, tranquil spirit;
> The first true gentleman that ever breathed!

After this pattern, we care not how many gentlemen we have in the church;—gentlemen who are not ashamed, like their master Christ, to be the friends of the poor. Who desire to live for them; to live among them; to learn their wants, to engage their affections, to be their counsellors and guides. Men who can understand and sympathise with the struggling children of poverty and toil, in villages and solitary places, and are therefore understood by them, and are beloved by them, and will follow them and make their precepts the rule of their lives and the precious hope of their deaths. Oh! what have not our clergy to answer for to God and to their country, that they are not such men; what blessings may they not become by being such! I know no men whose sphere of influence is more capacious and more enviable. It is the easiest thing in the world to become the very idol of the poor; there needs but to shew them that you feel for them, and they are all ardour and attachment. For the man who will condescend to be what Christ was, a lover of the poor, they will fly at a word over land and water in his service. He has but to utter a wish, and if it be in their power, it is accomplished. In the language of

Wordsworth, "it is the gratitude of such men that oftenest leaves us mourning." The parish clergyman has facilities of aiding the poor, that few other men have. At his slightest recommendation, the medical man is ready to afford them his aid; at his suggestion the larder and the wardrobe of the hall expand with alacrity their doors, and the ladies are ready to fly and become the warmest benefactresses of the afflicted. I am ready to admit that there are many such men already in England; but were it not for the cursed operation of this private patronage, there would be thousands more such. Numbers who now have no hope but of doing the drudgery of a curacy, would then be called by the voice of a free people, to a course of active usefulness. The land would be filled with burning and shining lights that are now hidden beneath the bushels of stipendiary slavery, and the effect on our labouring population would soon be auspiciously visible.

But what is the actual picture presented to us now under the operation of this detestable system? Look where we will, we behold the most gross instances of simony, pluralities, non-residence, and penurious remuneration of the working clergy. If every man were to declare his individual experience, such things would make part of his knowledge. In towns, where the clergy are more under the influence of public opinion, we see too many instances of lukewarmness, arrogance, and unfitness. I have seen gamblers, jockeys, and characterless adventurers put into livings by the vilest influence, to the horror and loathing of the helpless congregations—and that in populous cities; but in obscure, rural villages, the fruits of the system are ten-fold more atrociously shameful. There the ignorant, the brutal, the utterly debauched live without shame, and tyrannize without mercy over the poor, uncultivated flocks, whom they render ten times more stupid and sordid. Within my own knowledge, I can go over almost innumerable parishes, and find matter of astonishment at the endurance of Englishmen. I once was passing along the street of a county town in the evening, and my attention was arrested by the most violent ravings and oaths of a man in a shop. I inquired the occasion. "Oh!" said one of the crowd, who stood seemingly enjoying the spectacle, "Oh! it is only Parson ———; he has got drunk and followed a girl into her father's house, who meeting him at the top of the stairs in pursuit of his affrighted daughter, hurled him to the bottom, and the worthy man of God is now evaporating his wrath in vows of vengeance." From these spectators I found it was one of the commonest sights of the town to see this clergyman thus drunk, and thus employed. But why, said I, do not the parishioners get him dismissed? A smile of astonishment at the simplicity of my query went through the crowd. "Get him dismissed! Who shall get him dismissed? Why, he is the squire's brother; he is, in fact, born to the living. There is not a man in the parish who is not a tenant or dependant in some way on the family; consequently not a man who dare open his mouth." They have him, such as he is, and must make their best of him; and he or his brother will be sure to rear a similar prophet for the next generation.

I entered a village not five miles off. This I found a lovely retired place, with a particularly handsome church, a noble parsonage, a neglected school, and an absent clergyman. The living was 1800*l.* a year—the incumbent a desperate gambler. "Why," again I said, "don't you get this man dismissed?" I saw the same smile arise at my simplicity. "La! Sir, why he is his lordship's cousin!" It was a decisive answer—to the principle of private patronage this village also owed the irremediable curse of a gambling parson.

I went on.—In a few miles I entered a fine open parish, where the church shewed afar off over its surrounding level meadows of extreme fertility. Here the living was added to that of the adjoining parish. One man held them. Together they brought 2400*l.* a year. A curate did the duty at two churches and a chapel of ease, formerly for 80*l.* a year—now for 100*l.* a year. The rector was never seen except when he came and pocketed his 2300*l.* and departed. This man too was hereditary parson.

But in the parish which I know perhaps better than any other, a large and populous parish in Derbyshire, no one could recollect having heard of it possessing a decent clergyman. The last but one was a vulgar and confirmed sot. The last came a respectable youth, well married, but soon fell into dissipated habits, seduced a young woman of fine person and some property, who, in consequence, was abandoned by her connexions, married a low wretch who squandered her money, and finally died of absolute starvation. The clergyman's wife, heretofore a respectable woman, wounded beyond endurance by this circumstance, took to drinking: all domestic harmony was destroyed; the vicar began to drink too. A young family of children grew up amid all these evil and unfortunate influences: the parents finally separated; and as the pastor fell into years, he fell into deeper vice and degradation. I well remember him. I remember seeing him upheld, in a state of utter intoxication over a grave, by two men, while he vainly strove to repeat the burial service,— saying, " there is one glory of the sun, and another glory of the sun"—till they led him away, and closed the grave. I remember well his small, light person, his thin but ruddy countenance, and his singular appearance, as he used to trot at a quick pace up to the church, or down the village street back again,—for at that time he performed duty at three churches, each of which was three miles distant from the other. On one occasion, in winter, wishing to make great haste, he put on his skates and took the canal in his way; but it was not well frozen beneath the bridges, and the ice let him in. He hurried home, and changed his clothes, but left his sermon in the wet pocket, and arrived only to dismiss his long-expecting congregation. The old man, notwithstanding his vices, had much good-nature and no pride. He accepted every invitation to dinner at the weddings of his humblest parishioners, for his own dinners were, like those of the miser Elwes, generally cold boiled eggs and pancakes, which he carried in his pockets and ate as he went along. His hearers were many of them colliers; and in their cabins he has sometimes got so drunk that he has fallen asleep, and they have put him to bed with a slice of bacon in one hand, and one of bread in the other. I remember him meeting a labourer in the fields one Sunday as he returned from church, and seeing that the man had been nutting instead of to prayer, he said—" Ah, William! you should not go a nutting on a Sunday!—Have you got a few for me, William?" When he administered the sacrament to the sick, he advised them not to take much of the wine, lest it should increase their fever; but added charitably, he would drink it for them, and it would do as well. In short, he was not without redeeming qualities; but he is dead; or rather, was kicked out of the world by a horse, when he was in a state of intoxication. Another came in his stead; and such another! I see him now in fancy—he is

s

still the incumbent, or incumbrance of the parish, and may be seen by any one who lists—a hard-faced, vulgar-looking fellow, whom at a glance you know to have a heart like a pebble, a head full of stupid mischief, and a gripe like iron. I think it was Alderman Waithman who said in parliament, that of all tyrannies, none are so odious as the tyranny of a parish priest. And this fellow is a tyrant to perfection. To the poor he speedily shewed himself a fierce and arbitrary dictator; they must abide his pleasure as to the times of marrying, burying, and baptism; and he extorted from them the uttermost farthing. It is a coal district; and the coal had been got in the surrounding country, but had been left under the houses to prevent injury to them. This he claimed and sold. In getting the coal, he threw down a part of several houses,—cracked and undermined others, and would probably have thrown down the church, for the workmen were actually beginning to undermine it, when the churchwardens interfered. He bought farms, and borrowed money to pay for them; and when compelled to pay part of the interest, he persuaded the attorney to give him a memorandum of the receipt without a stamp, and then laid an information against him in the Exchequer. He got a commission to prove wills, and charged the poor ignorant people double, till some one more experienced informed the proctor, and got his occupation taken away. He was to be found at public-houses, and in the lowest company, till the very family who got him the living, absented themselves from the church; yet, with a very common kind of inconsistency, when the people complained, and asked if he could not be removed, this very family declined acting in it, alleging—it would be a great scandal for a clergyman to be dismissed from his living!! At length some unwise guardians, who had lent him the money of their orphan wards on his bare note, and the strength of his clerical character, have put him in prison; and the longer he lies, the greater the blessing to the people. The following is part of the report of the Insolvent Debtors' Court when he applied to be discharged:—"The Rev. gentleman's debts set forth in his schedule amounted to 8945*l*. 8*s*. 9*d*. It appeared that he had exercised certain lay vocations; speculated somewhat in land; dabbled a little in twist-lace machinery; worked a colliery; and now and then enjoyed a bit of horse-dealing. The insolvent's income was 246*l*. per annum, and his out-goings 500*l*. a-year."

Such is the ecclesiastical history of this one parish; such would be that of thousands were they related; and all this is the natural result of the absurd and iniquitous system of state and individual patronage. Till this scandalous mode—this mode so insulting to the people of a nation like this, of appointing parish ministers—be abandoned, vain is every hope of internal strength and life to the church. Let every parish choose its own pastor, and a new course will commence. The worthy and the talented will take heart,—piety will meet its natural reward, and work its natural works; the sot and the hireling incubus will disappear; the vicar will no more come and pocket his yearly 2000*l*. and leave his curate to do his yearly labour for 100*l*.; multitudes of needful reforms will flow into the heart of the church; a religious regimen and new life will animate its constitution.

The canons of the church must be revised; its articles abolished, or reduced to rationality; surplice fees done away with. It is a crying scandal and oppression, that none of the children of Heth are left who will say "bury thy dead out of thy sight—what is it between me and thee?—bury thy dead;" but the poor man cannot bury his dead except by feeing the parson to an amount that will cost him days of hard labour and months of privation. "To ask a fee of such," says Milton, "is a piece of paltry craft befitting none but beggarly artists. Burials and marriages are so little a part of the priest's gain, that they who consider well may find them to be no part of his function. It is a peculiar simony of our English divines only. Their great champion, Sir Henry Spelman, in a book written to that purpose, shews by many cited canons, and some of times corruptest in the church, that fees extorted or demanded for sacraments, marriages, and especially for burials, are wicked, accursed, simoniacal, and abominable."

## CHAPTER XIX.

### THE ENGLISH CHURCH—CONFIRMATION.

*I look on both sides of this human life—
Its brightness and its shadow.*

ONE of the most beautiful and impressive rites of the church, is the confirmation of young people as it is seen in the country. On some bright summer morning, you see troops of village boys and girls come marching into the town, headed by the village clerk, or schoolmaster. First one, then another little regiment of these rural embryo Christians, is seen advancing from different parts towards the principal church. All are in their best array. Their leader, with an air of unusual solemn dignity, marches straight forward, looking neither to the right hand nor to the left, but sometimes casting a grave glance behind at his followers. His suit of best black adorns his sturdy person, and his lappels fly wide in the breeze that meets him. His charge come on in garbs of many colours;—the damsels in green and scarlet petticoats; stockings white, black, and grey; gowns of white, bearing testimony to miry roads and provoking brambles; gowns of cotton print of many a dazzling flowery pattern; gowns even of silk in these luxurious days; long, flying, pink sashes, and pink, and yellow, and scarlet bunches in bonnets of many a curious make. The lads stride on with slouching paces that have not been learned in drawing and assembly-rooms, but on the barn-floor, beside the loaded wagon, on the heathy sheep-walk, and in the deep fallow field. They are gloriously robed in corduroy breeches, blue worsted stockings, heavy-nailed ancle-boots, green shag waistcoats, neck-handkerchiefs of red, with long corners that flutter in the wind, and coats shaped by some sempiternal tailor, whose fashions know no change. Amid the bustling, spruce inhabitants of the town, their walk, their dress, their faces full of ruddy health and sheepish simplicity, mark them out as creatures almost of another tribe. They bring all the spirit of the village—of the solitary farm—of heaths and woods, and rarely frequented fields, along with them. You are carried forcibly by your imagination, at the sight of them, into cottage life,—into the habits and concerns of the rural population. You feel what daily anticipations —what talk—what an early rising, and bustling preparation there has been in many a lowly dwelling, in many an out-of-the-way hamlet, for this great occasion. How the old people have told over how it was when they went to be confirmed. What a mighty place the church is; what crowds of grand people; what an awful thing the bishop in his wig and robes! How the fond, simple mothers have set forth their sons and daughters; and given them injunction on injunction; and followed them from their doors with eyes filled with tears of pride, of joy, and of anxiety. How the youthful band, half gay, more than half grotesque, but totally happy, have advanced over hill and dale. The whole joyousness of their holiday feeling is presented to you, as they progressed through bosky lanes and dells, through woods, over the open breezy heaths and hills,—the flowers, and the dews, and the green leaves breathing upon them their freshest influence; the blue, cheering sky above them, and the lark sending down, from his highest flight, his music of ineffable gladness. You feel the secret awe that struck into their bosoms as they entered the noisy, glittering, polished, and in their eyes, mighty and proud town; and the notion of the church, the assembled crowds, the imposing ceremony, and the awful bishop and all his clergy, came strongly and distinctly before them.

Besides these, numbers of vehicles are bringing in other rural neophytes. The carriages of the wealthy drive rapidly and gaily on to inns and houses of friends. Tilted wagons, gigs, ample cars, are all freighted with similar burdens; and many a strange, old, lumbering cart, whose body is smeared with the ruddy marl of the fields it has done service in, whose wheels are heavy with the clinging mire of roads that would make M'Adam aghast, rumbles along, dragged by a bony and shaggy animal, that if it must be honoured with the name of horse, is the very Helot of horses. These open conveyances exhibit groups of young girls, that in the lively air, and shaken to and fro by the rocking of their vehicle, and the jostling of chairs, look like beds of tulips nodding in a strong breeze.

As you approach the great church the bustle becomes every moment more conspicuous. The clergy are walking in that direction in their black gowns. Groups of the families of the country clergy strike your eyes. Venerable old figures with their sleek and ruddy faces; their black silk stockings glistening beneath their gowns; their canonical hats set most becomingly above, are walking on, the very images of happiness, with their wives hanging on their arms, and followed by lovely, genteel girls, and graceful, growing lads. As the rustics' aspects brought all the spirit of the cottage and the farm to your imagination, they bring all that of the village parsonage. You are transported in a moment to the most perfect little paradises which are to be found in the world—the country dwellings of the English clergy. Those sweet spots, so exactly formed for the "otium cum dignitate." Those medium abodes, betwixt the rudeness and vexations of poverty, and the cumbrous state of aristocratic opulence. Those lovely and picturesque houses, built of all orders and all fashions, yet preserving the one definite, uniform character of the comfortable, the pretensionless, and the accordant with the scenery in which they are placed;—houses, some of old, framed timber, up which the pear and the apricot, the pyracantha and the vine clamber; or of old, grey, substantial stone; or of more modern and elegant villa architecture, with their roofs which, whether of thatch or slate, or native grey stone, are seen thickly screened from the north, and softened and surmounted to the delighted eye with noble trees: with their broad, bay windows, which bring all the sunny glow of the south, at will, into the house; and around which the rose and jasmine breathe their delicious odours. Those sweet abodes, surrounded by their bowery, shady, aromatic shrubberies, and pleasant old-fashioned glebe-crofts—homes in which, under the influence of a wise, good heart, and a good system, domestic happiness may be enjoyed to its highest conception, and whence piety, and cultivation, and health and comfort, and a thousand blessings to the poor, may spread through the surrounding neighbourhood. Such are the abodes brought before your minds by the sight of the country clergy; such are thousands of their dwellings, scattered through this great and beneficent country,—in its villages and hidden nooks of scattered population,—amid its wild mountains, and along its wilder coasts;—endowed by the laws with earthly plenty, and invested by the bright heaven, and its attendant seasons, with the freshest sunshine, the sweetest dews, the most grateful solitude and balmy seclusion.

But the merry bells call us onward; and lo! the mingled crowds are passing under that ancient and time-worn porch. We enter,—and how beautiful and impressive is the scene! The whole of that mighty and venerable fabric is filled, from side to side, with a mixed, yet splendid congregation,—for the rich and the poor, the superb and the simple, there blend into one human mass, whose varieties are but as the contrast of colours in a fine painting,—the spirit of the *tout en semble* is the nobility of beauty. The whole of that gorgeous assembly, on which the eye rests in palpable perception of the wealth, the refinement, and the elevation of the social life of our country, is hushed in profound attention to the reading of the services of the day by one of the clergymen. They are past;—the bishop, followed by his clergy, advances to the altar. The solemn organ bursts forth with its thunder of harmonious sound, that rolls through the arched roof above, and covers every living soul with its billows of tumultuous music, and with its appropriate depth of inexpressible feeling, touches the secret springs of wonder and mysterious gladness in the spirit; and amid its imperial tones the tread of many youthful feet is heard in the aisle. You turn, and behold a scene that brings the tears into your eyes, and the throb of sacred sympathy into your heart. Are they creatures of earth or of heaven? Are they the every-day forms which fill our houses, and pass us in the streets, and till the solitary fields of earth, and perform the homely duties of the labourer's cottage—those fair, youthful beings, that bend down their bare and beautiful heads beneath the hands of that solemn and dignified old man? Yes, through the drops that dim our eyes, and the surprise that dazzles them, we discern the children of the rich and the poor kneeling down together, to take upon themselves the eternal weight of their own souls. There, side by side, the sons and daughters of the hall, and the sons and daughters of the hut of poverty, are kneeling in the presence of God and man—acknowledging but one nature, one hope, one heaven; and our hearts swell with a triumphant feeling of this homage wrung from the pride of wealth, the arrogance of birth, and the soaring disdain of refined intellect, by the victorious might of Christianity. Yet, even in the midst of this feeling, what a contrast is there in these children! The sons and daughters of the fortunate, with their cultured forms and cultured features—the girls just budding into the beauty of early womanhood, in their white garbs, and with their fair hair so simply, yet so gracefully disposed,—the boys, with their open, rosy, yet declined countenances, and their full locks, clustering in vigorous comeliness;—they look, under the influence of the same feelings, like the children of some more ethereal planet: while the offspring of the poor, with their robust figures and homely dresses; with their hair, which has had no such sedulous hands, full of love and leisure, to mould it into shining softness—nay, that has, in many instances, had no tending but that of the frosts and winds, and the midsummer scorching of their daily, out-of-door lives; and with countenances in which the predominant expressions are awe, and simple credence; these touch us with equal sympathy for the hardships and disadvantages of their lot.

Successively over every bowed head those sacred hands are extended, which are to communicate a subtle but divine influence; and how solemn is the effect of that one grave and deliberate yet earnest voice, which, in the absence of the organ-tones, in the hushed and heart-generated stillness of the place, is alone heard pronouncing the words of awful import to every youthful recipient of the rite. 'T is done,— again the tide of music rolls over us, fraught with tenfold kindling of that spirit which has seized upon us; and amid its celestial exultings, that band of youthful ones has withdrawn, and another has taken its place. Thus it goes on till the whole have been confirmed in the faith in which their sponsors vowed to nurture them, and which they have now vowed to maintain for ever. The bishop delivers his parting exhortation, and solemnly charges them to return home in a manner becoming the sacredness of the occasion and of their present act. Filled with the glow of purest feelings, breathing the very warmest atmosphere of poetry and religious exaltation, we rise up with our neighbours, and depart. We depart— and the first breath of common air dissipates the beautiful delusion in which we have been, for a short space, entranced. We feel the rite to be beautiful while we cease to think; but the moment we come to penetrate into the mind which lies beneath, it becomes an empty dream. We feel that did our after consciousness permit us to believe that he who administered this rite was filled with its sanctity, and relied implicitly on its efficacy,—that the youthful tribe of neophytes were rightly prepared by the ministry of their respective pastors, and possessed the simple credence of past ages to give vitality to the office— then, indeed, might it be in fact, what it can now only appear for an instant. We feel, moreover, taking yet lower ground than this, that were the clergy a body filled with the zeal of their calling, they possess in this ceremony a means of powerful influence. But I have hitherto spoken only of its poetical and picturesque effect, and that effect endures not a step beyond the church doors. At that point the habitual apathy of the clergy converts this rite into one of the most awful and hideous of mockeries. The bishop charges the recipients to return home in soberness and decorum; but he should charge their respective clergymen to conduct them thither. But where are the clergy? They are gone to dine with the bishop, or their clerical brethren; and what are the morals of the youth to good dinners? They have turned the children over to the clerks. And where are the clerks? They have some matters of trade to transact;—some spades, or cart-saddles, or groceries to buy—and what is the health of the children's souls to spades, and cart-saddles, and groceries?— they have turned the lambs of the flock over to the schoolmasters. And where are the schoolmasters? They, like their clerical lords, are gone to dine with their brother dominies of the town, having reiterated the injunction of the bishop with a mock-heroic gravity, as highly, but not as well assumed as that of the bishop himself, and with as little effect. While they sit and discuss the merits of the last new treatise of arithmetic or spelling, the work of some new Dilworth or Entick, their charges have squandered into a dozen companies, and each, under the guidance of some rustic Coryphœus, have surrounded as many ale-house fires. They are as happy as their betters. The loaf and cheese melt like snowballs before them; the stout ale is handed round to blushing damsels by as many awkward, blushing swains. Hilarity abounds—their spirits are kindled. The bishop, and the church, and the crowd all vanish—or rather, their weight is lifted from their souls, which rise from the abstracted pressure with a double vivacity. Already heated, they set forward on their homeward way. At every besetting ale-house the revel is renewed. Over hill and dale they stroll on, a rude, roistering, and disgraceful rabble. For the effects of this confirmation let any one inquire of parish overseers, and they will tell him, that it is one of the most fruitful sources of licentiousness and crime. The contagion of vice spreads under such circumstances, with the fatal rapidity of lightning. Young and modest natures which otherwise would have shrunk from it and been safe, are surprised, as it were, into sin, and shame, and misery. Instead of a confirmation in Christianity, it becomes the confirmation of the Devil. And this clergymen know; and yet with the same apathy whence the evil has sprung, they continue to suffer its periodical recurrence; and thus, for want of a little zeal, and a little personal exercise of the good office of a shepherd, they convert one of the fairest rites of their church into one of the worst nuisances that afflict our country.

## CHAPTER XX.

### THE ENGLISH CHURCH.

Yet thus is the church, for all this noise of reformation, left still unreformed.  *Milton.*

Thus have we traversed the field of the world. We have waded through an ocean of priestly enormities. We have seen nations sitting in the blackness of darkness, because their priests shut up knowledge in the dark-lanterns of their selfishness. We have seen slavery and ignorance blasting, under the guidance of priestly hands, millions on millions of our race, and making melancholy the fairest portions of the earth. We have listened to sighs and the dropping of tears, to the voice of despair, and the agonies of torture and death; we have entered dungeons, and found their captives wasted to skeletons with the years of their solitary endurance; we have listened to their faint whispers, and have found that they uttered the cruelties of priests. We have stumbled upon midnight tribunals, and seen men stretched on racks; torn piecemeal with fiery pincers; or plunged into endless darkness by the lancing of their eyes; and have asked whose actions these were—and were answered—the priests! We have visited philosophers, and found them carefully concealing their discoveries, which would suddenly have filled the earth with light, and power, and love,—because they knew the priests would turn on them in their greedy malice, and doom them to fire or gibbet. We have walked among women of many countries, and have found thousands lost to shame, rolling wanton eyes, uttering hideous words; we have turned from them with loathing, but have heard them cry after us, as we went—" Our hope is in the priests,—they are our lovers, and defenders from eternal fire." We have entered for shelter from this horror the abodes of domestic love, and have stood petrified to find there all desecrated—purity destroyed—faith overthrown—happiness annihilated;—and it was the work of priests! Finally, we have seen kings, otherwise merciful, instigated by the devilish logic of priestcraft, become the butchers of their people; queens, otherwise glorious, become tyrants and executioners; and people, who would otherwise have lived in blessed harmony, warring on each other with inextinguishable malice and boundless blood-thirstiness; and behold! it was priestcraft, that, winding amongst them like a poisonous serpent, maddened them with its breath, and exulted with fiendish eyes over their horrible carnage. All this we have beheld, and what is the mighty lesson it has taught? It is this—that if the people hope to enjoy happiness, mutual love, and general prosperity, they must carefully snatch from the hands of their spiritual teachers, all political power, and confine them solely to their legitimate task of Christian instruction. Let it always be borne in mind, that, from the beginning of the world to this time, there never was a single conspiracy of SCHOOLMASTERS against the liberties and the mind of man: but in *every age*, the priests, the SPIRITUAL SCHOOLMASTERS, have been the most subtle, the most persevering, the most cruel enemies and oppressors of their species. The moral lesson is stamped on the destinies of every nation,—the inference is plain enough to the dullest capacity. Your preachers, while they are preachers alone, are harmless as your schoolmasters;—they have no motive to injure your peace; but let them once taste power, or the fatal charm of too much wealth, and the consequent fascinations of worldly greatness, and like the tiger when it has once tasted blood, they are henceforth your cruellest devourers and oppressors.

We may be told that there is no such pernicious tendency now in our establishment,—that it is mild, merciful, and pious: my attention may be triumphantly turned to the great men it has produced; and the number of humble, sincere, and exemplary clergymen who adorn their office at the present day.

Much of this I am not intending to deny; but if it be said, there is no evil tendency in the church, I there differ. The present corruption, the present admission, even of the clergy, of the necessity of reform, is sufficient refutation; and if it does not now imprison, burn, and destroy, we owe it to the refinement of the age, as the history of the past world will amply shew. Human nature is for ever the same; it is the nature of priestcraft to render the clergy tyrants, and the people slaves; it always has been so; it always will be; the only preventive lies in the general knowledge of the community. That the church has produced great men, who will not admit, that remembers that Plato of preachers—Jeremy Taylor, Selden, Tillotson, Hooker, and others? but that it would have produced far more such men, had it been more thoroughly reformed, placed on a more broad and Christian basis, is equally certain.

That there are numbers of excellent clergy, I as readily admit. I honour and love the good men who, in many an obscure village, in the midst of a poor and miserable population, spend their days with no motive but the fulfilment of their duty; cheerfully sacrificing all those refined pleasures,—that refined society which their character of mind, and their own delightful tastes, would naturally prompt and entitle them to. Who do this, badly paid, worse encouraged; compelled by their compassion to despoil themselves of a great part of their meagre salaries, to stop the cries of the terrible necessities by which they are surrounded;—who do this, many of them, at the expense of remaining solitary, unallied individuals; unmarried,—childless: or if husbands and fathers, expending their wives' comforts, their children's education on the poverty, which the wealthy incumbents neither look on, nor relieve. When I observe them do this, and all the while see their parishes drained by some fat pluralist, or sinecurist, who scorns to take the cure of souls whom he never goes near, except to take the living, and appoint his journeyman—when I see them look on wealth, dignities, and preferments showered on the well-born, well-allied, or well-impudenced, while there is a gulph between themselves and their attainment as impassable as that between Dives and Lazarus,—then do I indeed love and honour such men; and it is for such that I would see the church reformed; and the road to greater comfort and more extensive usefulness thrown open. I would not, as the bees do, appoint a killing day for the drones, but I would have no more admitted to the hive.

There are many excellent men, we admit; but are the multitude such? We shall undoubtedly be told so. The whole body will be represented as the most disinterested, holy, beneficent, industrious, wonder-working, salvation-spreading body imaginable. In their own periodicals and pamphlets, they are, in fact, represented so. Whether they be so or not, let one of the greatest intellects of the age, and one of their own warm friends testify—

> The sweet words
> Of Christian promise, words that even yet
> Might stem destruction, were they wisely preached,
> Are muttered o'er by men, whose tones proclaim
> How flat and wearisome they feel their trade:
> Rank scoffers some; but most too indolent
> To deem them falsehoods, or to know their truth.
>                                         COLERIDGE.

And let one great truth be marked.—The *prevalent character of a public body* stamps itself in the public mind as faithfully as a man's face in a mirror. There may be exceptions to a body, and they may be considerable: but when that body becomes *proverbial;* when it is, as a whole, the object of the jokes, the sarcasms, and contempts of the people, that body is not *partially*, but *almost wholly corrupt*. Now such is the character of the church of England clergy, in the mind of the British people. We may be told it is the vulgar opinion, and the vulgar are wrong. In judgments of this kind the vulgar, as they are called, are *right*. They always were so: but this too will be denied. A body in its corruption, never did, and never will admit it; its only feeling will be anger, not repentance. When the Romish church was utterly corrupted; when its priests and monks were the scandal and the scorn of all men, did the church admit it? Did it reform them? When Luther's artillery was thundering against it, and shaking it to its foundations, did it admit the justice of his attack? No! it only turned in rage, and would have devoured him, as it devoured all other reformers. When he had knocked down many of its pillars, blown up many of its bastions, laid bare to public scorn and indignation its secret fooleries and horrors, it relaxed not an atom of its pretensions, it abated not a jot of its pride, it stayed not its bloody arm, shunned not to proclaim itself still holy, invulnerable and supreme. While Dante and Bocaccio laughed at its errors, or declaimed against its abuses in its own territories; while Erasmus in the Netherlands, Chaucer in England, and Sir David Lindsay, the Chaucer of Scotland, were pouring ineffable and everlasting ridicule on its monks, its priests and pardoners, they were told that theirs was but the retailing of vulgar ignorance and envy;—but what followed? Time proclaimed it TRUTH. The corrupted tribes were chased away by popular fury and scorn, and have left only a name which is an infamy and a warning.

From age to age, the great spirits of the world have raised their voices and cried, Liberty! but the cry has been drowned by the clash of arms, or the brutish violence of uncultured mobs. Homer and Demosthenes in Greece, Cicero in Rome, the poets and martyrs of the middle ages, our sublime Milton, the maligned, but immoveable servant and sufferer of freedom, who laid down on her altar his peace, his comfort, and his very eyesight, our Hampdens and Sidneys, the Hofers and Bolivars of other lands, have, from age to age, cried, Liberty! but ignorance and power have been commonly too much for them. But at length, light from the eternal sanctuary of truth has spread over every region; into the depths and the dens of poverty it has penetrated; the scholar and the statesman are compelled to behold in the marriage of Christianity and Knowledge, the promise of the establishment of peace, order, and happiness, —the reign of rational freedom. We are in the very crisis in which old things are to be pulled down, and new ones established on the most ancient of foundations,—justice to the people. To effect safely this momentous change, requires all the watchfulness and the wisdom of an intelligent nation. The experience of the world's history, warns us to steer the safe middle course, between the despotism of the aristocracy and the mob, between the highest and the lowest orders of society. The intelligence, and not the wealth or multitudes of a state, must give the law of safety;—and to this intelligence I would again and finally say—be warned by universal history! Snatch from your priesthood all political power; abandon all state religion; place Christianity on its own base—the universal heart of the people; let your preachers be, as your schoolmasters, simply teachers; eschew reverend justices of the peace; very reverend politicians; and right reverend peers and legislators, as you would have done the reverend knights, and marquises, and dukes of the past ages. They must neither meddle with your wills, nor take the tenth of your corn; they must neither tax you to maintain houses in which to preach against you, and read your damnation in creeds of which no one really knows the origin; nor persecute you, nor seize your goods for Easter offerings and smoke-money. The system by which they tax you at your entry into the world; tax you at your marriage; tax you at your death; suffer you not descend into your native earth without a fee, must be abolished. The system by which you are made to pay for everything, and to have a voice in nothing—not even in the choice of a good minister, or the dismissal of a vile and scandalous debauchee; by which you are made the helpless puppet of some obtuse squire, and the prey of some greedy and godless priest, must have an end.

On this age, the happiness of centuries—the prosperity of Truth depends;—let it not disappoint the expectations, and mar the destinies of millions!

THE END.